# MAHLER'S FORGOTTEN CONDUCTOR

# Mahler's Forgotten Conductor

*Heinz Unger and His Search for Jewish Meaning, 1895–1965*

HERNAN TESLER-MABÉ

UNIVERSITY OF TORONTO PRESS
Toronto Buffalo London

Toronto Buffalo London
utorontopress.com
Printed in Canada

ISBN 978-1-4875-0516-5 (cloth)
ISBN 978-1-4875-3167-6 (EPUB)
ISBN 978-1-4875-3166-9 (PDF)

---

**Library and Archives Canada Cataloguing in Publication**

Title: Mahler's forgotten conductor : Heinz Unger and his search for Jewish meaning, 1895–1965 / Herman Tesler-Mabé
Names: Tesler-Mabé, Hernan, author.
Description: Includes bibliographical references.
Identifiers: Canadiana (print) 2019020270X | Canadiana (ebook) 20190203358 | ISBN 9781487505165 (cloth) | ISBN 9781487531676 (EPUB) | ISBN 9781487531669 (PDF)
Subjects: LCSH: Unger, Heinz, 1895–1965. | LCSH: Conductors (Music) – Canada – Biography. | LCSH: Conductors (Music) – Germany – Biography. | LCSH: Jewish musicians – Canada. | LCSH: Jews – Identity.
Classification: LCC ML422 U54 T47 2020 | DDC 784.2092 – dc23

---

University of Toronto Press acknowledges the financial assistance to its publishing program of the Canada Council for the Arts and the Ontario Arts Council, an Ontario government agency.

Canada Council for the Arts
Conseil des Arts du Canada

Funded by the Government of Canada
Financé par le gouvernement du Canada
Canada

*Dedicated to my father Eduardo, who passed away too soon to read this book, and to my dog Murray, who lay at my feet until it was done.*

# Contents

# Illustrations

# Acknowledgments

Transforming my initial ideas into a finished book has taken many years of reading, researching, fretting, planning, chatting, debating, presenting, writing, and rewriting. I could not have done any of this without the help of a great many family members, friends, and colleagues. A sincere thank you to all who have borne this with me, and an apology to those I have not mentioned in full here.

In particular, I wish to thank the following people and institutions: Pierre Anctil for supervising the dissertation upon which this book is based; the University of Ottawa and the adjudicators of the Ontario Graduate Scholarship for providing support during the initial rounds of research; my mother Rosa, Horatio Kemeny, and the Vered Jewish Canadian Studies Program for the financial support without which I could not have published this work; Lynn Lafontaine and Jean Matheson and the many other helpful staff at Library and Archives Canada for their help in finding (and re-finding) material and for answering every question, no matter how large or small; the many colleagues who helped me refine my ideas in so many ways and who provided me with valuable feedback; my wife Mandy for reading (and rereading) this work and listening to me speak about it for years; Robert and Susy Kemeny, who asked about my research every single time I saw them; Jean Wulkan for introducing me to her late husband David's evocative pictures and allowing me to use them here; the thoroughly professional staff and editors at University of Toronto Press, who helped me refine my work in its final stages (especially my copy editor Ryan Perks, without whom this book would have read much less well); and last but certainly not least, Len Husband at University of Toronto Press for his patience and guidance throughout the long process of bringing this manuscript to press.

# MAHLER'S FORGOTTEN CONDUCTOR

# Introduction

"The hero ... suffers three blows of fate, of which the third fells him like a tree." This is how Alma Mahler apocryphally described the extra-musical significance of the three hammer blows in the finale to Gustav Mahler's Symphony no. 6 (*Tragic*). These words, meant as commentary on the tragedies in the composer's life, could also describe those of one of his most committed followers, the German Jewish conductor Heinz Unger (1895–1965). Unger, three times a victim of fate, failed to complete his recording of Mahler's *Tragic* symphony after suffering a fatal heart attack in 1965. This blow was but the second struck him: in 1933, the conductor was exiled from his native Germany after Hitler's rise to power. The third and final blow – his posthumous neglect by both the wider musical community and a Jewish community to which he remained tied throughout his life – still resounds today.

Heinz Unger was born in Berlin on 14 December 1895 and died in Toronto on 25 February 1965. In the seven decades that separate these two dates, he lived through turbulent times filled with all kinds of triumph and tragedy. This book chronicles Unger's life and aims in part to restore the musician's professional achievements to their rightful place in the public consciousness.

But the reasons for writing this work transcend this most simple plane. Indeed, any historian who aims to write a microhistory must be acutely aware that they are more than merely recounting a life, however enamoured they may become with their historical subject.[1] Rather, they must recognize that writing what might be seen by some as a biography represents a choice that must be made only after careful deliberation over what this historical subject contributes to our general understanding. Why was *this* person selected? And what do they represent as a historical subject? I hope the answers to these questions become clear in the course of this book. But by way of an introduction, the next few pages lay out the reasons why I have chosen to write this work as I have, as well as identify its main themes.

## I. Heinz Unger's Life Presents an Opportunity to Better Understand the Course of Modern Jewish History in the Diaspora

Heinz Unger was born in a Berlin that near the turn of the twentieth century had become a cosmopolitan centre where German Jews intermingled with non-Jewish Germans on a daily basis. This close interaction between Jewish and non-Jewish segments of the population allowed German Jews to negotiate their identities in a meaningful space and to come to a fuller understanding of who they were and, perhaps more importantly, who they wanted to be.

German Jews had by this time undergone a process of modernization first begun in the eighteenth century by the father of the Jewish Enlightenment, Moses Mendelssohn (1729–1786). But the distance between Moses Mendelssohn – the grandfather of the composer Felix Mendelssohn (1809–1847), who would embody the many changes Jews underwent in the nineteenth century – and twentieth century Jews was enormous. From the midpoint of the eighteenth century, German Jews were swept up in the same cultural, intellectual, and social changes begun in the Enlightenment, expressed during the course of the French Revolution, and negotiated thereafter as part of the invention, birth, and subsequent definition of the modern nation-state. By the time of the German Reich's founding in 1871, German Jews were no longer a distinct people but had officially become Germans, possessing the same rights and opportunities (in principle if not in practice) as any other German in the newly minted liberal state. Looking at Unger's early life, we will see how far this process had come by the end of the nineteenth century and how its success affected one individual's identity.

But a grey cloud hung over the "success story" of Jewish emancipation. Significant segments of the non-Jewish German population rejected these "Germans of the Mosaic Faith" as their brethren and continued to discriminate against them in subtle (and sometimes unsubtle) ways. By the late nineteenth century, however, this discrimination no longer relied upon religious motivations, as in the past, but was instead buttressed by an even more threatening Social Darwinism that mixed dangerously with lingering Romantic notions of *Volk.* This potent mix transformed the sporadic anti-Jewish outbursts of the past into a much more pervasive and systemic modern articulation of antisemitism.

But this was not only a matter of how Germans – and Central Europeans more broadly – understood the German Jews that lived in their midst.

Rather, it was as much about how Germans Jews viewed themselves and understood their identities in a period of great change. And so, while at the beginning of the twentieth century German Jews still bore a Jewish identity that they could not forget, they often struggled to find a means of expressing this latent Jewish identity. In Heinz Unger's case, he achieved an understanding of his Jewish identity via his passion for Gustav Mahler's music, though even then only with the passage of time and by way of a process of reflection that took him beyond the bounds of traditional Jewish community affiliation. In focussing less on communal Jewish expressions to help better understand the full and complex identity of German Jews, my hope is that this work will serve as a corrective to a scholarship that often privileges the accomplishments and utterances of intellectuals such as Gershom Scholem and Franz Rosenzweig as representative of German Jewish sentiment in the first half of the twentieth century.[2] Building upon more recent studies, I posit that German Jewish modernity is composed not of a symbiosis between the German and the Jewish elements but rather a mutually reinforcing and inseparable modernity that existed within German Jews and was manifest and experienced in a number of different ways that exceed the traditional bounds of intellectual history.[3]

Of course, one man cannot represent the course of an entire people and to assert as much would open oneself up to powerful and entirely justified attacks of misrepresentation. Still, ground-breaking microhistories such as Carlo Ginzburg's *The Cheese and the Worms* have shown us that a properly constructed and articulated study of a single historical subject can open up an entire universe of understanding that otherwise would have remained unexplored.[4] In consciously positioning my work as a *contextual biography*, I aim to not only chronicle Heinz Unger's life but to place him in context and examine the manner in which he negotiated his own German Jewish identity, thereby allowing us not only to exhibit his life in a fuller manner but also to better convey the complex, non-monolithic nature of German Jewish identity.[5]

## II. Heinz Unger's Later Years in Canada Allow Us to View Canadian Jewry through a Different Frame

The story of Canadian Jewry begins not with their arrival in the New World but in the Old World from where Canada's Jews had come, most stemming from the eastern fringes of the European continent. This Eastern European Jewry existed within an illiberal and highly stratified general milieu that changed far less than its Central and Western European antipodes over the course of the nineteenth century. As Gershon Hundert points out, Eastern European Jewry negotiated its own course into the modern era, retaining significant features of their pre-modern "shtetled" lives and changing little with the arrival of the twentieth century.[6] In essence, much of Eastern European Jewry remained embedded behind ghetto walls and in *shtetls* for far longer than had European Jews to the west.

Nonetheless, the arrival of modernity near the end of the nineteenth century forced Eastern European Jews to confront the outside world, and they did so in two key ways that would remain an important feature of Eastern European Jewish immigrant culture as it moved through the Diaspora. The first, Zionism, was a movement that aimed toward the creation of a Jewish homeland. Theodor Herzl (1860–1904) was an assimilated Austrian Jewish journalist who, in covering the Dreyfus Affair near the end of the nineteenth century, came to the conclusion that, no matter how far Jewish emancipation progressed, bouts of antisemitism would always mark Jews as distinct and that sudden and disastrous setbacks were not only possible but inevitable. Seeking the creation of a state that would act as a refuge for European Jews, Herzl searched the world over – petitioning British politicians for the use of Uganda, attempting to purchase land in the undeveloped Argentine hinterland, and meeting with the Ottoman sultan in the hopes of obtaining the Ottoman-controlled lands of Palestine – to create a Jewish homeland founded not upon religion but a liberal secularism akin to that employed in the modern nation-state.

The second ideology that greatly impacted Eastern European Jewry was Bundism. In illiberal Eastern Europe (and particularly in the Russian Empire), socialist ideologies resonated strongly among the many Jews who lived a meagre urban existence shaped by frequent pogroms (often tacitly supported by local and central governments) and chronic economic exploitation at the hands of more affluent, enterprise-owning Jews. The birth of the Bund in 1897 – the same year in which the inaugural Zionist Congress was held in Basel – granted the Jews of Eastern Europe what they viewed as a realistic solution to many of their socio-economic problems. The Bund rapidly evolved into a vibrant form of community affiliation possessing nationalist tendencies.[7] The Bund's cultural vibrancy – including the development of Yiddish as a linguistic-cultural foundation – persisted until the tragic demise of much of Eastern European Jewry in the Holocaust.

Not all of Europe's Jews, however, disappeared with the disaster that overwhelmed Europe in the late 1930s and the first half of the 1940s. At the turn of the century, large numbers of Jews from Eastern Europe – motivated to flee their homes in the wake of pogroms such as the Kishineff massacre of 1903 – left their communities to start anew in settings such as Canada that they hoped would be an improvement over the intolerant conditions in which they had lived.[8] These Jews, arriving with few if any linguistic skills and a legacy of *shtetl* life, chose to form or were forced into closed communities in Canada's largest urban centres, such as Montreal, Toronto, and Winnipeg. In these communities, they recreated the contours of their previous lives, working primarily in the garment industry and creating a vibrant, rich community whose borders were, at times, porous yet still clearly visible and, often, closely guarded from both within and without. Canada's large Jewish communities recreated their social structures on their own, growing organically but also maintaining the flavour of the communities left behind in Eastern Europe.[9]

This was the landscape and the circumstances with which Unger and many of his German Jewish compatriots were confronted upon immigration. Often unable to find common ground with vast segments of an existing Jewish community with which they seemed to have little in common, they often sought out association with Canadians or German-speaking Canadians that only furthered the distance between German Jews and their Eastern European co-religionists. In place of a meaningful dialogue with many members of the Canadian Jewish community, these newly Canadian German Jews embedded themselves in Canadian culture while also maintaining a network of affiliation that transcended borders, linking together like-minded and assimilated Jews according to common interests and codes of already deeply entrenched behaviour and thought across the Diaspora.

Yet the Canadian Jewish community was itself undergoing a general process of change in the post-war period, allowing Unger and his ilk to establish a dialogue with Canadian Jews aware of their place within an ever more pluralistic Canadian society. In these circles, Unger did not seem as great a threat as he did to more traditional-minded Canadian Jews still questioning the wisdom of extending the parameters of Jewish identity. Among Canada's upwardly mobile and increasingly affluent Jews, Unger's Jewish identity was not so deeply questioned, and his affiliation with Mahler's music – as well as high culture more broadly – as a locus of Jewish understanding made perfect sense.

Put another way, the failure of German Jews to embed themselves in Canada's more traditional Jewish communities does not mean that these recent immigrants from Central Europe had "lost" their Jewishness. Instead, they negotiated their Jewish identity in a manner that reflected their assimilationist German Jewish experience and that put them at odds with the political and cultural positions of more traditional-minded Canadian Jews. The way in which German Jews negotiated their Jewishness, however, is often erroneously confused with an ambivalence to their Jewish identities. The chapters that follow will examine one such articulation of German Jewish identity, positing that the manner in which Unger explored his identity and constructed his life across space and time sheds new light on notions of marginalized Jewish identities in a Canadian context and in the Diaspora more generally. In the course of this work, we will follow Unger's interaction with and negotiation of ideologies, trends, and personalities that bore a special significance for German Jews. Ultimately, I argue that any understanding of Canadian Jewish identity must take into account the historical experience of German Jewry – an admittedly small group – in order to fully and accurately represent the true pluralism of Canadian Jewry.[10]

## III. Heinz Unger's Engagement with Music Allows Us to Arrive at a Richer Understanding of What Constitutes Jewish Music and How Gustav Mahler's Music Represents a Key Site for the Formation and Maintenance of Jewish Identity

Heinz Unger was vitally interested in the dissemination of Gustav Mahler's music. In this book, I argue that Unger's performance of Mahler's music – what in the final chapters I call a "performative rite" – opens up a new way to understand German Jewish identity that would go unnoticed were one to only focus on more-orthodox expressions such as speech and writing.[11] Putting aside for the moment the musical worth of Mahler's oeuvre and focussing instead on Unger's dedication to the dissemination of Mahler's music, I advance the thesis that Mahler's music represents a key site of German Jewish identity and that Unger's allegiance to this music therefore represents an evolving "performativity" of his Jewish identity.[12]

This claim, however, requires some clarification. In 1952, Israel Rabinovitch (1894–1964), the highly influential editor of Montreal's Yiddish-language daily *Keneder Odler* (the Canadian Eagle) published *Jewish Music, Ancient and Modern.* In this work, Rabinovitch stated that "Jewish music began only then when Jewish musicians consciously devoted themselves to its creation."[13] In this way, he effectively delimited the bounds of Jewish musical expression for an entire community, discounting the work of Jewish composers who did not "consciously" attempt to create Jewish music but who were still writing music that was either suffused with a Jewish sensibility or that reflected their own cultural experience. Coming from one of the community's leading intellectuals and foremost writers on music, Rabinovitch's view functioned as a key component in the community's self-definition, patrolling its boundaries and determining what was allowed entry into this world.

If the position held by Rabinovitch had been the view of some marginal figure, we might be able to discount it and instead conceptualize Jewish music in a more holistic manner. But Rabinovitch's view was neither unique nor insignificant, dovetailing as it did with the views of other Jewish thinkers intimately linked to Jewish community structures and predisposed to reaching conclusions consistent with their lived experience that failed to do justice to the complexity of Jewish musicology and Jewish art more generally. Whether conscious or not, this bias reflected the manner in which these mostly Eastern European commentators defined their own relationship to Judaism as religion and culture. Moreover, it also led to the marginalization of a whole set of musicians and music that, despite being of Jewish origin, failed to meet the stringent criteria of *Yiddishkeit* set out by orthodox musical commentators. In such a structure, only those Jewish composers who reflected the critics' perceptions of what constituted a thoroughly Jewish life were considered able to endow music with a Jewish ethos.

So limiting a line of argumentation – however well-intentioned – is disconcertingly similar to the first articulations of a Jewish musicology launched, paradoxically, not by Jewish musicians or intellectuals themselves but with the German composer Richard Wagner's (1813–1883) antisemitic tract "Das Judenthum in der Musik."[14] This article, first published in September 1850 in the highly regarded and influential German music journal *Neue Zeitschrift für Musik* (Leipzig) and written by Wagner under the pseudonym K. Freigedank ("K. Freethought"), seems at first glance to be little more than a searing, vitriolic attack on the German Jewish composers Felix Mendelssohn and Giacomo Meyerbeer (1791–1864). Even a cursory read, however, shows that Wagner was not aiming solely to attack these composers but, rather, to argue that they represented an affront to "genuine" Germans and distorted their understanding of music and culture on account of – in Wagner's own term – their "Jewhood." It is not, therefore, Wagner's attack on these two composers but rather his linking of their shortcomings to alleged Jewish deficiencies (i.e., highlighting Jews as unable to conform to European characteristics or speech) that marks his tract as antisemitic.

I argue that the exclusionary tactic, if not the reprehensible language, that Wagner employed in "Das Judenthum in der Musik" is reflected in many Jewish musicological explorations of what constitutes Jewish music.[15] In these works we see the same exclusionary rhetoric, albeit employed as an instrument to cast out certain composers not only for their failure to consciously synchronize their artistic efforts with what are considered to be genuine expressions of Jewish feeling, but sometimes also because the composer simply stemmed from a milieu deemed insufficiently "Jewish."

These studies of Jewish music bear a further similarity to Wagner's polemic: just as Wagner's work can be viewed as a particularly brutal attempt to delineate the bounds of German music, Jewish musical studies were attempts at the self-definition of a cultural group in a period marked by strong currents of epistemological uncertainty. That is, they are attempts to work through issues of collective identity and to delimit that cultural group's sense of itself during major historical crises. Wagner's "Das Judenthum in der Musik" was a tract written in the wake of the revolutionary year of 1848, when German-speaking Central Europeans were undergoing a series of upheavals (the rise of the liberal state, for instance) that brought into question their identity as they negotiated the strains of a period that would culminate in 1871 with the creation of the German Reich. In the case of Jewish musicology, meanwhile, the latter part of the nineteenth century to the mid-twentieth century was a historical period marked by a series of upheavals (the rise of modern antisemitism, pogroms, collective displacement, and the Holocaust) throughout which Jews were constantly reappraising their identities. It comes as no surprise, then, that a great many studies of Jewish music undertaken by Jewish scholars bore intentions and goals similar to those of their nineteenth-century German-speaking counterparts: to define music and conscript it as an ally in the quest for a sense of self that would serve as an element of identity-building.

It is this very impulse that lies at the heart of Israel Rabinovitch's treatise on Jewish music. It also informs Abraham Idelsohn's pioneering 1929 work of Jewish musicology, *Jewish Music: Its Historical Development.* In this work, Idelsohn – a Russian-born Jewish musicologist who systematically collected an enormous body of Jewish melodies that would serve as a source of inspiration for numerous Eastern European Jewish composers seeking to create a new Jewish national art music in the first decades of the twentieth century – intended to follow Jewish music's "history as a tonal expression of Judaism and of Jewish life."[16] Idelsohn's idea of "Jewish life" had a very clear meaning, built upon a value-laden hierarchy that moved from the Temple, to the ghetto, and on to the general society in which assimilated Jewish musicians practised their art. Combined with a bias that favoured Eastern European Jewry at the expense of developments in Central and Western Europe, Idelsohn's book was bereft of anything more than a cursory examination of the interplay between Jewish music and what he considered European art music. As such, he largely dismissed the work of assimilated Jewish composers, rejecting, for instance, the Swiss-American Ernest Bloch's (1880–1959) compositions despite the composer's strong attachment to his Jewish heritage and the fact that his music was suffused with traditional Jewish modes and motifs.[17] Idelsohn's work did little to establish pluralism in Jewish music; instead it advanced an analysis reflecting *his* time and place that, by way of its particularism, patrolled and more deeply entrenched a narrow understanding of the bounds of Jewish music.

Yet not all Jewish musicologists and scholars have been so quick to dismiss the plurality of Jewish culture and experience. Israel Rabinovitch, for instance, accepted Ernest Bloch's bona fides as a Jewish composer despite holding many views in common with Idelsohn.[18] Moreover, in the last few decades Jewish studies has experienced a paradigm shift, leading Jewish scholars to examine their subject in a way that erodes limiting definitions, dismissing the once-common reliance on community structures and bringing back into the narrative the experiences of individuals that transcend communal definitions and modes of conduct.[19] Musicologists in Jewish studies also began to reframe their questions, abandoning the frustrating model of inclusion/exclusion inherited from a century and a half of musicological inquiry and embracing the idea that all spaces represented different yet still equal negotiations of Jewish identity.[20]

This fresh approach serves an important function, recognizing cultural plurality and moving us away from a Jewish musicology that for too long ignored the strains of Jewish (musical) identity from across the Diaspora. By opening up the parameters of the debate, we arrive at a more broad-minded and inclusive definition of Jewish music. In this new scheme, far greater latitude is allowed for the manner in which composers exhibit their "Jewishness" as well as how other musicians and audiences looked to their music(s) as a form and reflection of their own Jewish identity.

Building upon this recent understanding of music as a site of identity formation, expression, and maintenance, this book looks at how Unger's allegiance to Gustav Mahler rests upon an understanding of the composer as a critical – and evolving – site of German Jewish identity. Born 7 July 1860 in the small Bohemian town of Kalischt (Kaliště), Mahler was raised in Iglau (Jihlava) before moving to Vienna in 1875 to complete his musical studies. Mahler then moved throughout the German-speaking world, securing conducting posts in ever more important musical centres before obtaining the position of court conductor of the Vienna Opera in 1897. He did so, however, only after his conversion to Catholicism, a step he believed to be "necessary for self-preservation."[21]

Yet Mahler's conversion did little to curb an antisemitism that to varying degrees would continue to plague him for the balance of his life. And so, despite having had a thoroughly German upbringing and partaking in the nationalist culture of the period, he nevertheless struggled to escape from antisemitic insinuations, reproaches, and attacks, a state of affairs that led him – or his wife Alma, depending on the version – to famously declare, "I am thrice homeless, as a native of Bohemia in Austria, as an Austrian among Germans, and as a Jew throughout the world. Everywhere an intruder, never welcomed."[22]

Perhaps Mahler's experience of feeling like an intruder in the world made him compose a body of work that situated itself uncomfortably in the German symphonic repertoire, at once indebted to past masters such as Beethoven and Brahms while also borrowing popular tunes and idioms to create highly unusual symphonic structures. And so, despite claims made by Franz Kafka's erstwhile editor Max Brod and taken up by American musician Leonard Bernstein, it is not only the Jewish "folk" elements (such as the klezmer music that appears in the third movement of his First Symphony) that marks Mahler's music as "Jewish," nor is it only the "intellectual voice" that, according to Theodor Adorno, expresses Mahler's Jewishness.[23] Rather, it is how these elements coalesced to create what was seen as a musical "instability" suggestive of discomfort not only with the symphonic form but also with society, reminding us of Kafka's characteristic quip that "[most Jews] who began to write German wanted to leave Judaism ... but with their little hind legs they were still glued to the Jewishness of their fathers and with their little front legs they found no new ground."[24] The conflict that existed within Mahler's music – as well as perhaps within the composer himself – is not, therefore, the composer's "Jewishness" but, rather, an expression of the highly destabilizing social and cultural reality experienced by Jews in this period.

Mahler's music only truly became a part of the general Jewish sphere in the second half of the twentieth century, after his cause was taken up principally by Jewish musicians and musicologists who came to see the composer's art as bearing a post-Holocaust Diasporic meaning; indeed, some scholars have gone so far as to suggest that the nexus between Gustav Mahler and Jewishness is little more than an anachronistic fiction built to serve as part of an uplifting psychological narrative.[25] Yet Mahler's music had since its inception found its greatest concentration of support among the many German Jews who shared a social and cultural position very similar to his own. In the field of conducting, a great many of his staunchest supporters (Bruno Walter, Otto Klemperer, Klaus Pringsheim, as well as Heinz Unger) were the product of that same emancipated and assimilated Jewry as Mahler. Leading defenders of Mahler's musical *weltanschauung* such as Franz Schreker (1878–1934), Paul Bekker (1882–1937), Richard Specht (1870–1932), and Alfred Einstein (1880–1952) were also Jewish. In sum, Mahler's music seems to have borne a cultural meaning for German Jews that created a particularly strong devotion in Mahler's disciples, however little they may have understood or reflected on why this might be. In turn, this attachment suggests that Mahler's music was in some vital way a forum in which German Jews negotiated and expressed their multifaceted and overlapping identities.

But we should also note here that cultural and artistic articulations of identity are not constant. As such, the strands that connect Jewish identity with cultural expression are not evenly distributed through one's life and they reflect circumstances as much as the inevitability of aging. Indeed, much as we often see people become more religious as they age, Unger also began to connect more explicitly with his Jewish identity in his later years. Unger's return to Berlin in 1956, followed by the centenary of Mahler's birth in 1960, played a key role in all this, causing Unger to reflect increasingly on why Mahler had meant so much to him over the years. So, too, did what Adam Sacks has recently called the "overbiographical" myth, which cast Mahler "as the ultimate victim who suffered horrendously through his brief fifty-one years," appeal to an embittered and embattled Unger in his later years; this view, culminating in Bernstein's view of Mahler "as a latter-day Jewish prophet for the catastrophes and violence of the twentieth century," would also inform Unger's understanding of his own relationship with Mahler and with the Jewish people more generally.[26]

On the whole, then, the biography of Heinz Unger and his affiliation with the music of Gustav Mahler – the story of a thoroughly assimilated yet avowedly Jewish musician being inspired by a composer of Jewish birth who became a key figure in the German musical world – presents us with a wonderful opportunity to problematize the relationship between Jewish music and identity. In essence, Unger's biography allows us to witness first-hand the way in which Mahler and his music became a vital site for German Jews to understand as well as express their hybridized and evolving identities.[27]

## IV. Heinz Unger's Accomplishments Deserve Recognition

This book attempts to do more than provide new insights into Jewish identity among German Jews, the Canadian Jewish context, or to develop a richer understanding of Jewish music. As suggested earlier, at its most basic level it is an attempt to tell a story about a musician's life and his accomplishments. Heinz Unger forged a successful career in both Europe and the Americas, if one punctuated by a series of setbacks that undermined his legacy. A large part of this biography is devoted to bringing to light the conductor's achievements in the hope of helping readers recognize his impact upon the evolution of musical culture – Jewish and otherwise – in disparate parts of the world.

But music is an ephemeral phenomenon, and the many unrecorded concerts over which Unger presided in his lifetime have remained only in the memory of those who witnessed them first-hand. As a consequence, any understanding of Unger's professional success is largely reliant upon the music critics around the world that the conductor consistently impressed with his performances. The sheer volume of positive assessments reflects very well on the conductor, demonstrating that he was a talented musician. However, recognizing that the talents, dispositions, and expertise of musical critics – to say nothing of their potential political and cultural motivations – range across time and space, I have, where possible, attempted to provide background information on the critics who must play an important role in our understanding and assessment of Unger's musicianship.

All that being said, in my research I discovered that many of Unger's recordings have been collecting dust at Library and Archives Canada. These musical documents represent not only the achievements of a particular artist, but also register the premieres and early performances of important music in Canada. Indeed, Unger is singlehandedly responsible for the premiere of many of Mahler's symphonies in Canada, an achievement that was recognized at the time but is now completely forgotten. The fact that the tapes of these historic performances languish in closed archives does a serious disservice to our cultural legacy and prevents musicologists and other experts from studying Unger's work first-hand. I hope that this book will help to generate sufficient interest in Unger to encourage the dissemination of these valuable sonic resources among researchers and music lovers (and especially Mahlerites).

~

The story of Heinz Unger's life as told in the following chapters is structured more or less chronologically, that approach being perhaps the clearest way of conveying the sweep of a life filled with movement.

The first chapter covers Unger's early life, beginning with his birth in 1895 and ending with his exodus from Germany in 1933. Here I cover Unger's youth, his service in the German Army during the First World War, the emergence of his love of Gustav Mahler's music and his decision to become a conductor, his first successes as a conductor in Berlin, his first travels to the Soviet Union, and his emigration from Germany at the beginning of the Nazi period.

The second chapter begins in 1930, a mere handful of years before Unger was forced to depart Germany. From this starting point, I follow the conductor through his time in the Soviet Union until 1937, when his stint there was cut short due to ideological and artistic differences with the authorities. I then discuss Unger's life after he chose to settle with his young family in England after 1933, the conductor's activities during the Second World War, his early – and, to some, contentious – travels in Spain after 1945, and his successes in the Spanish-speaking world.

The third chapter focuses on Unger's move to Canada. As such, it begins with a discussion of his first appearances on Canadian soil in the late 1930s. But my main focus in this chapter is Unger's endeavours to create anew a career for himself after his permanent move to Canada in 1947. After a discussion of the musician's work with community orchestras and the joyful circumstances surrounding the founding of his York Concert Society, the chapter ends with Unger's emotional return to Berlin in 1956.

The fourth chapter looks at some of the central episodes in Unger's life, reconstructing the conductor's activities during the latter half of the 1950s and ending in 1960, the year of the centenary of Gustav Mahler's birth and one that possessed a particular German Jewish meaning for Unger. But despite Unger's pleasure at being a part of the Mahler centenary, his happiness was blunted by an ongoing antagonism with the Israel Philharmonic; this raised the ire of this Jewish musician who was cast aside, his "Jewish" credentials questioned by those who held sway in Jerusalem. That messy affair notwithstanding, this chapter also shows Unger's international recognition as a leading Mahlerian, as demonstrated by his reception of a Mahler medal and the first in a string of Canadian premieres of Mahler's symphonies that brought to the conductor a joy dented only by the affair with the Israel Philharmonic. In this chapter I also explore Unger's relationship with parts of the Jewish world – highlighting, for example, Unger's role in the "Chicago Affair" of 1949, an episode that caused a deep and permanent fissure between Unger and significant portions of the American Jewish community and ensured that he would never achieve success in an American context, despite the advocacy of influential Jewish supporters in the United States.

The concluding chapter recounts Unger's final years, beginning with the circumstances surrounding the cancellation of the York Concert Society's 1961 season. I then continue with an exploration of Unger's troubled last years, riddled with repeated setbacks that caused him bitterness despite his receiving further accolades from the Gustav Mahler society and leading the Canadian premiere of Mahler's final completed symphonic utterance, his Ninth Symphony. I end with a discussion of Unger's ultimate demise, which occurred, fittingly, while working toward the Canadian premiere of Mahler's Symphony no. 6 (*Tragic*).

I end this exploration of Unger's life with a postlude that revisits the key themes discussed in the course of this chronicle. I then close with a brief discussion of Unger's forgotten musical legacy – a legacy that, it is hoped, this book will go some way toward rehabilitating. I also once more touch upon the main ideas pertaining to German Jewish identity surveyed herein.

*Chapter One*

# A Thoroughly German Youth, Early Trips to the Soviet Union, and an Unfortunate Exile (1895–1933)

Heinz Unger was born 14 December 1895 in the picturesque Berlin suburb of Charlottenburg, home to Berlin's largest surviving royal palace and an independent city until 1920, when it was incorporated into Gross-Berlin (Greater Berlin). His birth certificate, dated 21 December 1895, exhibits no surprises.[1] His liberal, middle-class parents, Jakub Unger and Karolina Unger (née Kann), are identified as being of the Mosaic faith, an appellation used to convey the Jewish identity of German Jews in a culture wherein the majority of Jews had accepted their status as German citizens whose only difference from the remainder of the populace, at least in theory, was religious.[2] Remarkably, the name that Unger's mother assumed upon marriage suggested, almost prophetically, the central role that music would play in Unger's life: legend has it that it was the singer Karolina Unger who placed her hand upon Ludwig van Beethoven's shoulder and delicately turned the long-deaf composer around at the 1824 Viennese premiere of his Ninth Symphony so that he could see the ovation that his work received.

Little else is known about Unger's childhood except that he was raised as an only child after his parents lost their first born at the age of five from a sudden illness.[3] However, since this family tragedy occurred before Unger's birth, it is doubtful that it would have affected him in any significant way, except to provide him with over-indulgent parents. All told, his family life and upbringing seem to have borne all the trappings of a comfortable, upper-middle-class existence, with Unger's father being a "highly respectable lawyer" and his mother an "accomplished pianist, but not a professional musician."[4] Both were also surely keen on ensuring for their surviving child a comfortable home.

A product of a thoroughly *Mittelstand* milieu, Heinz Unger's childhood coincided with a period during which the great gains made in Jewish emancipation over the course of the nineteenth century allowed for an ever-fuller Jewish participation in German life. During the Franco-Prussian War of 1870–1, German Jews allied themselves not with their co-religionists across the border but with their own countrymen.[5] The subsequent unification of Germany under Otto von Bismarck did nothing to reverse this trend, but instead marked the moment German Jews were finally granted the same legal rights as their countrymen. And while the Dreyfus Affair of the early 1890s exposed an alarming racialist rhetoric in Germany as well as across Europe, the advancements in social status achieved by Jews went a long way to allaying fears arising from this event.[6]

Still, the German branch of the racialist rhetoric brought to light during the Dreyfus Affair could not be entirely dismissed. In Germany, many nationalist groups, even those whose membership consisted largely of the intelligentsia and students, were markedly racist and displayed an eagerness to blame any perceived social ills on the Jews in their midst. Surprisingly, a great many of these nationalist groups included numerous Jewish members, who saw these ideas as part of a perfectly reasonable discourse that correctly interpreted their contemporary circumstances and compelled them to redouble their efforts to become an integral part of the *Volksgemeinschaft.* Moreover, many members of these fraternities, if they were troubled by the aggressive language they heard, were assuaged by the fact that these groups sought primarily to create a strong national ethos, a goal with which many Jews identified.

At his father's insistence, Heinz Unger early on embarked upon a course of study that would lead him toward a career in law. As a youth, he undertook studies at the Mommsen-Gymnasium in Charlottenburg. As expected of the university-bound son of a respected professional, he completed his *Gymnasium* studies, obtaining his school-leaving diploma in 1914. He then commenced his post-secondary education, beginning his legal training at the Friedrich-Wilhelms-Universität of Berlin, continuing at the Ludwig-Maximilians-Universität in Munich, before finally returning to Berlin to obtain his doctorate in law from Berlin's Wilhelm II University in October 1917.[7]

But Unger's life course was fundamentally altered by a single event. In November 1915, while a law student in Munich, he attended a concert featuring Gustav Mahler's *Das Lied von der Erde,* conducted by the composer's close friend and disciple, Bruno Walter (1876–1962). That single evening – that single event that could not have lasted much more than two short hours – marked the first entry in a personal mythology that he would construct and cling to for the rest of his life. As he would often recount, enraptured by the performance that he witnessed, Unger decided that he could not follow in his father's footsteps and assume the "highly respectable" legal career toward which he had been working. Instead, he decided at that very moment to devote his life to music-making and to sharing Mahler's music with the rest of the world.

Heinz Unger's impulsive decision to alter his life's direction was met with little enthusiasm from his parents. While music and the arts were seen as a fundamental aspect of the *Bildung* (self-development) process so integral to the development of a well-educated citizen, a life in music was not deemed a suitable career for the only son of a respected, and respectable, lawyer. As Unger's future wife Hella would recall many years later:

> His parents were against their son's decision to become a professional musician. This was not thought of as an "up to the mark" livelihood for the only son of well to do parents.[8]

As a means of compromise and to avoid familial disharmony, Unger promised his parents that he would complete his law degree and only afterwards pursue a course of musical studies, thereby having a stable career to fall back on if his interest in music did not develop in the manner he envisioned. And he remained true to his word, if only in the strictest sense: he completed his legal studies before beginning his musical training, though years later his wife would note wryly that "his musical education and studies took up the major part of his time as a student."[9] Away from his parents' watchful eyes, Unger had already approached conductor Bruno Walter and cultivated a friendship that consisted of long walks on which they would discuss music, much as Walter had done with Gustav Mahler himself years earlier in Vienna. In this instance, though, the friendship had been won through sheer persistence, Unger carrying Walter's music case to and from rehearsals until being allowed into his confidence. The two men would remain friends for the rest of Walter's life.[10]

In the summer of 1914, Europe descended into war after the assassination of Austrian archduke Franz Ferdinand heightened tensions that had been building on the continent since 1870. Like so many of his Jewish compatriots, Unger joined the German war effort, proud of the opportunity to display his loyalty.[11] Responding to the enthusiastic cries of the Central-Verein and the Verband der deutschen Juden for German Jews to "devote [their] faith and bravery to the fatherland above and beyond the call of duty [and] rush to the flag!," Unger served his country proudly, and was honoured with an Iron Cross for his service in the Brandenburg Battalion in the last two years of war – this despite the Ministry of War's decision, motivated by the shrill cries of antisemitic nationalists, to conduct a headcount (*Judenzählung*) to determine whether German Jews were contributing to the war effort in sufficient numbers.[12]

His commitments to his parents and his fatherland met, Unger was at the end of the First World War free to pursue his chosen path and openly work toward a career as a musician. He thus embarked upon the formal musical training that his new vocation required, undertaking private musical studies in Berlin with Wilhelm Klatte and Theodor Schoenberger in theory and Eduard Mörike and Fritz Stiedry in conducting, obtaining a State Music Teacher's Diploma of Prussia.[13]

Fresh from his musical formation, Unger was now ready to make his professional debut. His first conducting experience had come in 1915, when he led a Berlin-based amateur orchestra – consisting principally of doctors and dentists – in a reading of a part of Beethoven's Fifth Symphony.[14] Leading a professional orchestra like the Berlin Philharmonic was another matter altogether. Increasing the pressure was the fact that, given his lack of experience, Unger had only obtained this opportunity by paying the orchestra in advance. Undaunted, Unger marked his debut by leading the Berlin Philharmonic in the challenging works of his favoured composer Gustav Mahler. A first concert, showcasing Mahler's First Symphony, took place on 13 September 1919 and a second, in which he conducted *Das Lied von der Erde*, occurred on the nineteenth.[15] In the wake of the First World War, Bruno Walter would joke that Unger's ambitious debut was "as unthinkable as that [French prime minister George] Clemenceau should send a note to Germany tomorrow, renouncing war reparations and giving back Alsace Lorraine."[16] Walter's words so touched Unger that he kept them written on a card that he brought wherever his life took him; to him, this was no jest but a critical moment he would always remember.

Unger immediately proved himself a conductor of great promise with these two performances. The critics of the day responded with reviews that revealed great enthusiasm for Unger's art. Writing in the *Signale für die musikalische Welt*, critic and musicologist Max Chop noted that Unger was "a young lawyer [who] undertook to prove his capability to perform as an orchestra conductor, and show that the artistic talent in him is an applicable elemental force swelling with imperious force."[17] The respected musician, pedagogue, and critic Leopold Schmidt, writing in the *Berliner Tagenblatt* – a newspaper for which he had written since 1897 – echoed Chop's praise for Unger's achievement, noting that Unger's treatment of "Wagner's Faust Overture and Mahler's Symphony in D major prove his musical maturity and capability to create ... with the characteristics of an experienced conductor and self-conscious security." He would end by writing, "Dr. Unger, actually a lawyer, is supposed to be conducting an orchestra for the first time. If so, then we found a very strong talent."[18]

Believing since 1915 that music was his true calling, such acclaim must have come as a great relief to Unger and his family. The extent of his triumph, moreover, assured him the support of the venerable Berlin Philharmonic, a state of affairs that would lead to a close affiliation with that esteemed organization over the next thirteen years. The beginning of the 1920s signalled an ever-closer relationship, with engagements in the Berlin Philharmonic's *Konzerte des Anbruch* series between 1920 and 1922.[19]

Further successes were to come. Even with the constellation of talent assembled in Berlin at the time – a roster that included Wilhelm Furtwängler, Otto Klemperer, and Bruno Walter – Unger was able to not only eke out a living conducting but also establish himself as an increasingly recognizable figure in the Berlin musical world. By mid-decade, he was a permanent fixture at the Berlin Philharmonic, the orchestra – formed as an autonomous collective wherein the musicians administered the orchestra's activities – having sufficient faith in his abilities and drawing power to devote to Unger an entire concert series. These concerts, established under the auspices of the Gesellschaft der Musikfreunde, began in 1925 and remained a fixture of the Berlin Philharmonic's season until 1933, when Unger was suspended due to a new set of cultural policies and regulations laid out by the Nazi regime.

During this period, Unger's allegiance to Mahler's works remained central to the development of his career and coincided with a broader emerging interest in the composer's music. Following on the heels of his professional debut in Mahler's First Symphony and *Das Lied von der Erde*, Unger's next performances with the Berlin Philharmonic (save for a single excursion into Mozart on 20 March 1920) were of Mahler's Fifth Symphony and the song cycle *Lieder eines fahrenden Gesellen* in a concert held on 29 April 1920.[20] This concert was followed by a repeat performance of Mahler's Fifth Symphony on 9 September 1920, that program also including the *Kindertotenlieder* song cycle.[21]

So great was Unger's devotion to Mahler that he was at once recognized as a pivotal figure in the dissemination of Mahler's music. He was thus invited to the Mahler-fest held in Amsterdam between 6 and 19 May 1920 and hosted by another of Mahler's disciples, the Dutch conductor and director of the Concertgebouw Orchestra, Willem Mengelberg.[22] The Mahler festival represented the first integral cycle of Gustav Mahler's symphonies but it was much more than a series of concerts; it was also a gathering where leading figures in the Mahlerian universe (musicologists, musicians, and admirers) came together to reflect upon and

1.1 Heinz Unger (circa 1923). By the time this picture was taken, Unger had embarked upon his professional career as a musician. Source: Library and Archives Canada, MUS 56, File 16.

discuss the meaning of Mahler's art in a venue suffused with the strains of the composer's still largely unfamiliar music. It also represented one of the first major musical gatherings after the cataclysm of the First World War. Music critic and author Oskar Bie noted the special extra-musical significance of the event:

> We were intoxicated. Was this still the same bloodstained world? At some point we will all return to our homes, yet we will not forget this moment.

> When we speak about the war, we who were once enemies experience the same scornful twitch in face and hands. But when we think back to the moment of Amsterdam, our eyes light up with that glowing expression through which we understand and unite.[23]

Unger breathed deep in this rarefied company, honoured to have been invited to the event and carried away by both the music in which he was enveloped as well as the spirit of peace that figured so prominently at the event.

In the wake of the Mahler-fest, Unger was buoyed by the timely coincidence of a rising interest in Mahler's works and his growing reputation as a Mahler specialist. He was soon given a further opportunity to prove his talents to the Berlin Philharmonic when he was contracted to conduct two more performances of Mahler's works in 1921. The first concert, held on 11 February, was devoted to the Seventh Symphony while the second, held on 2 December, was an early performance of Mahler's *Das klagende Lied.*[24] From early on, Unger's burgeoning directorial career was built primarily, explicitly, and even self-consciously on his expertise in the Mahlerian sound-world.

In the midst of this professional success, an altogether different yet equally significant event occurred. In October 1923, Unger married his childhood friend Johanna ("Hella") Wolff.[25] The simple civil ceremony that marked their union was not unusual by this point, many German Jews having lost their explicitly religious affiliation. Still, the very fact that Unger married a Jewish woman that he had known since his youth – the two had met during their "first dancing lessons together in a family circle when [they] were both very young" – constitutes a marked affiliation with a Jewish culture and milieu when a great number of German Jews, instead of marrying denominationally, were choosing to intermarry with non-Jews.[26]

Free from financial woes as a consequence of his wife's dental practice and happily married, by the mid-1920s Unger was living a contented life in the musical capital of Germany.[27] He had established himself professionally in Berlin, not only featuring regularly on the podium of the Berlin Philharmonic but also founding and directing the Caecilienchor, an in-house choir that he and other conductors used in concerts requiring greater numbers of voices.

Along with his ever-expanding commitments with the Berlin Philharmonic and the Caecilienchor, the energetic young conductor also began to travel, conducting concerts across Europe as well as in other parts of Germany.[28] None of these voyages, however, could compare with the simultaneous excitement and trepidation Unger felt in

1.2 Heinz and Hella Unger (circa 1915). The pair wed in 1923 and remained married until Heinz Unger's death. Source: Library and Archives Canada, MUS 56, Box 14.

receiving an invitation from what he called "the cultural State Institute of the Ukraine" to conduct a series of concerts in the Ukrainian cities of Kiev, Kharkov, and Odessa.[29] Years later, in a memoir of his time in the Soviet Union entitled *Hammer, Sickle and Baton*, Unger would recount how his first "thirty-six-hour journey from Berlin to Kiev" aboard a train in the dead of winter gave him "the impression ... of travelling into the unknown ... Neither then nor at any time afterwards could I rid myself of the feeling when travelling eastwards that I was giving myself up to something incalculable."[30]

By 1924, the Russian Revolution that changed the course of Russian and world history appeared to be at its end: the Union of Soviet Socialist Republics had been founded in December 1922 and the horrifically bloody civil war that pitted "Red" supporters of the revolution against foreign-backed counter-revolutionary "White" forces had concluded.[31] The young Soviet Union, however, was far from a prosperous or contented land. Indeed, on his first walk through the streets of Kiev, Unger witnessed with horror the plodding march of a people beaten down by the hardships of the past decade:

> What had I seen? A grey mass moving through the town; driven by some invisible force. Could these be human beings? I tried to look into their faces, and shrank back. They had the grey faces of tired, beaten animals, and seemed eyeless – and yet it was perhaps the eyes which were the most tragic feature. They were tired eyes that desired to see no more; they were smileless, joyless. There was nothing human in them.[32]

Unger's belief in the spirit of humanity was, within the hour, virtually shattered. He quickly "fled back to the hotel, vowing never to set foot in the streets again."[33]

And yet Unger, despite this distressing first exposure to the Soviet Union and his distaste for the hypocrisy he witnessed in the supposedly classless system in which only some could buy luxury, would return to the Soviet Union on an almost annual basis for the next thirteen years. Unger would explain that his decision to return had much to do with his conviction that music could be a truly uplifting experience and that a concert – as "an expression of the human spirit" – could bring relief and joy to the mass of downtrodden and miserable people he had seen.

But there is another possible explanation for Unger's choice to return to the Soviet Union over so many years: that he bore sympathies that spurred him to return to the USSR to help build socialism. In early spring 1926, Unger would make his second trip to the Soviet Union, this time dividing his time between Leningrad and Moscow.[34] And on this trip, Unger would see the May Day celebrations, witnessing these seemingly spontaneous expressions first-hand and years later recounting how he had been swept away by the "genuine enthusiasm" that he thought he had seen. Yet even this – "the first really favourable impression which I received in Russia" – would be spoiled a mere twenty-four hours later.[35] Invited to the house of an old and trusted Russian musician friend, he learned that the euphoric scenes he had witnessed – a celebration in which "the entire population seemed to be taking part" – had been made "to order." His friend – who Unger quite astutely never named – explained to him the sinister truth, informing him that "as every institution, great or small, provides its own procession – every factory, hospital theatre, waterworks, and so on – it's easy enough to check up on those who take part."[36] Unger, for the first time overjoyed with the life he thought he had seen in the Russian people, had his hopes dashed:

> I shuddered. Something that had appealed to me as a demonstration of organized spontaneity was now proved to be one of organized compulsion, and my companion's last words hinted at an abyss of fear and suspicion that haunted every citizen in the country.[37]

He then asked himself a question that goes some way toward revealing why he may have travelled to the Soviet Union in the first place: "Was this the free land I had fancied?"[38] Unger's every attempt to see the Soviet system in a positive light was being ruined by what he saw and heard there.

Unger's negative impressions were reinforced by the musical dogma of the day. Here, too, he was unsettled by the way musical history was being recast and revised to ensure that all music performed was deemed sufficiently "revolutionary." True, there were new works – such as Alexander Mosolov's *Iron Foundry* (1927) and Arthur Honegger's *Pacific 231* (1923) – that easily fit the bill, filled as they were with cacophonous sounds befitting of the revolution and modernity. But new music could not alone fill the programs of Soviet orchestras, lest audiences stay away from these novelties.[39] Thus, the music of earlier times was seized upon as "being beyond time and politics" and therefore acceptable. The music of "the last half of the last century or so," however, posed a greater threat, and this "forbidden zone of dangerous or bourgeois music" (including the music of Wagner, Brahms, Mendelssohn, Tchaikovsky, and Chopin) was initially forbidden until popular outcry forced a reconsideration – and a reformulation – by which the composers of the era were recast as revolutionaries. As Unger put it in his Soviet memoir:

> Every epoch had had its open and secret revolutionaries. If this was so, then even the last century, rotten with capitalistic slavery as it was, must have had them ... Why not seek out the revolutionary spirit in the art of the past, in the works of composers – even in their lives? Not a few of these had amazed their contemporaries by introducing new elements into music that were likely to be understood only by a later generation. Were they not all revolutionaries in the true sense, and therefore worthy to be hailed as heroes of the Soviet Union?[40]

Unger was far from pleased by an inventiveness that proved to be an all-too-obvious instance of ideological manipulation. Feeling that "politics had encroached on the domain of art," and that this ran categorically counter to his view that art should be free of such political interference, Unger concluded that he could no longer work in such a climate.[41] He therefore left the Soviet Union after his scheduled six appearances in Leningrad – which included a rare performance of Anton Bruckner's Ninth Symphony – and a further concert in Moscow, convinced that he would not return to the USSR again. Heading away from the Soviet-Finnish border, he felt that he was – in his own words – "a rotten individualist."[42] Unger had decided that the break with the Soviet Union and its regime was to be final.

As once before, however, Unger second-guessed himself and returned to the Soviet Union. His decision to do so was buoyed by a rediscovered optimism for the Soviet Union and its leadership. Unger expressed his "surprise and relief that economic recovery and growing political security ... were having their effect on the country's culture" and that consequently "political tyranny in matters of art was being relaxed."[43] As Unger was seeing first-hand, the second half of the 1920s was an immensely rich period in Soviet culture. Inspired in part by the revolution but also by the foreign artists that brought with them new ideas, Soviet artists sought to capture this enthusiasm, writing original (and often quite adventurous) works that looked expectantly toward a promising future.[44] Unger summarized his views on the period by calling it "the most marvellous period I ever experienced in Russia."[45]

Yet even in this effusive praise, a vein of criticism can be perceived. Unger conceded that this "golden age" of opportunities applied only to "foreign engineers, architects and artists" whose political creed was paid no heed.[46] But Unger remembered all this occurring while Soviet leaders "had purged away nearly everyone who could not prove that his very grandmother had been in the revolutionary movement."[47] Unger therefore identified the fundamental contradiction of the period: that the creative freedoms he witnessed were being achieved against a backdrop of repression and persecution.

Intriguingly, however, Unger – displaying what in hindsight seems a remarkable naivety – would argue that such freedom of artistic expression had stemmed directly from Stalin himself:

> At a time which proved to be decisive in this thriving period, Stalin is said to have made the momentous remark that his favourite opera was Tchaikovsky's "Queen of Spades." The remark was momentous because up to then, as has been said, Tchaikovsky had been regarded as the most bourgeois of composers ... These words were to become a landmark in the Soviet art policy of those days. They sanctioned a state of affairs which ... definitely released the Arts from the political bonds which had hitherto imprisoned them. These words meant, in effect, that all music was open to performance.[48]

Unger's characterization of this period as one of complete artistic freedom is not, of course, accurate; all sorts of limits were placed on the arts, and indeed on life. Even he would encounter interference in the summer of 1928. In that season, Unger returned to the Ukraine to conduct a series of concerts in Kiev and Kharkov. At one of the Kharkov engagements, he was asked to reverse the final two movements of Tchaikovsky's Sixth Symphony (*Pathetique*) so that the concert would not "end with such a destructive and pessimistic slow movement as the lamentable fourth one of this symphony."[49] The conductor, unwilling to rewrite Tchaikovsky's work, settled on a compromise:

> As for Tchaikovsky's "Pathetique" ... it was of course performed in its proper order, but it had changed its place in the programme, and now came at the beginning instead of at the end of the evening: an arrangement which apparently made it ideologically more digestible.[50]

Unger's positive view of Soviet matters in 1928 – the *Pathetique* episode notwithstanding – helped him decide to return to the Soviet Union the following summer. This time, however, his trip took him neither to the cosmopolitan centres of Leningrad or Moscow, nor to western Ukraine, but to the Azerbaijani capital of Baku. In August 1929, Unger conducted a total of ten concerts in the city in just over a fortnight. Unger also took the opportunity to visit Tiflis, Georgia on this trip, from which he came away duly impressed, not by the city but by its people:

> I discovered that Tiflis was the only place in the whole of the Soviet Union where one could look at one's fellow-men without being repelled by what one saw. Here were no grey masses moving dully along grey streets ... Here

> for the first and only time I saw that I was surrounded by other human beings ... Here every face, whether you liked it or not, wore its own personal look; and everyone you met in the street, even the most ragged, appeared to be, if not a personality, at least an individual.[51]

In this part of the Soviet Union, the air, to say nothing of the streets, was filled with a humanity that had seemingly been lost in other parts of the Soviet Union.

It should come as no surprise, then, that Unger expectantly looked forward to the prospect of returning to the Caucasus. In the summer of 1930, he was engaged to conduct ten concerts with the Leningrad Philharmonic in the spa town of Kislovodsk. So pleased had he been with the previous year's trip that he was eager to share this corner of the world with his wife. And so she accompanied him for the first time on a trip to the Soviet Union. But what had been planned as a relaxing working holiday soon became memorable in a very different manner altogether: after the fifth concert, Unger fell terribly ill. A good thing it was, then, that he was accompanied by someone who could take care of him, for he soon discovered that his illness was no ordinary cold but scarlet fever, a disease that had been ravaging Kislovodsk for weeks and that, in this underdeveloped part of the world, bore the distinct possibility of proving fatal. As it was, Unger persevered, not because of the hospital in which he was treated – he would quip that he had found the facility wonderful, "the wonder being in this case that I left it alive" – but because of his wife's care and what he rather boastfully claimed was his strong constitution.[52]

Despite surviving the ordeal, Unger's bout with scarlet fever left him with two serious conditions that would plague him for the balance of his life. First, it seriously weakened his heart, leading to the cardiac problems that would manifest themselves later in his life. Second, it had the almost catastrophic professional effect of causing him partial deafness, a serious liability for a musician. Nevertheless, Unger persevered and continued his work for a further three and a half decades, his hearing compromised but his skill in leading an orchestra more than overcoming any auditory shortcomings.

But in the years that followed, any events of a musical or personal nature would inevitably be overshadowed by politics. In 1929, the stock market – driven by post–First World War optimism and speculation – had crashed, sending shock waves around the world. The steps taken by governments – increasing tariffs and pursuing other protectionist initiatives – had brought on a world-wide depression and signalled the beginning of an era – the Great Depression – in which millions were left deprived of their livelihoods and forced to eke out an existence as best they could.

Germany was perhaps hardest hit by all this, its economy virtually coming to a standstill as international loans were recalled, leaving millions unemployed. Germans' desperation exposed a dangerous current of antisemitism that had always been present but had failed to resonate during sound economic times. The sharp downturn in the circumstances of the average German, however, left them reeling and looking for both answers as well as scapegoats to blame for their problems. The ideals of the Nazi Party, a platform that once had truly appealed to only a fringe of the disenfranchised and desperate, now resonated with a force that must have sent shivers down the spines of all German Jews. In sum, the economic crisis led to a sharp rise in the popularity of the National Socialist (Nazi) Party, a popularity that built on the existing base of antisemitic rhetoric, even as German Jews – now significantly integrated into the fabric of German life – had ascended to the heights of political, cultural, and intellectual leadership of the Weimar Republic. In fact, their continued devotion to the liberal Weimar structures worked against German Jews, who could now be singled out by Nazis and other antisemites as having directed Germans toward their misery.

Heinz Unger had returned to Germany from the Soviet Union a frail man. Seeking to recover from his bout with scarlet fever, he embarked on a cruise to the Azores, Madeira, and the Canary Islands in late summer 1930. On this trip, he once more met the "well-dressed, educated people" of the type he felt he had almost forgotten during his dark years in the Soviet Union. But on what should have been an idyllic cruise, Unger felt ill at ease; years later, he would recall how he felt that things were changing, writing that "these glorious days filled me with an instinctive dread that never again should we enjoy such a happy, light-hearted time together."[53]

Unger could not have been more correct in his assessment of the changes to come. In the September 1930 Reichstag elections, the National Socialist Party led by Adolf Hitler achieved a great upsurge in popularity. Still aboard the cruise, Unger's sense of dread was confirmed when he received word that "the Nazi Party had gained new seats in the Reichstag, bringing the number to over one hundred."[54] Unger's fellow passengers seemed, in his eyes, rather unconcerned by the results, making "their choice between dream and reality."[55] But Unger, already sensitive to the dangers of totalitarianism from his time in the Soviet Union, reflected with sadness upon Germany's new course, recognizing at once that these events signalled a significant change for the worse in his homeland. And yet, in his last three years residing in Germany, his career continued to develop. Often at work at the podium of the Berlin Philharmonic, Unger continued to conduct works both old and new.[56]

Hitler's rise continued unabated during this period of political and economic uncertainty. The tremendous popularity of the Nazi Party and its leader, already displayed in the 1930 elections, would be confirmed in the years that followed. In the presidential elections held on 13 March 1932, the incumbent – and ailing – Great War legend Hindenburg received the greatest number of votes (18,651,497, or 49 per cent of the vote). However, President Hindenburg's failure to secure an absolute majority meant that an electoral run-off was required between himself and the second-place candidate, Hitler, who had secured 11,339,446, or 30 per cent of the total. The run-off occurred on 10 April 1932 and the outcome confirmed Hindenburg's popularity, as he obtained 19,359,983 votes (53 per cent of the total) and the majority that he required to remain in charge. But that election also confirmed the rise of the National Socialists as Germany's second party: Hitler now increased his share to 13,418,547 votes, or 36.8 per cent of the total. Hitler's popularity signalled the demise of the Weimar Republic, for as the economic situation worsened and Hindenburg proved unable to maintain control of Germany, Hitler would be the man to whom Hindenburg would turn to help restore order. Events in the coming months would show the folly of Hindenburg's belief that he could control Hitler and exploit him for his own – and Germany's – gain. By the beginning of 1933, Hitler had outmanoeuvred the aging Hindenburg, assuming the seat of power on 30 January of that year.[57]

The first month of 1933 marks the commencement of what was supposed to be Hitler's thousand-year Reich. It also marks the midpoint of Unger's final season with the Berlin Philharmonic, the beginning of his last year residing in the country of his birth, and a most ironic twist of musical fate: on the first day of 1933, the German Jewish musician would conduct the Berlin Philharmonic in a New Year's Day concert of arias by Hitler's favourite composer, Richard Wagner, sung by another Jewish musician, the bass Wilhelm Guttmann.[58]

Indeed, the 1932–3 season was to be a significant one for the conductor, and if music could reflect reality, then Unger's final Berlin season represented his trajectory up to this point. The season began on 13 October 1932, with Unger leading a rousing all-Mahler concert consisting of three orchestral songs and Mahler's final completed symphonic statement, his Ninth Symphony.[59] Half a year on – on 2 March 1933 – Unger conducted his farewell concert with the Berlin Philharmonic. On this occasion, three works were performed. The middle work on the program was Weber's *Konzertstück* no. 1. Bracketing this composition were two works that now seem so reflective of the times: the concert began with what must have been one of the last pre-war German performances of the Austrian Jewish composer Arnold Schoenberg's *Pelleas und Mélisande* and ended with two pieces by Richard Strauss – *Burleske* and *Till Eulenspiegels lustige Streiche* – a composer who would be intimately linked with the Nazi regime. Moreover, the programming of *Till Eulenspiegels* – a work wherein an impish character mocks the pretensions of those around him and thereby erodes their authority – takes on an extra meaning in light of contemporary events.

And so ended Unger's time in Germany. With the rising Nazi influence on the country, and with the coming apocalypse written in very clear language for all to see, Unger gathered his family and left Germany, the country in which he had been born and raised, the country that he had served, respected, and loved. And the country that betrayed him and all those like him. The future for Unger lay not in Germany, but in the Soviet Union, England, Spain, Canada, and beyond.

*Chapter Two*

# European Exodus: USSR, England, Spain, and the World (1933–1954)

On 30 January 1933, German president Paul von Hindenburg appointed Adolf Hitler chancellor of Germany. Heinz Unger, still months away from his final pre-war German concert but displaying a prescient awareness of the act's significance, began to consider quitting his native land. His hollow optimism aside – as he would quip, "political developments in my home country unexpectedly provided me with considerable spare time in 1933" – Unger would soon be left homeless and without direction.[1]

Invited in 1933 to conduct a series of summer concerts in Moscow, Leningrad, Kiev, and Baku, he therefore returned to the USSR, but only after considering the offer carefully and deciding that it provided him the "splendid opportunity of surveying artistic conditions in Soviet Russia as a whole, and of learning something of what had been accomplished there during the two years which had passed since I had last seen it."[2] What Unger failed to note was that this invitation also meant an opportunity to work after being exiled from Berlin and the Philharmonic.

Unger's return to the USSR came in the wake of the 1932 party resolution "On the Reconstruction of Literary and Artistic Organizations." The resolution had aimed to curb the excesses of the Russian Association of Proletarian Musicians (or RAPM), which since the late 1920s had attempted to "consolidate its position as the leader of the cultural revolution in music" and create a new proletarian music directed by the common man.[3] Unger's reappearance in the Soviet Union – a "Russia [that] had become ... a very remote place" in the three years since his last visit – came during a brief period in which a new level of artistic freedom had been achieved.[4] Unger would go on to describe this two-month tour as "the most agreeable surprise in every respect which I experienced in all the years of my work in that country." It was a positive episode that erased, at least for the moment, many of the setbacks and disappointments he had experienced in his earlier travels to the Soviet Union.[5]

At the end of this tour, Unger was offered not one but three permanent positions simultaneously: as music director of the State Opera in Tiflis; as conductor of the Radio Orchestra in Kiev; and as conductor of the newly founded Leningrad Radio Orchestra.[6] Had these offers come in one of his many periods of disillusionment with the Soviet Union or at a time when he could have returned to Germany, perhaps Unger would have refused them outright. Coming as they did when he was no longer able to work in Germany and in the wake of a highly satisfactory trip to the Soviet Union, he decided that here were opportunities surely deserving consideration. And so after careful deliberation, he decided on the position with the Leningrad Radio Orchestra – "the least interesting of the posts offered." As he would write in his memoir, "the international situation being what it then was, it seemed to me better to be as near a western frontier as possible, so that in the case of any emergency it would be easier for me to rejoin my family, who had just made their home in England."[7] Unger was ultimately pleased with his decision. Not only was he given the opportunity of overseeing the growth of a new orchestra, he was also conscripted into working with a number of other local organizations, including the Leningrad State Choir, the Opera-Studio section of the Leningrad Conservatory, and the Leningrad Philharmonic.[8] In sum, the variety of work that Unger undertook soon washed away any lack of enthusiasm he had initially felt for the position.

Ironically, the one area in which he was underworked at the beginning of his tenure in Leningrad was with the Radio Orchestra itself. The reason for this rather surreal turn of events stemmed from a characteristic example of bureaucratic disorder in which the orchestra was created before any consideration had been given to where it might perform. And because his "old friends of the Leningrad Philharmonic Orchestra ... were doing all they could to prevent certain halls being at the disposal of the Radio Direction for public performances," Unger was forced to wait a year and a half to conduct the Leningrad Radio Orchestra in its first public concert.[9]

The hurdles the conductor faced in trying to develop the orchestra did not, however, prevent him from filling his schedule with wide-ranging and meaningful work. Indeed, his time in Leningrad proved a fertile artistic period:

> At that time I was conducting on average about ten times a month in the different Leningrad institutions, and whatever the difficulties to be overcome, was not the mere fact of these ten nights a thing to rejoice at? Whatever the stupidity and the prejudice which I might have to fight, every time I lifted my baton I was nearer to fulfilment. To have arrived at last to conducting for

> the masses almost everything, from Bach's "Matthew Passion" to Beethoven's "Ninth Symphony," from Mozart to Mahler, from Berlioz to Strauss, and from Scriabin to Delius was something of a triumph; and at last I had achieved the state of mind in which I could hope to make my work a lasting success.[10]

Yet Unger's happiness did not last long. In 1936, the artistic climate in the Soviet Union darkened after Stalin attended a performance of Dmitri Shostakovich's opera *Lady Macbeth of Mtsensk*, a work that had received its triumphant premiere in Leningrad on 22 January 1934.[11] Scandalized by the theatrical goings on (including an on-stage violation of the heroine and her ultimate demise as she throws herself into a river) and the music written to express these events, Stalin walked out of the performance. Shortly thereafter an article appeared in *Pravda* that not only signalled the end of the opera's run and resulted in a harrowing period of terror for the composer, but also brought into question what kind of music best reflected Soviet ideology.[12] The answer, it turned out, was music written in an idiom that could be grasped easily by Soviet concertgoers. Unger neatly summarized the new dictates as a "war against modernity."[13]

But this war was not waged on the artistic level alone. The war against "modernity" in music (it really was, more precisely, a campaign against modernism) was only a part of a general campaign of Stalinist repression following the 1 December 1934 assassination of Leningrad Communist Party leader Sergei Kirov. Kirov's murder launched a chain of events that would result in a series of purges that ravaged Soviet society and brought with it terror and paranoia, culminating in a state philosophy of Soviet nationalism that was both aggressive and xenophobic in nature.[14]

Unger had already encountered such a climate once before in Nazi Germany and his memoirs point out the similarities he saw in these ideologically opposed yet equally repressive, and dangerous, regimes:

> At first one heard phrases which reminded one of the Germany of 1933 ... Whereas the Nazis had turned such slogans as these upon people who had been their fellow-citizens, the Soviets used them against the thousands of foreign experts from all over the world, who were now working in their country. Years ago they had travelled miles to seek them out. Glowing promises had been made to induce engineers, artists, architects, etc., to help to build up a new civilisation and a new culture for Russia. These times were now over.[15]

Unger knew well where the rhetoric and the resulting prohibitions of the time would lead. Having seen what had become of his German homeland, he was highly sensitive to pronouncements of excessive nationalist pride and also well aware of the infringements on his freedom, on both the artistic and personal level, that he had already faced and would continue to face were he to remain in the Soviet Union.

And so, his patience at its end, Unger had transformed into a ticking bomb by 1937, ready to go off at the slightest affront. The inevitable explosion came one day as he entered the hall of the Leningrad Radio building in which he had worked for years and where, despite their familiarity, the guards continued to insist upon seeing his credentials daily, a protocol that left Unger feeling "increasingly humiliated" and a "human being no longer."[16] On a day otherwise like any other, Unger rejected this choreographed ritual, entering into a physical confrontation with a guard "as if he were the personification of all the stupidity against which I had striven for thirteen years."[17]

Unger's outburst signalled the end of his relationship with the Leningrad Radio Orchestra and the Soviet Union. Near the end of April 1937, the conductor was still carrying a contract for a series of twenty summer concerts in Moscow, Baku, Kislovodsk, and Sochi. But he had seen enough and decided that he did not wish to remain in the Soviet Union.[18] Reunited with his family in England a few weeks later, he found himself relieved "that the Soviets had refused [him] a visa to return to their country."[19] Whatever initial zeal he had borne for the adventure and whatever joy he may have experienced, the years of surreal oversights and of absurd, politically motivated prohibitions at the hands of the Soviet government and cultural institutions were over. A chapter in Unger's life, at once rewarding and frustrating, had come to an end.

But what was he to do? Exiled from his native Germany in 1933 and barred now from the Soviet Union as well, Unger now settled with his family in London. In a setting free of the totalitarian strains of Germany and the Soviet Union, Unger once again got down to the business of rebuilding his career in a new country.

Unger's first engagements in England proved to be the first tentative steps in a successful relationship with British concertgoers that would last until his move to Canada following the Second World War. While his first appearance on English soil had been with the London Philharmonic Orchestra in 1934, Unger conducted his first concert with the Leeds-based Northern Philharmonic Orchestra on 21 November 1936 in an evening of standard symphonic fare that included Mozart's Symphony no. 35 (*Haffner*), Edouard Lalo's *Symphonie Espagnole* for Violin and Orchestra, the Polka and Fugue from Jaromir Weinberger's opera *Schwanda the Bagpiper*, and Tchaikovsky's Fourth Symphony.[20] Unger's debut with the Northern Philharmonic put him in elite company;

in that same season, the balance of the orchestra's Saturday concerts were conducted by notable British conductors John Barbirolli (1899–1970), Sir Hamilton Harty (1879–1941), and Malcolm Sargent (1895–1967).[21] And then, fresh from his debut with the Toronto Symphony Orchestra, Unger returned to England to conduct a second Northern Philharmonic Orchestra concert in January 1938, "renew[ing] the excellent impression made on his previous visit early last season" in a concert that included Schubert's Overture in the Italian Style in C major (D. 591), Liszt's Piano Concerto no. 1, Beethoven's Symphony no. 7, the Mahler-completed Entr'acte from Weber's opera *Die Drei Pintos*, and Bizet's *L'Arlésienne Suite No. 2*.[22] Unger would parlay these early successes with the Northern Philharmonic Orchestra into not only steady employment as a guest conductor but a leading position as well, becoming the orchestra's principal conductor and music director in 1940.

As the war years loomed, however, much work remained to be done before Unger would become a recognized figure in Britain. His efforts to secure his position as part of the British cultural landscape were aided by the publication of his memoir of life in Soviet Russia (*Hammer, Sickle and Baton*), a book that underlined – and perhaps even played up – the liberal views that Unger shared with the English. Unger's mockery of the Soviet system was well received in late-1930s Britain, the *Daily Telegraph* calling it "an excellent book, well-written, humorous and truthful, [that] cannot fail to delight all who have not sold their birthright for a mess of ideology."[23] The views expressed in the book signalled Unger's status as a proponent of liberal values and an outspoken enemy of authoritarian regimes such as those that had arisen in Nazi Germany and Stalinist Russia. That these regimes would go on to formalize their relationship in the Nazi-Soviet non-aggression pact that very year – a step that positioned the USSR as a potential adversary in the coming apocalypse – underscored the warnings that Unger provided in the work. Unger's opinions and world view, evolving out of his experience in the Soviet Union – and despite stemming not from a Briton but from a German Jew settled only by circumstance in England – led him to an apolitical liberalism that overlapped with the British cultural climate of the time. This quickly transformed into a mutual understanding that would solidify Unger's place in the British artistic world of the period.

Just as significantly for the conductor, *Hammer, Sickle and Baton* resonated in corners of the Jewish world. In June 1939, the *Jüdische Welt-Rundschau* covered the book, the reviewer's interest piqued by the travails of the Jewish conductor in his contest with Soviet authorities over musical ideology.[24] More interesting still, the reviewer placed particular emphasis on Unger's battles on behalf of Gustav Mahler's music, ending the piece by asking Unger to present Mahler's music in Palestine: "Es wäre gut, Unger in Palestina, dessen Menschen ganz geöffnet fur die seeliche Welt Mahlers sind, Mahler spielen zu hören." (It would be good to hear Unger in Palestine, whose people are completely open to Mahler's soulful world.)[25] Even so early on, Unger's battles for the acceptance of Mahler were already beginning to be understood as part of a broader Jewish cultural self-understanding.

In the fall of 1939, Europe descended into war for the second time in the century. While Hitler's aggressive foreign policy had been ominously pointing toward war for years, the apocalypse was triggered by Nazi Germany's invasion of Poland in September. For the next six years, Europe and the rest of the world would be plunged into a conflict that would destroy millions of lives.

Having been a target of Nazi discrimination since 1933, Unger knew the extent of Hitler's ambitions and the profound dangers they posed. And though he seldom spoke out about the period, it is clear from his later writings that he considered Nazi Germany an abomination thrust upon the real Germany. In 1965, as he was being honoured with the West German Commander's Cross just weeks before his death, he spoke of "those years of darkness," a period during which

> those who held power temporarily in the country which I, like generations of my ancestors, had considered home, deprived me on account of my race of the right to continue in my profession, and when I, to escape worse, left the country with my family. Every tie broke in those evil years.[26]

Unger clearly saw this period as an aberration, a break from both the pre- and post-war Germanies that was entirely devoid of legitimacy.

Unger quickly mobilized to confront this existential threat, his sympathies – as well as his identity – clearly in evidence as he tried to help those most acutely affected by the war. It should therefore come as no great surprise that his actions brought him close to the Jewish community of both his former *heimat* and his newly adopted home. In the winter of 1940, Unger formed the West London Amateur Orchestra, a group of some forty musicians that was, according to the *Synagogue Review*, "composed of a majority of German Jewish Kulturbund workers, talented refugee amateurs and a few English music students."[27] The orchestra held its rehearsals every Tuesday in Stern Hall at the West London Synagogue – Britain's oldest Reform congregation – and staged at least three concerts in its short-lived existence. The first of these concerts, held on 28 January 1940, was a concert in which more than six pounds was raised for the West London Hospitality Committee for Refugee Children.[28] The community-based orchestra's premiere outing included a standard set of works from the Central European musical canon: Schubert's Overture in the Italian Style (D. 591), two Mozart serenades, Beethoven's First Symphony, and Brahms's *Zigeuner Lieder*, the latter sung – according to the *Synagogue Review* – "with consummate artistry" by Erika Storm, a singer who devoted herself between 1941 and 1943 to performing Lieder recitals that almost exclusively featured the songs of Jewish composers "forbidden" (*Entartete*) in Nazi Europe: Gustav Mahler, Ernst Krenek, Wilhelm Grosz, Arnold Schoenberg, and Egon Wellesz.[29] And while Unger's West London Amateur Orchestra was clearly an amateur ensemble – its inexperience revealed by its "wrong entries" – any signs of the orchestra's rawness could be overlooked by concertgoers who recognized that the group did not aim at being a first-class ensemble but, rather, served as a community association meant to relieve the strains and stresses of Central European émigrés adjusting to a new life in England and provide relief to refugees and those impacted by the war.[30]

To that end, the West London Amateur Orchestra continued its policy of staging concerts for charity, with two further engagements held on 4 February and 27 July 1940. The particular associations that would benefit from these events were determined by Unger's sympathies. The orchestra's February concert in support of the Finland Fund closely resembled the program from the first concert but added what must have been, considering the circumstances, a stirring rendition of Sibelius's *Finlandia* in defiance of the Soviet attack on Finland on 30 November 1939.[31] As had been the case with the charitable organization in whose name the first concert had been held, Unger chose to contribute to a cause that he felt dearly toward – the plight of the small nation of Finland against the Soviet juggernaut that he had come to detest after his many years of working in the repressive Soviet system. The proceeds from the July concert (a total of ten pounds, six shillings) went to the Selbsthilfe Deutscher Ausgewanderter – an initiative undertaken by German immigrants to help fellow exiles in need.[32]

Along with these concerts for charity, Unger attempted to alleviate the general suffering of others by providing succour with his music-making. During the war years, he carried on an intensive schedule, travelling in his adopted country of England to conduct concerts with an array of the finest orchestras in the land. His primary orchestral instrument, however, remained the Northern Philharmonic. As noted, Unger had by 1940 become the orchestra's principal conductor and music director. Alongside concerts in the orchestra's home city of Leeds, the conductor regularly led the orchestra around England, holding concerts in large and small cities alike by way of a government grant – administered

2.1 On 4 February 1940, Heinz Unger led the West London Amateur Orchestra in a concert in support of a Finland facing Soviet aggression. Source: Library and Archives Canada, MUS 56, Box 2, File 74.

through the Council for the Encouragement of Music and the Arts – that encouraged orchestras to stage concerts in communities that would have otherwise been left wanting in terms of culture.[33]

The 1942 season was the year during which Unger solidified his reputation as a major artist in Britain. On the local scene, he had galvanized the Northern Philharmonic Orchestra into a solid musical troupe able to express its creativity under his leadership. Speaking about one of the many successful concerts of that season – in this case a rendition of Tchaikovsky's Fourth Symphony in a concert that also included Mendelssohn's Overture to *A Midsummer Night's Dream* and Clifford Curzon performing Mozart's Piano Concerto no. 27 in B flat – the *Yorkshire Post* would report:

> Mr. Heinz Unger's conducting from memory added visible proof of a mastery of this work that was amply demonstrated in sound by the clarity of his orchestral effects. There were moments of abandon which, with an

> orchestra less sure of its ground, would have verged on recklessness. That they were carried off with such élan is of itself a tribute to the quality of Mr. Unger's direction.[34]

By the end of 1942, Unger had become a source of community pride as a conductor taking concertgoers away from the hardship and misery of war. Moreover, his travels with the Northern Philharmonic during the war years helped fulfil the cultural needs of a nation defiantly opposing Nazi terror and aggression.

Unger did not, however, limit his conducting activities to leading the Northern Philharmonic. His growing reputation also meant that ever greater opportunities would come his way. By the middle of the war, he was a frequent guest conductor with storied orchestras such as the London Philharmonic Orchestra (LPO).[35] In the winter of 1943–4, he led the LPO on a twenty-concert cross-country tour (with nine concerts held in January alone) that included stops in Coventry, Nottingham, Leicester, and London.[36]

These visits to large and small cities were greeted enthusiastically by both press and audience alike.[37] Even the orchestra was impressed by Unger's musical instincts, a point not missed by English critics like the *Musical Courier*'s Hugh Liversidge:

> After one of Dr. Unger's rehearsals the orchestra applauded him enthusiastically. Such demonstrations are generally reserved for the actual concert and are then made by the audience and not by the orchestra.[38]

Unger's rising star in the British musical firmament also allowed him to devote ever greater energy to Gustav Mahler's music. In his first English appearance in 1934, he had performed Mahler's First Symphony with the London Philharmonic. By 1941, a full two decades before the Mahler revival of the 1960s, Unger was advocating Mahler's cause by including the composer's works in his programs. But the conductor introduced audiences to Mahler's art cautiously: instead of overwhelming them with the composer's longer symphonic works in their entirety, he would include shorter pieces or selected movements from the less familiar symphonies. On 21 February 1942, at a Northern Philharmonic concert that was particularly well attended because of the presence of renowned British pianist Dame Myra Hess (1890–1965), Unger closed the program with the Andante from Mahler's Second Symphony.[39] In September of that same year, he conducted the London Symphony Orchestra in a concert that included Mahler's highly emotive orchestral song cycle *Songs of a Wayfarer*.[40] That performance of Mahler's music was greeted with great acclaim to a packed house, the *Cavalcade*'s music critic brazenly asking for "more Mahler, please."[41]

As the war neared its end, Unger's persistent advocacy for Mahler and his own increased repute allowed him the opportunity to present Mahler's more profound works in their entirety. But these concerts were not all greeted with the same enthusiasm. In March 1945, Unger led the Liverpool Philharmonic Orchestra in a performance of Gustav Mahler's *Das Lied von der Erde* that met with mixed reviews. While the *Yorkshire Post*'s music critic was moved by "this most intricate, but lastingly beautiful, score" by "the most authoritative representative Mahler has in this country,"[42] segments of the Liverpool media were less impressed by the performance, some lamenting that "it was lacking of the sunset radiance, the subtlety of atmospheric detail, the depths of passionate and poetic emotion which saturate Mahler's score."[43]

But already by 1944 Unger was working toward what would be one of the highlights of his career: the British premiere of Mahler's Fifth Symphony. He approached this goal in the same manner that he had used to pique British interest in Mahler earlier in the war, by introducing portions of the work in his concerts. By the 1944–5 season, he was regularly programming the Adagietto from Mahler's Fifth Symphony into his concerts with the LPO.[44] In total, Unger performed the Adagietto at least nine times before premiering the entire work, underlining the conductor's belief that this movement was the emotional centrepiece of the entire symphony.

On 21 October 1945, Unger premiered the symphony to a thrilled though disappointingly small audience (the hall was only "three-fourths full") and a curious critical community at London's Stoll Theatre.[45] Though earning an ovation, the work's success was limited by the audience's unfamiliarity and an orchestra straining under the burden of a complex work still new to them.[46] Despite the enthusiasm that his performances of Mahler's music generated in quarters of the audience and among members of the critical community, English audiences and music critics were clearly not yet fully attuned to Mahler's idiom.[47]

By the end of the war, Unger had established himself as a leading musician in England. Alongside his place at the head of the Northern Philharmonic, he was a regular guest with the London Philharmonic Orchestra as well as a highly respected guest with other orchestras such as the London Symphony Orchestra, the City of Birmingham Orchestra, and the Liverpool Philharmonic. His campaign for the acceptance of Gustav Mahler's music, while not entirely successful, also played a part in redefining mid-century British musical tastes. Indeed, Unger's status in Britain had developed to such an extent that he was contracted by Decca to record a program of mainstream classical works – Mendelssohn's *Ruy Blas* Overture and Beethoven's Third Symphony (*Eroica*). At the close of the war, Unger was safely ensconced within Britain's cultural community, one reviewer of the Decca recording going so far as to call him "a first-class conductor whom we can ill afford to lose."[48]

Yet even with this critical acclaim and popular success Unger remained troubled. After living through a harrowing decade during which Europe had been ravaged by the Second World War, and with the continent now poised to become a new battleground for the ideological struggle between capitalism and communism, Unger began to weigh the possibility that Europe might never again be able to offer him or his family peace and stability.

But Unger, not yet able to rupture the ties that bound him to the continent that had always been his home, remained in Europe for a further two years. Those years were filled with concerts given not in his adopted home of England but in Spain, a country whose people had impressed him with their warmth and enthusiasm for his art before the war. In the mid-1930s, Unger had held concerts in both Valencia and Madrid, leading the Valencia premiere of Beethoven's Ninth Symphony in 1935 and returning to the Spanish capital the following year, making a favourable impression before cutting short his tour due to the outbreak of the Spanish Civil War in 1936.[49]

In late fall 1945, Unger travelled again to Spain, this time to a country still attempting to recover from the three-year-long civil war that had set Spain alight and in which thousands had died for their political beliefs. Spain was a country in need of unification, uplifting, and amity. It was also a country in desperate need of legitimacy due in no small part to its wartime complicity with Nazi Germany.[50] Shortly after the end of the Second World War, in the fall of 1945, Unger accepted an official invitation from the Spanish government – vetted and approved by the British government – to travel there as a "cultural ambassador."[51]

Unger's acceptance of this role might be seen as a compromise and a collaboration with a dictatorial regime that brings into question both his morality and his adherence to liberal values. Such a position, however, discounts a number of important factors that informed Unger's decision. First, the invitation had met with the approval of the British government, a government that, much like the rest of the Western world, was coming to see Franco and his regime as a significant member of an anti-Communist block necessary to prevent the expansion of the Soviet Union's influence into Western Europe.[52] Second, following a concerted campaign waged by Franco's government in the final years of the war and in the immediate post-war period to highlight its positive actions in respect to Jewish support and aid during the Holocaust, significant elements in the Jewish world had come to endorse such a view; even the president of the British chapter of the World Jewish Congress, Rabbi Maurice Perlzweig, was convinced of Spain's positive wartime record of providing assistance to Jews.[53] And while Spanish overtures toward the soon-to-be-created State of Israel would be rebuffed in the late 1940s and early 1950s – a function of Israel's attempt to position itself "morally" in the first years of its existence – even within Israel a significant segment of the Sephardic Jewish population was also calling for closer ties with Spain.[54] All things considered, then, it should come as no surprise that Unger would not have seen his work in Spain as an "immoral" act.

Given Unger's status as a cultural ambassador, it is surprising to see that his first concerts were held not in Madrid but in Valencia with the recently established Orquesta Municipal de Valencia.[55] Whatever the case, Unger's first Valencian concerts during the winter of 1945 did not disappoint; the audience and the press – guided perhaps by the official nature of the visit – greeted him rapturously, proclaiming him "one of the greatest conductors ... that we have had the occasion of hearing in our lifetime."[56] These concerts included not only the standard symphonic works by Beethoven and Brahms but also the Spanish premieres of English "novelties" such as Arthur Benjamin's "Overture for an Italian Comedy" and Gordon Jacob's "Passacaglia."[57] Valencian audiences responded enthusiastically to Unger's readings of music both familiar and unfamiliar and sent him off with "an impassioned, affectionate and extended farewell ovation."[58]

Following his concerts in Valencia, Unger proceeded to the Spanish capital, where he appeared in a further sequence of concerts with the Orquesta Sinfónica de Madrid and the Orquesta Nacional de España.[59] As in Valencia, the Madrilenian press and audiences expressed a great enthusiasm for Unger. For example, Antonio Fernandez-Cid (1916–1995) – one of Spain's foremost music critics and, not coincidentally, critic for *Arriba*, the official Francoist organ of the period – opined that "the Madrilenian public has known to lend the most enthusiastic and unconditional reception to Heinz Unger, the admirable conductor, whose concerts will remain for a long time as a model difficult to copy."[60] Whatever political capital Spain may have gained by his visit, it also seems clear that Unger's work was greatly appreciated by Spaniards hungry for cultural nourishment.

But by no means was the admiration one-sided. Upon his return to England, Unger would note that the Orquesta Nacional was a "conductor's dream" and that the musical success of Spanish musicians lay in the fact that they "play with their hearts as well as their heads."[61] More interesting still was Unger's naive verdict that the Spanish government pursued a policy of non-interference in cultural matters. As Hugh Liversidge put it after his discussion with the conductor,

> Dr. Unger said that in Spain music is still the free expression of the individual and not a vehicle for propaganda. He was both surprised and pleased to hear the Secretary of the "Comisaria de la Musica" in a Falangist Government suggest a performance of a work by the Soviet composer Shostakovitch [*sic*].[62]

Admittedly, Unger was a musician who saw the world through that lens first and foremost, allowing him to easily overlook the transgression of rights and freedoms that would continue to take place to varying degrees under Franco's watch until 1975. Moreover, the conductor's need for acclamation left him unprepared to question the warm reception that the Spanish government, press, and audiences accorded him. Nonetheless, his familiarity with the Nazi and Soviet regimes – wherein culture was regularly and heavy-handedly conscripted into ideological battle – makes him a sufficiently reliable source to judge how different Franco's regime was to those of Nazi Germany and the Soviet Union. Franco's post-war Spain – while being, in the words of Spanish historian Antonio Cazorla-Sanchez, a "brutal police state" – was a very different creature from the fascist and communist dictatorships further north and east.[63]

In late March 1946, Unger returned to Spain. On this trip, as on the previous journey, the musician conducted in both Valencia and Madrid, his hosts allowing him to adventurously program Gustav Mahler's First Symphony in concerts with both the Orquesta Nacional and Orquesta Municipal de Valencia held during the late winter and spring.[64]

Encouraged by his early post-war triumphs and his experiences on both trips, Unger would make Spain an annual pilgrimage for the remainder of his life. In the first year after the Second World War, he spent two entire months (essentially the entirety of the 1946 fall season) in Spain, conducting orchestral concerts in Valencia, Madrid, and Barcelona.[65] Appearing still as a cultural ambassador, those concerts on occasion included British works such as Ernest John Moeran's (1894–1950) *Overture for a Masque.*[66] As Unger solidified his reputation in Spain, however, the number of British works in his concerts steadily fell, replaced by works that lay within his standard repertoire – the Central European musical canon.[67] Indeed, Unger was becoming a sufficiently vital character in the Spanish cultural world that even more honorary engagements began to come his way. On 14 November 1946, for example, he appeared at the Universidad Literaria de Valencia for a gala celebration of the fourth centennial of one of Spain's most important cultural figures, the author

FOTO
Martin Vidal

2.2 (opposite) and 2.3 (above) In the post-war period, Heinz Unger was a regular visitor to Spain and particularly to Valencia. Here he is pictured at work and in repose during the 1950s. Source: Library and Archives Canada, MUS 56, Box 11.

Miguel de Cervantes, leading the local orchestra in a stirring rendition of Richard Strauss's *Don Quijote.*[68]

After a brief return to England in the winter of 1946, during which he appeared as guest conductor with the City of Birmingham Orchestra,[69] Unger would again travel to Spain in the spring of 1947, appearing once more with Spain's leading orchestras.[70] These events were interrupted only by rare concert appearances in his home country of England, such as on 21 October 1947, when Unger appeared at the helm of the Philharmonia Orchestra in a concert that featured Clara Haskil performing Mozart's Piano Concerto in A major (K. 488) and ended with Tchaikovsky's Fifth Symphony.[71]

Such concerts, however, came ever less frequently as the war years faded into the past. Instead, Unger mined the prospects provided by his numerous visits to Spain. Building upon his increased exposure in the Spanish-speaking world, Unger seized the opportunity to conduct concerts in Latin America. After a further winter and spring season in the sunny climes of Spain – where his new-found fame allowed him to program Mahler's Fourth Symphony in Valencia and Madrid – Unger departed for Cuba. In the summer of 1948, he appeared with the Orquesta Filarmónica de la Habana on four occasions, leading that ensemble to considerable acclaim in a series of concerts showcasing the works of Berlioz, Beethoven, Smetana, Richard Strauss, Rossini, Chopin, and Tchaikovsky.[72] On the back of these concerts, Unger continued to develop his reputation in Latin America. In November 1948, Unger travelled to Mexico, where he would conduct the Sinfónica Mexicana in a concert that included Brahms's First Piano Concerto and Tchaikovsky's Fifth Symphony.[73]

The next few years proved a busy time in Unger's career. On the one hand, he occupied himself with building his reputation in his new Canadian homeland (as we will see in more detail in chapter 3). At the same time, he spent many felicitous moments in Spain, a site of refuge from the challenges and frustrations that were such a key feature of his first years in Canada. By 1951, Unger was so confident in the Valencian musicians that he felt prepared to program Mahler's more challenging symphonies with the Orquesta Municipal. On 21 February 1951, Unger performed the Spanish premiere of Mahler's Second Symphony (*Resurrection*) at Valencia's Teatro Principal, the event proclaimed, in the words of music critic E.L. Chavarri, "a complete success."[74] The Spanish press reflected the crowd's enthusiasm at the concert:

> Last night, Valencia ... sensitive to the tremendous effort of the distinguished maestro Unger, the Municipal Orchestra, Coral Polifónico and the Orfeón de Godella, the contralto and soprano soloist ... that is to say, corresponding to the admirable task of an ensemble of two hundred and fifty executants ... greeted the eminent conductor with unanimous applause and a clear display of affection and admiration.[75]

The performance was highly praised and the work was greeted with such enthusiasm that the concert was repeated four days later. In another new setting, Unger was proselytizing for Mahler's music and gaining the composer new supporters.

After a further spring and summer spent trying to consolidate his Canadian reputation, Unger once again returned to the Spanish-speaking world. This time, his travels took him to Buenos Aires, that most European of Latin American cities. The Argentine capital in the early 1950s was a city in which Spanish mixed with German, and where even English was heard in the streets, the *Buenos Aires Herald* serving as

2.4 Heinz Unger conducted the Spanish premiere of Gustav Mahler's Second Symphony (*Resurrection*) in front a sold-out house in Valencia on 21 February 1951. Source: Library and Archives Canada, MUS 56, Box 11.

the English-speaking community's mouthpiece. So, too, was the Buenos Aires of the 1950s experiencing its golden age, a time when Evita Peron wielded tremendous influence and buttressed the presidency of her general-husband Juan Peron. This was the classic Argentina, where *gauchos* in traditional dress rubbed shoulders with European émigrés in sharp tailored suits, and where a native culture intermingled with the high culture imported by immigrants from both before the war and after.

Arriving in such a cultural mecca, Unger could not help but be fascinated by the city and its cosmopolitan culture. Imbued with the optimism of the era, he seized his opportunity firmly with both hands, leading the Orchestra of the State Radio in a series of concerts held at the Faculty of Law and Social Sciences of the Universidad de Buenos Aires in August and September 1951 that mixed the familiar with the unknown, blending the classics of the European canon with twentieth-century works by Spanish and Argentinian composers. On 23 August, Unger crafted a program consisting of Berlioz's *Le Carnaval Romain* Overture, Brahms's *St. Anthony Variations*, Spanish composer Joaquin Turina's *Fantastic Dances*, and Tchaikovsky's Fifth Symphony; his 30 August program was more adventurous still, including Mozart's Symphony no. 41 (*Jupiter*), Argentinian composer Alberto Ginastera's (1916–1983) "Canto de Estío" and "Marcha fúnebre" from *Palambo,* the local composer Troiani-Bandini's *Cueca,* and Berlioz's *Symphonie fantastique.* His final program in the arranged sequence of concerts – held on 6 September – not only included Mendelssohn's Fourth Symphony (*Italian*) and the *Creole Overture* by the Argentinian composer Ernesto Drangosch (1882–1925) but also Mahler's First Symphony.[76] By the end of these of concerts, the music critic for Argentina's leading newspaper, *La Nación,* would write that Unger "favourably impressed, as much with his authority and mastery of technical matters as with the expressivity and animation that he communicated in his interpretations."[77] Unger's success in these concerts resulted in the rapid addition of two further concerts on 20 and 22 September 1951 to deal with the crowds clamouring to see the conductor. In these two concerts, Unger returned to Beethoven, leading the composer's *Egmont* Overture and his Fifth and Sixth Symphonies.[78] Unger's success in Argentina was even reported back in his adopted Canadian homeland, the *Globe and Mail* noting that "the queue for tickets for the final Beethoven concert extended five blocks."[79]

Three years later, Unger was asked to return to Buenos Aires. This time, the Orchestra of the State Radio ensured that its *Porteño* audience would be provided with the opportunity of hearing him conduct. The directors of the orchestra booked Unger in an entire cycle of concerts that would survey the entirety of Beethoven's symphonic oeuvre. These concerts, held weekly between 16 September and 10 October, were almost unanimously praised, Argentinian critics and audiences alike calling attention to the conductor's clarity and direction.[80] So impressed was the orchestra's management that they invited Unger to repeat the entire cycle as well as perform the Ninth Symphony two more times, with as many as twenty-five thousand people having attended Unger's 1954 Beethoven cycle.[81]

Despite his successes there, Unger never returned to Argentina. This was not a result of any antipathy but merely a consequence of the fact that Unger's career would take a different direction in the years to come. In the decade following the end of the Second World War, Unger had taken to travelling the world. As time passed, however, health issues began to take a toll on his career and he spent his dwindling strength not on seeing the world but on advancing his career in Canada. His contact with the Spanish world did not end, however. Instead, Spain – and Valencia in particular – became an oasis from the harsh Canadian winters and from the frustrations that he would face in his adopted homeland. But that is to move too far ahead. For the moment, Unger busied himself with expanding his activities in Canada.

*Chapter Three*

# Early Life in Canada and a Return to Germany (1937–1956)

Heinz Unger immigrated to Canada in 1948. But the story of his time in Canada does not begin there, dating back instead to his first North American concert appearance before the Second World War. In the fall of 1937, Unger travelled to New York aboard a Cunard White Star Line vessel, arriving by the end of October. Unger's appearance in the Americas may have simply been an opportunity to leave behind the maelstrom in Europe for a short while and embark on a long sea voyage – something that he enjoyed his entire life. At least for a few fleeting moments, the trip enabled him to unburden himself of the emotional turmoil of the preceding years.

But it is also possible that the trip was more than an isolated foreign engagement. Indeed, given his recent break with the Leningrad Radio Orchestra, it is entirely conceivable that Unger may have been on a reconnaissance tour to determine whether any prospects existed to fill the void resulting from his Soviet debacle, a disastrous episode in the conductor's life that had recently ended in an undignified physical altercation with a guard and the rather predictable cancellation of his contract for the 1938 season.

His bitter disappointments in the Soviet Union fresh in his mind, Unger's early forays into the North American public eye often involved denouncing Soviet political interference in cultural matters. Journalists, for their part, encouraged the musician to recount his time in the USSR, their appetites whetted by stories from a distant and mysterious land. In an interview appearing in the *New York Post* in October 1937, he mocked the Soviet authorities openly:

> The Soviet officials came to me about one of the concerts. They said the slow movement of Tchaikovsky's Sixth Symphony should be altered so as not to end slowly and morbidly. Would I just speed it up a bit? they said.

> I couldn't agree internally. Or there was Mahler's Fourth Symphony! ... They wanted me to have the soloist sing it in a parodistic style![1]

Unger and *Post* reporter Earl Lewis also made light of the reason for his exile from the Soviet Union as well as from his native Germany:

> He has been refused a visa – kicked out. Ironically, the official explanation offered the man who since has become conductor of the British Broadcasting Company Orchestra is that he is a German – "although" he said, spiritedly, "because I am a non-Aryan, I have not been welcome in Germany for years!"[2]

However much Lewis attempted to record Unger's good-natured comments, the journalist effortlessly saw through the forced joviality, describing the conductor as a "solemn, frowning man of forty-two."[3]

Unger did not stay long in New York. Despite publicly praising the United States and its artistic climate in his interview with the *Post* ("The country you have here is so wonderful ... because in it an artist can breathe"[4]) and in a further interview with the *New York Times*,[5] he confessed to his wife that he found American culture not to his liking.

By the beginning of November, Unger had moved on to Canada, where he discussed matters both light and profound with journalists prior to his debut with the Toronto Symphony Orchestra (TSO), an opportunity that, according to his wife, had arisen thanks to their English neighbour and fellow musician Benjamin Dale's friendship with the TSO's music director, Sir Ernest Macmillan (1893–1973).[6] In an interview with the correspondent from the *Globe and Mail*, Unger tried to convey his appreciation for the "American" lifestyle – playing up his love of both movies and jazz music – as well as his respect for the continent's freedom:

> Here in America I love the air I breathe. Everything seems so much more human. The freedom of movement and expression enjoyed by the people of America is new to me.[7]

In the same interview, Unger, still stinging from the shock of dislocation, passed on the opportunity to discuss at length his reasons for leaving Germany, noting instead that "the times speak for themselves."[8]

Despite his best attempts to make light of his circumstances, Unger could not maintain this tenor for long. In an interview conducted by the *Evening Telegram*'s C.B. Pyper just two days later, Unger reflected on the difficult times through which most of Europe was passing while also reiterating his stance on artistic freedom:

> When politics meddles with art, art dies ... In Germany, where the objection is to work by non-Aryans, and in Russia, where it is to work by individualists, the result is the same. Art cannot live.[9]

These interviews were conducted at the Westminster Hotel, where Unger was staying during his brief sojourn in Toronto. His main site of activity was Massey Hall, where he was preparing to lead the TSO – founded in 1922, it is one of Canada's oldest and most distinguished musical ensembles – in Hector Berlioz's *Symphonie fantastique*, a work the group had never performed and that Ernest Macmillan's biographer Ezra Schabas would later describe as an "especially demanding work even for a virtuoso orchestra."[10] Unger, who liked to talk to the orchestra members about matters beyond the score itself, insisted on three rehearsals to familiarize the orchestra with the score and acquaint them with his vision of this intensely emotional piece.[11]

Unger's Toronto debut took place on 9 November 1937, the event divided between Unger, who conducted the aforementioned Berlioz work as well as Mozart's Symphony no. 35 (*Haffner*) that opened the evening, and Ernest Macmillan, the orchestra's regular conductor, who assumed directorial duties in a performance of Tchaikovsky's Violin Concerto with Mishel Piastro as soloist.[12] And while the TSO's long-time conductor was much loved by Toronto concertgoers, the next day's newspapers were filled instead with talk of Unger's conducting, calling attention to his role in stimulating the TSO to what they called "new heights":

> It was the guest conductor – Heinz Unger – that did it, of course. For if there was any doubt about that when the Mozart was finished, the playing of the Berlioz settled it forever. For if the Mozart was revelation of an orchestra's latent power the Berlioz was positively revolutionary. The number might be called a test piece for orchestral virtuosity. It is full of effects – tone painting and rhythm torturing – fire and fury – charm and ugliness – the bitter and the sweet – the nightmare and the religious rhapsody. Small wonder that the audience cheered Mr. Unger and couldn't recall him often enough at the end of the concert ... It must be said that it was a new-born orchestra, and guest conductor Heinz Unger was the miracle worker. When comes their [*sic*] such another?[13]

Unger then returned to Europe on the Cunard White Star Line's RMS *Queen Mary* on 15 December 1937.[14]

In light of the positive reception of Unger's performance with the TSO, it should come as little surprise that he was invited back for a second concert. On 11 November 1938, he once again set sail for the

Americas, this time bypassing the United States and steaming directly to Canada for his eagerly anticipated return.[15] And if Unger had enjoyed a positive critical assessment the previous year, the response to his second concert with the TSO – consisting of Brahms's Fourth Symphony, Liszt's *Les Préludes*, Wagner's "Siegfried's Rhine Journey" from *Götterdämmerung*, and Tchaikovsky's *Romeo and Juliet* – bordered on the rapturous. Hector Charlesworth, writing in *Saturday Night*, noted that Unger "more than justified the golden opinions he won a year ago," while the *Globe and Mail*'s reviewer also praised Unger, commenting on how "our distinguished European visitor made the orchestra sing divinely in his profoundly beautiful and moving reading of [Brahms's] great work, especially in the heavenly andante."[16] Augustus Bridle was also lavish in his praise, noting how "in a complete programme conducted by a master of spiritual interpretation [concertgoers] were conscious of a high intellect working to bring out subtleties of mood and meaning through a marvellously expressive sincerity of technique in conducting, and a highly responsive orchestra."[17] In sum, the majority of Toronto's musical press, along with many concertgoers, were impressed a second time by Unger's mastery of the orchestra.

Despite these successes, Unger would not return to Canada for another ten years. A major reason for this was surely the commencement of the Second World War, which made sea travel particularly dangerous. But there was also Sir Ernest MacMillan, the long-serving director of the TSO who had been responsible for Unger's initial invitation to the city. As conductor of the TSO since 1931 (he would continue in this role until 1956), principal of the Toronto Conservatory of Music between 1926 and 1942, and an accomplished composer in his own right, Macmillan had become one of the most important figures in the development of Canadian music in the first half of the twentieth century. Unger's successes in 1937 and 1938 could not have but caused MacMillan consternation, especially during a period when he had begun to question whether he even wanted to remain at the TSO's helm.[18] Riddled with anxiety and indecision, Macmillan may have been relieved that circumstances had arisen that would prevent Unger from returning to Canada for many years.[19]

~

By 1945, the world was tired of war and conflict. The Second World War was the bloody bookend of a thirty-year period during which Europe had been wracked by war, conflict, and instability. Tens of millions had died in two apocalyptic wars and millions more had been driven from their homes and forced to begin life anew. The first half of the twentieth century – with very short respites – had been an era of unremitting pain, desperation, and death for too much of Europe and the rest of the world.

Unger had not been free of this anguish. He had served in the First World War, experienced the years of hyper-inflation, the Depression, and growing antisemitism in Germany, run afoul of Soviet authorities, and lived through the Blitz on London. Even at the end of the war, Unger saw no future in Europe, a continent that he feared would soon be overrun by Stalin – an eventuality that would have plunged Europe into the grasp of yet another totalitarian and repressive dictatorship that he knew all too well from his time in the Soviet Union. Exhausted by the constant worry of further conflict and dislocation and eager to start anew, he decided that his and his family's future lay not in the cauldron that was Europe but in the New World.

And so Unger began to plan his exodus to the Americas. The question of exactly where, though, had yet to be decided. During the 1930s, Los Angeles had become a significant Jewish émigré outpost as more and more Jewish artists, exiled from Central Europe on account of an increasingly intolerant and antisemitic climate, moved to the United States in search of safety and a new life free from persecution.[20] Despite the attraction that this tight-knit community might have held, Unger – perhaps out of a fear of too much competition for too few posts – decided against settling there. Nor did New York appeal to him any more than it had before the war; a year spent amidst what Leopold Stokowski called "disturbed and crowded conditions" failed to convince Unger that his future lay in the United States.[21] Years later, his wife would recount how both she and her husband "hated it" and that they had become "so English-orientated that we didn't like that atmosphere."[22]

Unger therefore continued on to Toronto, a Commonwealth city that must have seemed comfortably familiar to someone who had called England home for over a decade. Nor can one discount Unger's memories of his artistic triumphs in his two pre-war concerts with the Toronto Symphony Orchestra. Indeed, these memories may have led him to think that he would quickly rebuild his career, or perhaps even assume directorship of the TSO. In fact, his return to Canada was initially a favourable one; in his first post-war Canadian appearance, on 15 July 1948, Unger led the Toronto Philharmonic Orchestra – an orchestra composed of many of the musicians from the TSO that played through the spring and summer months – in a Proms concert at Toronto's Varsity Arena, the concert being a collection of mostly lighter fare in the Proms tradition.[23] Reviews of the concert were favourable, if not as rapturous as those of the conductor's appearances with the TSO a decade earlier.[24]

However, despite his pre-war Toronto successes and his arrangement of a concert upon his move to Canada, Unger failed to effectively establish himself within the Toronto musical scene as well as in the city's wider social milieu during the first years of his life in Canada. This is due to a number of personal reasons that also have implications for the wider social understanding of Unger as a German Jew trying to integrate into his new Canadian context.

These personal reasons are the easiest to lay out, if not to understand. Engaged to conduct four Proms concerts, Unger fell ill and was unable to complete his contract. More difficult to understand and especially problematic was an ever more discernible tendency toward self-pity and defensive posturing that seems to have emerged during the war years – a tendency that Helmut Kallman, the former director of the Music Division of Library and Archives Canada, and even Unger's own daughter, confessed often aroused the ire of potential friends and supporters. This nexus of negative emotion and an increasingly acute narcissism and sense of entitlement – whether or not a function of a decade and a half of persecution, displacement, loss, and death – translated into a clumsy negotiation of the realities of his new adopted Canadian homeland.

But a further problem lies at the heart of Unger's inability to integrate himself into Toronto society: his relationship with Ernest Macmillan. As suggested earlier, in attempting to secure for himself employment in the wake of his dismissal from the position of music director of the Leningrad Radio Orchestra, Unger had approached his pre-war concerts with the Toronto Symphony Orchestra not as one-off engagements but as an opportunity to impress upon the orchestra's directors that he should be considered as MacMillan's successor. This proved a serious misstep. In his authoritative biography of Macmillan, Ezra Schabas briefly recounts the situation:

> When Unger had been in Toronto in 1938, he and some avid supporters had heard some rumours that MacMillan might be leaving the TSO (it was the time of MacMillan's despondency with the orchestra) and had made some inappropriate and tasteless proposals to the TSO that he be MacMillan's successor. MacMillan had gotten wind of this, and from then on was wary of Unger. Unger had written to MacMillan from England during the war to try and clear himself, but MacMillan's responses had been guardedly cool. He rarely judged people unkindly, but thought Unger a flagrant opportunist and, worse, an ingrate. He had, after all, given Unger his first chance in North America.[25]

Macmillan never forgave Unger for this perceived duplicity, leaving him marginalized even before his post-war move. Indeed, he would become a key feature of the conductor's frustrations in the first decade of his life in Canada.

Yet the matter is not as clear as it seems, for Unger had – as noted by Schabas – not only written to Macmillan during the war but would later also note that the enmity between them had arisen not on account of a "flagrant opportunism" but as a result of a miscommunication on the part of influential agent Arthur Judson (1881–1975). Judson, manager of the New York Philharmonic from 1922 to 1956 and agent to many leading classical musicians of the day (including John Barbirolli, Van Cliburn, Clifford Curzon, Benjamino Gigli, Zino Francescatti, Jascha Heifetz, Yehudi Menuhin, Eugene Ormandy, Fritz Reiner, Rudolph Serkin, and Helen Traubel), had suggested to Unger that Macmillan would be leaving Toronto.[26] As Unger warned his friend Harry Newstone many years later,

> Careful with Judson! After my first great success in Toronto in 1937 I saw him in New York and he told me that MacMillan was leaving Toronto (!), which was incorrect, but caused me to make a lot of wrong moves (the damage of which lasted for many years).[27]

Thus, while Unger may have exhibited poor judgement in not directly approaching MacMillan to determine the veracity of Judson's account, it would be unfair to cast Unger solely as a "flagrant opportunist."

More importantly, Macmillan also seems to have come to terms with Unger over time, their relationship eventually losing its antagonistic edge. After all, when Unger established the York Concert Society some years later, MacMillan and his wife served as patrons. In due course, the two men developed a peaceful coexistence, never becoming friends perhaps, but learning to deal with one another's idiosyncrasies.

But the initial bitterness between Unger and MacMillan – albeit dimming over time – suggests a larger reason for why Unger may have struggled to establish himself in Toronto in his early years there. Heinz Unger was a German Jew – a German *and* a Jew – and his arrival in Canada in the immediate post-war years may have directly contributed to an isolation from both the Canadian Jewish communities for being German and from a more general Canadian context wherein being neither a Jew nor a German were particularly coveted.

In regards to the Canadian Jewish community, we must remember that Unger stemmed from a Central European milieu in which the contours of identity and the integrationist impulses established among German Jewry during the course of the nineteenth century were at odds with the very different understandings of Jewishness and communal self-sufficiency possessed by the vast majority of Canadian Jews who had arrived from Eastern Europe.[28] And while post-war Canadian Jews, in the words of Franklin Bialystock, "were bent on advancing from the fringes of the Canadian mosaic into the mainstream of Canadian society," the contours of the community would have still been informed by its antecedents.[29] In other words, the preconditions for what Canadian historian Harold Troper has called the "whitening of Euro-ethnics" could not have entirely discarded the self-understandings accrued over the course of centuries in the old country as well as in the half-century of life in Eastern European Jews' adopted new homeland of Canada.[30] In welcoming far fewer German Jews in the post-war period than its neighbour to the south, Canada remained a space wherein the views of Eastern European Jewry continued to dominate the contours of a national Jewish ethos in the process of negotiating its own space in the evolving Canadian mosaic. In this context, the German Jewish immigrants of the immediate post-war period were as islands in a stream, having come from a different milieu than the majority of Canada's Jews who, while undergoing a process of liberalization after the war and breaking many of the bonds of a formerly parochial community, continued to view themselves – and just as importantly be viewed by other Canadians – as part of a distinct community within Canada, however much they may have "gained the acceptance of most Canadians."[31]

Moreover, we cannot discount the rather obvious fact that German Jews bore distinctly German features. For, while German Jews remained Jews, the manner in which they expressed themselves often contained elements – everything from their more formal mode of dress to their preferences in music, literature, and the arts, and their decidedly German-inflected speech – that served as painful reminders for Canadian Jews who had very recently seen, in their eyes, the vilest manifestation of the very culture that German Jews carried within them.[32] In short, how could Canadian Jews stomach the cultural expressions of German Jews who seemed to them eerily similar to the very people who had perpetrated the Holocaust?

All this being said, Unger was not entirely ostracized by the Toronto Jewish community. While his bifurcated German Jewish identity may have contributed to some of the difficulties he faced in his first years in Canada, he still advanced his career in ways that brought him pride and helped forge a dialogue with segments of Toronto's Jewish community. Thus, though Unger made but one appearance with a professional ensemble in his first years in Canada – the aforementioned Proms concert with the Toronto Philharmonic in 1948 – he still managed to make a series of new acquaintances that would propel his Canadian career in the years to come. Indeed, the main thrust of his career in these years lay with the Forest Hill Village Community Orchestra. His work with this ensemble culminated on 12 November 1951 at the Forest Hill Community Centre in an adventurous program consisting of Ernest Bloch's Concerto Grosso for Strings and Piano Obbligato, a commissioned work composed by Leo Smith entitled *Occasion for Strings,* and Tchaikovsky's *Serenade for Strings.*

The 1951 concert with the Forest Hill Village Community Orchestra, an ensemble that mixed professional and amateur musicians, was the peak of an effort to build up an orchestra that during the summer of 1950 had been described by even the decidedly provincial *Forest Hill Journal* as being in a "very rudimentary state."[33] It was also a consequence of Unger managing to embed himself within a Forest Hill that was quickly becoming home to a number of upwardly mobile Canadian Jews who were all too happy to welcome into their midst a Jewish conductor of reputation to serve as a community flag-bearer and reflect their civic pride.[34] Unger, once a regular conductor with the Berlin Philharmonic, was now the leader of a community orchestra in Toronto. But his move also marked the beginnings of a relationship – albeit a tenuous and selective one – with Canada's Jewish community.

Unger embraced his modest position with an enthusiasm that suggests not only a sincere desire to succeed in his new Canadian home but also his deep respect for a role wherein he could help cultivate the development of Canadians, Jewish or otherwise, according to a *Bildung* sensibility that was intricately interwoven into his German Jewish world view.[35] As early as July 1950, he had held a public rehearsal with his then six-month-old Forest Hill Orchestra, partly in an attempt to display their achievements and presumably also in the hopes of creating more interest in his enterprise and luring further support. At the rehearsal, held at Forest Hill's Central School, Unger's ensemble of some seventy musicians, "although the drum and percussion instruments were entirely missing and some other sections too thinly populated," impressed the small audience assembled to hear the new group's first endeavour. Just as significantly, Unger outlined the orchestra's main goals, stressing the ensemble's pedagogical purpose in a speech that remained always true to the elements of *Bildung* with which he himself – as a German Jew – had been inculcated and had increasingly come to appreciate in his new home in a faraway land.[36]

By the fall of 1950, Unger had expanded his pedagogical goals, creating the Forest Hill Training School devoted to ensemble playing. By 14 November, the group was prepared to make its official public debut in a concert that included Weber's *Oberon* Overture, Schubert's Eighth

Symphony (*Unfinished*), Beethoven's *Egmont* Overture, and Mozart's Serenade no. 12 for eight wind instruments. Assembled to hear the performance were many critics, the *Toronto Star's* Hugh Thomson, for example, noting that

> Many in music circles eyed [Unger] askance when he announced he would produce a fine orchestra in Forest Hill, playing the best music at short notice. Some 50 professionals and amateur instrumentalists flocked to his colour, and in their limited time, worked hard learning at the feet of this maestro how the classics should be interpreted.
>
> The hall was packed to hear the finished product. Some must have come with doubt in their minds, but by the time Dr. Unger had led his orchestra through classical staples (not the lighter chestnuts) everybody was applauding, with shouts of "Bravo!" heard through each ovation.[37]

Unger surely delighted in reading such a positive review of the orchestra's work, but his own talk, delivered at the concert's intermission, made explicit that this small group's performance represented more than a musical achievement:

> Tonight you are here because we wish to show you the progress made since last spring. I remarked in June that I was a firm believer in the possibilities of cultivating music on a "civic" basis, the word "civic" implying collaboration of instruments as members of a community and irrespective of the fact of their being either professionals or amateurs. Our ensemble here is a living example of what can be done on this basis.[38]

Unger was speaking to the gathered audience about his adherence to civic values not only because these words could serve as a means of generating further support for his project but because they were a reflection of the pedagogical and artistic principles in which he believed.

Unger's success with the Forest Hill Orchestra paid dividends immediately. Shortly after the concert, the Toronto Department of Parks and Recreation swooped in to secure the conductor's services, contracting him to improve the level of playing of the Beaches Orchestra, based out of the Malvern Collegiate Community Centre. In his first years in Canada, Unger was quickly earning a living if not a reputation as an amateur orchestra builder.

Moving from the summit of European musical culture with the Berlin Philharmonic to creating a community orchestra in a sleepy Toronto suburb seems a tremendous fall from grace. Indeed, it would be naive to think that Unger was neither aware of this reversal in his professional fortunes nor disappointed by his inability to establish himself in the mainstream of Toronto musical life immediately upon his arrival in Canada. As Paul Helmer would put it, Unger's "Canadian experiences are understandably marked with bitterness": he was, after all, one of the many émigrés who had "reached significant high points in their lives before they arrived and could not find opportunities to match their experience and expectations."[39] That said, Unger had been granted the opportunity to teach a new generation of musicians the values that he had learnt and he was free to conduct his rehearsals at the leisurely pace he preferred.

And then in 1951 and 1952, Unger's hard work and patience began to pay off. As he continued to serve community orchestras in the Greater Toronto Area, increased opportunities began to come his way, beginning with two Proms concerts in late spring 1951.[40] He also continued in his progress with the City Parks Department–sponsored Community Centre Orchestra, holding an all-Mozart concert – consisting of *Les petit riens* Ballet Suite (K. 299b), Violin Concerto no. 4 in D major (K. 218), Serenade no. 12 for Winds (K. 388), and the *Haffner Serenade*, no. 7 (K. 250) – on 29 January 1952 at the Oakwood Collegiate Auditorium that was praised for blurring the distinction between an amateur and a professional ensemble.[41] Unger also marked his debut nationwide broadcast with the Canadian Broadcasting Corporation (CBC) on the *CBC Wednesday Night* program on 23 January 1952, leading Arnold Schoenberg's *Transfigured Night.*[42]

The months that followed saw the conductor's domestic standing continue to grow. February brought Unger the opportunity to conduct at the thirty-third-annual Toronto Police Association concert, an enormous Pops event held at the Maple Leaf Gardens and attended by more than seven thousand people.[43] March, meanwhile, signalled his debut with the London Chamber Orchestra (based in London, Ontario) in a program that included a selection of works by Mozart, Handel, and César Franck.[44] Unger's initial success with the London Chamber Orchestra in turn led to further engagements with that ensemble – for example, leading the opening concerts of the Bach Festival in April 1952, at which he conducted a variety of works, including *Brandenburg Concertos* nos. 3 (BWV 1048) and 4 (BWV 1049), the Harpsichord Concerto in F minor (BWV 1056), and Bach's Cantata BWV 51 ("Jauchzet Gott in allen Landen").[45]

In two consecutive weeks in October 1952, Unger led the recently constituted CBC Symphony Orchestra in concerts for CBC Radio. The first, broadcast on 6 October, was a performance of the second movement of Mahler's Third Symphony, followed by Richard Strauss' *Till Eulenspiegels lustige Streiche* and Mahler's *Songs of a Wayfarer.* The second, broadcast on 13 October, began with Vincenzo Tommasini's 1916 *Good Humoured*

3.1 Extreme measures were sometimes taken to advertise York Concert Society events in Toronto. Here, a placard reminds motorists about an upcoming YCS concert (circa April 1958). Source: Library and Archives Canada, MUS 56, Box 14.

*Ladies* Suite (*Le donne de buon umore*) and continued with Brahms's Fourth Symphony.[46] On 20 October 1952, Unger was once again at the helm of the London Chamber Orchestra, conducting a mixed program of works by Handel, Schubert, and Beethoven, while two days later the conductor returned to lead his Community Centre Orchestra in a program devoted to works by Schubert and Beethoven.[47]

Following this very busy October in Canada, Unger again returned to Europe, conducting extensively in Spain and also in England. But while his international career comprised a prominent part of his professional life during the 1950s, it was in Canada where the most significant developments would arise. In his new home, Unger was steadily building a network of supporters that recognized his talent and wished him to have an orchestra upon which he could impress his artistic vision. In 1953, a group of music lovers and supporters came together to help organize the York Concert Society (YCS). The YCS was to be a new type of ensemble on the Canadian landscape. Culled from the ranks of the TSO and holding most of its concerts at Toronto's Eaton Auditorium, the YCS was created by a group of enthusiasts referred to as "admirers of Unger's art" with the purpose of allowing him the opportunity to conduct in Canada on a regular basis. The ensemble's activities were limited to four concerts held every spring to supplement the regular TSO events.

The creation of the YCS was greeted with much enthusiasm in the Toronto area, the press lauding the society's goal of "adding to Toronto's musical life during the gap between the Toronto Symphony Orchestra Subscription Series and the Promenade Symphony concerts."[48] The newly formed society also proved popular because it aimed to provide greater opportunities for home-grown talent. In its twelve-year existence, the YCS encouraged notable Canadian soloists such as Lois Marshall, Maureen Forrester, Greta Kraus, and Lubka Kolessa. But while the twin aims of cultivating Canadian talent and providing Toronto musicians with additional work did nothing to hurt the YCS from a purely financial standpoint, these were by no means cynical goals aimed only at furthering Unger's career. It was, rather, an extension of the same philosophy of cultivating learning and culture at a civic level that Unger had already shown in his time with the Forest Hill Orchestra.

The constitution of the YCS as an orchestra that would stage its concert season each spring not only provided local musicians with much-needed work but also afforded Unger the time to continue his regular concert tours of Europe and beyond during each winter season. Simultaneously, the YCS, because of its affiliation with the TSO and the CBC Symphony Orchestra, allowed the conductor to remain close to the nerve centre of the Toronto and Canadian music scenes an affiliation that would pay dividends in the coming years and lead to numerous engagements.

The organization of the YCS also allowed Unger one further liberty: despite its musicians being culled from the Toronto Symphony Orchestra, the York Concert Society was a fully autonomous entity, allowing the music director to freely choose its programs. And while early music played a major part in the programming due to the logistics of the smallish orchestra and the preferences of its soloists, Unger was also able to expand the orchestra on select occasions to program the music of those composers closest to his heart. Not surprisingly, Gustav Mahler's music would figure prominently in YCS program, the ensemble becoming the vehicle for the Canadian premiere of many of the composer's works.

In its first season, the York Concert Society concerts displayed a variety that was to remain a fixture going forward. The orchestra's premiere, held on 23 April 1953, was devoted to Beethoven's works, with the Ukrainian-born Lubka Kolessa as soloist in Piano Concerto no. 3 in a program shaerd with the Coriolan Overture and Symphony no. 7.[49] The second concert, held on 6 May, was an all-Bach program (Overture in G minor, Harpsichord Concerto in F minor, Air from Suite in D, *Brandenburg Concerto* no. 3, and the Suite in B minor) with Greta Kraus as soloist.[50] The third concert – held on 14 May – was organized thematically as a "Serenade Programme," including Mozart's *Haffner Serenade*, Berlioz's Serenade from *Harold in Italy*, Hugo Wolf's (orch. Reger) *Italian Serenade*, and Tchaikovsky's *Serenade for Strings*.[51] The final concert of the YCS's inaugural year consisted of a selection of Mozart's works, Schubert's Sixth Symphony and – beginning a tradition of including at least one Mahler work per season – the Adagietto from Mahler's Symphony no. 5 and two orchestral songs from *Des Knaben Wunderhorn* sung by the Canadian soprano (and, in her later singing years, mezzo-soprano) Lois Marshall.[52]

This first season was highly praised in the media. After the society's debut concert, John Kraglund of the *Globe and Mail*, known for his extreme reserve – biographers Alan H. Cowle and Kenneth Winters would note that "a measured enthusiasm from Kraglund was the equivalent of panegyric from a colleague" – declared the performance

> a triumph for Heinz Unger and the small orchestra's outstanding musicians ... Dr. Unger's conducting has an individual angularity that is rare in Toronto. It is an almost violent quality, but one obviously suited to the music and there was no feeling of wasted effort. For the audience there is an impelling magnetism that translates the music into an easily understood idiom of deceiving simplicity ... There was about the whole concert a vibrant vitality that fully justified the rounds of applause that kept calling the dynamic conductor back to the podium.[53]

Edward Wodson mirrored Kraglund's enthusiasm, praising the thirty-seven-member chamber orchestra and Unger's leadership.[54] The second all-Bach YCS concert met with the same positive response. On this occasion, the unusually small ensemble of some twenty players performed admirably, Kraglund echoing his enthusiasm for the first program by calling the performance "close to perfection."[55] In short order, the York Concert Society became a significant part of the Canadian musical landscape, its immediate success marking it as the central pillar of Unger's post-war Canadian resurrection.

But the mid-1950s represent a fertile period in Unger's artistic life, one marked by more than the establishment of the York Concert Society. After a very successful string of concerts in Argentina, Unger returned to Canada to conduct two concerts with the CBC Symphony Orchestra, both of which would air on the CBC Radio network. The first program, broadcast on 6 December 1954, consisted of Wagner's *Siegfried Idyll*, and Beethoven's Symphony no. 6 (*Pastorale*), while the second, on 13 December, contained Gustav Mahler's Fourth Symphony.[56] The program was a major milestone for the conductor and the CBC alike, representing as it did Unger's first leadership of a complete Mahler symphony in Canada as well as the first time that a Mahler symphony was broadcast in its entirety on the CBC. And while the reading failed to totally impress – Ezra Schabas and Stuart Nall calling it "a sympathetic if not exquisite performance of this beautifully irridescent [*sic*], almost naïve work" in their co-authored review in the *Musical Courier* – the very fact that the CBC had called upon Unger to lead this radio premiere must have brought the conductor great pride as well as kindled a hope that this would be but the first of many Mahler performances.[57]

Indeed, as the leading musical authority on Mahler resident in Canada, Heinz Unger would soon begin to receive the accolades and opportunities that such a reputation merited. Reflecting a rising interest in Mahler's music, the CBC began to devote ever more airtime to the composer's works. On 30 March 1955, *CBC Wednesday Night* devoted an entire program – what Ezra Schabas would call "one of the most interesting two and one half hours our CBC Wednesday nights have had in quite a while" – to a biography of the composer, with all the musical excerpts (the *Songs of a Wayfarer* and *Kindertotenlieder*, the first movement of Symphony no. 3, and the first two movements of *The Song of the Earth*) conducted by Unger.[58]

However important was his work expanding the understanding of Mahler's singular voice and his devotion to the still-young York Concert Society, one of the highlights of this period in Unger's career was his return to the TSO podium after years of yeoman's work.[59] In 1955, Unger was officially invited back to conduct the Toronto Symphony Orchestra, a full seventeen years since his last appearance with the orchestra and seven years since he first began living in Toronto.

After his years away from one of Canada's pre-eminent orchestras, Unger knew full well the significance of his return to the TSO; he therefore set to work immediately, his attention squarely placed on the three concerts scheduled for early November 1955. On 4 November, Unger led the TSO in a Pops concert that mixed lighter fare with the Adagietto from Mahler's Fifth Symphony.[60] On 8 and 9 November, he returned

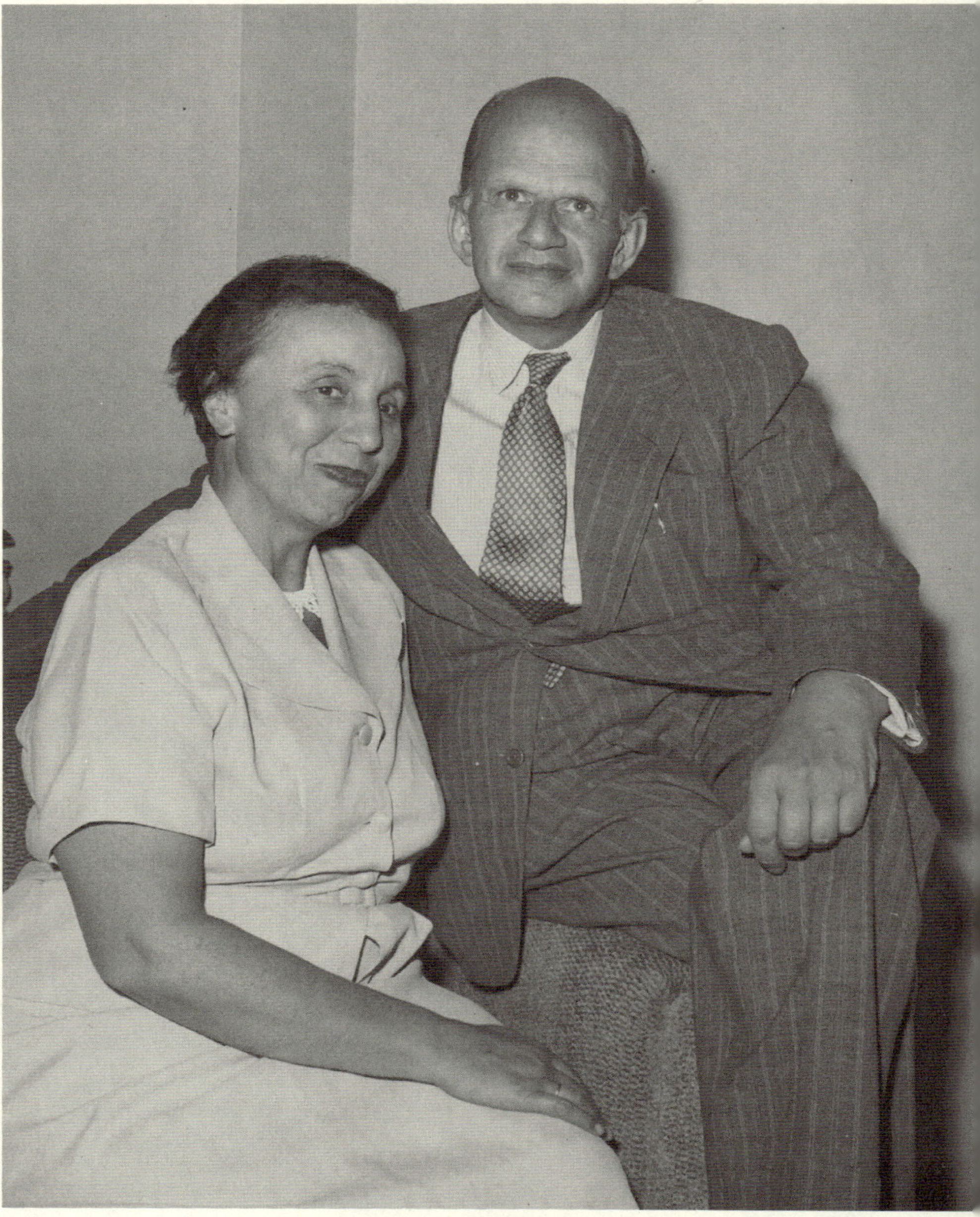

3.2 Heinz Unger conducted in Vancouver over three consecutive summers in the mid-1950s. Unger is here pictured on one of these trips, accompanied by his wife Hella. Source: Library and Archives Canada, MUS 56, Box 14.

to the helm of the TSO, this time leading the orchestra in weightier symphonic fare: Berlioz's *Le Carnaval Romain* Overture, the Adagietto from Mahler's Fifth Symphony, Beethoven's Symphony no. 8, and Tchaikovsky's Fifth Symphony.[61] The critical response to these performances was just as positive as it had been almost two full decades earlier, John Kraglund writing that

> Last week's pair of concerts marked the first time Heinz Unger has appeared with the TSO on the Subscription Series since he took up residence in Toronto. The results were little short of spectacular for all concerned. Clarity was the outstanding characteristic, not only in the softest pianissimos of the introduction to the Berlioz "Roman Carnival" Overture, but also in the towering climaxes of Tchaikovsky's Symphony no. 5.[62]

Music critics Hugh Thompson and George Kidd also praised the concerts, regaling the conductor and orchestra with similar plaudits.[63]

Unger conducted two more performances in Canada in December 1955, both with the CBC Symphony Orchestra and both broadcast on the CBC network. The conductor chose interesting repertoire that was underappreciated in Canada but spoke to both his continuing attachment to the Central European canon of art music as well as his embrace of new music discovered during his travels. The second concert, held on 26 December 1955, consisted of Anton Bruckner's Symphony no. 4 (*Romantic*), a work Unger had not conducted in years but was a mainstay of the symphonic repertoire. The performance the week prior, however, was more unusual; as well as the beautiful *Les Nuits d'Été* of Hector Berlioz (with Elizabeth Benson-Guy as vocal soloist), he programmed the Argentinean composer Alberto Ginastera's *Variaciones Concertantes,* a piece premiered as recently as 1954 by the Russian conductor Igor Markevitch (1912–1983) that Unger had surely unearthed on his recent travels to Argentina and now saw fit to premiere for Canadian audiences.[64]

In the New Year, Unger commenced a lengthy concert tour of Europe, beginning in Scandinavia with a series of dates that underlined his ongoing devotion to Mahler. Following a concert with the Filharmonisk Selskaps Orchester (State Radio Orchestra) of Oslo at which he programmed Mahler's Fourth Symphony as the centrepiece,[65] he then continued his work in Norway by leading the Oslo Philharmonic Society in a performance of Mahler's Second Symphony.[66]

Despite this Mahler-filled sweep through Scandinavia, Unger's 1956 winter tour of Europe was dominated by a pair of concerts that would prove to be among the most significant events of his life. On this trip, the German Jewish musician returned to the city of his birth to conduct the Berlin Philharmonic for the first time since his 1933 exodus.

The invitation had come from none other than Wilhelm Furtwängler (1886–1954), the Philharmonic's music director, who before his death the previous year had asked Unger to return to his native city to conduct the orchestra with which he had experienced his first artistic triumphs.

Heinz Unger made his return to Berlin in a pair of concerts performed on 22 and 23 February 1956. That the program chosen for these concerts did not include any Mahler would have surely disappointed a musician whose career had been so fundamentally built on his reputation as a Mahler specialist since his professional debut at the beginning of the 1920s. But this honour was reserved instead for Klaus Pringsheim (1883–1972), a musician who had an even closer connection to Mahler. Having studied with the composer, Pringsheim played a vital role in the Mahler renaissance in the 1920s as well as in the decades that followed his move to Japan, and he had also returned to conduct the Berlin Philharmonic as a guest in the 1956 concert season.[67] But Unger's program was still filled with extra-musical meaning, beginning with the overture to Smetana's *The Bartered Bride*, continuing with arias from *The Bartered Bride* and Dvořak's *Rusalka*, moving on to the tone poem "Die Moldau" ("Vltava") from *Má Vlast* (*My Homeland*), and ending with Dvořak's Symphony no. 9 (*From the New World*).[68]

The program thus ended with two works that spoke to Unger's sense of having returned to his own homeland from the New World: perhaps he had not had the opportunity to again conduct Mahler in his native city, but he did fulfil "his secret yearning to do a native's return and conduct, after an absence of 22 years from his home city, the Berlin orchestra again."[69] Unger's return to his childhood city was bittersweet, to be sure – as he put it, "it was a little saddening" to find it "reduced to rubble."[70] That sadness, however, could not detract from his joy at discovering that he had not been forgotten. Indeed, he "was delighted and touched to discover standing audiences for both Berlin Philharmonic concerts he conducted, and 'overwhelming ovations.' "[71] Heinz Unger's return to Berlin would mark the beginning of a new and vital period for the musician – a veritable resurrection and a newfound understanding of his German Jewish identity that played a key role in the rest of his life.

*Chapter Four*

# A Jewish Renaissance: Life in Canada, the Israel Philharmonic, and the Mahler Centenary (1956–1960)

The late 1950s were an important time in Heinz Unger's life. Professionally, the conductor's career was looking ever more promising, both domestically and abroad. Within Canada, his York Concert Society was gaining a greater reputation as a quality ensemble. On the international stage, too, Unger's concert tours were filled with artistic successes.

But whatever happiness these developments brought him, critical reflection also loomed on the personal horizon. Unger's 1956 return to Berlin had exposed an essential part of his identity that he had kept locked away for decades. Returning to Germany, he reconnected with his German Jewish identity – an element that seems to have played but a peripheral role in his life for a number of years – in a profound manner. The depth of his German Jewish rebirth was made manifest in the rapidly approaching 1960 centenary of Gustav Mahler's birth, the composer that represented a nexus of German Jewish identity for Unger and whom the conductor viewed as a kindred emotional spirit. Moreover, significant events in the Jewish world during this period – including an evolving engagement with the Holocaust – were to inform Unger's understanding of himself and his place in that milieu. Over the course of this chapter and the next, we will witness the many manifestations of this German Jewish renaissance as they appear and reappear during a period of intense professional and personal activity. In sum, we will see how Unger's final decade of life was marked by a return to an interest in Jewish issues, at least as they impacted on his thoughts and feelings, if not religiosity.

~

Heinz Unger's concertizing in 1956 and in the years that followed reveals how important Mahler's music – and other core works of the

Central European art music canon – was to the German Jewish conductor. Indeed, as his reputation grew and the corresponding professional opportunities expanded, he would begin to regularly program this music to such an extent that it is tempting to consider this a "performative rite" – a ritualized expression of his German Jewish identity during a period of intense personal reflection brought upon by personal, professional, and external factors. Illustrating this is the fact that, beginning in 1956, a major Mahler work was performed by Unger in virtually every year until his death a decade on. Other works that shared a Mahleresque sensibility – in some way imbued with a glorification of nature – also made up an important element of his performative expression of a German Jewish identity heavily informed by Romanticism.[1]

The fourth and final concert of the 1956 York Concert Society season, held on 15 May, is a case in point. On this occasion, Unger selected a program that began with Weber's *Oberon* Overture and ended with a traversal of Schubert's Symphony no. 9 (*The Great*). In between, the YCS presented less familiar fare, beginning with the Canadian premiere of Riccardo Zandonai's (1883–1944) arrangement of *Sogno*, by the Italian composer Alfredo Catalani (1854–1893).[2] The concert's essence, however, lay in Mahler's *Songs of a Wayfarer* and the Entr'acte music from Weber's *The Three Pintos* (completed by Mahler and first performed in Leipzig on 20 January 1888).[3] John Kraglund, aware of the importance that Mahler held for Unger, devoted the majority of his review to the Mahler works on the program, praising in particular the *Wayfarer* songs as understood and executed by both the conductor and his guest soloist, the highly acclaimed, Montreal-born contralto Maureen Forrester:

> Gustav Mahler's music is high on Dr. Unger's list of favourites. His enthusiasm seems to have been passed on to Miss Forrester and the orchestra, for one of the evening's highlights was the interpretation of Mahler's Songs of a Wayfarer. Both words and music of this youthful cycle of unhappy love songs were written by the composer, resulting in a well-balanced whole.
>
> The balance was retained in performance. Miss Forrester skilfully evoked contrasts, even in the almost unalloyed despair of the opening song, resorting frequently to the depths of heavy, contralto coloration. Then with the same ease the soloist's voice soared lightly and grace-fully to soprano heights in the gayer, swinging rhythm of the second piece.
>
> Dr. Unger displayed his ability to get the most out of singer and orchestra in the third song. The instrumental music served by turns as contrast, support and exaggeration for the singer, now voicing dramatic protest, then depressed acceptance. And as a fitting climax there was the more harmonious mood of a resigned peace, verging on joy, in the expressive finale.[4]

Unger's ability to capture and convey the varied moods of a work so unknown to Canadian audiences speaks to his – and Forrester's – skill at conveying the meaning of a music so dear and important to him.[5] Unger's performance of Mahler's music was a personal revel meant to be shared with his audience.

In the summer of 1957, Unger continued to program the work of composers that expressed his musical-cultural creed. Among them was even Richard Strauss (1864–1949), a composer who had been closely linked to the Nazi regime – as president of the Nazi musical institution Reichsmusikkammer starting in 1933, composer of the anthem for the 1936 Summer Olympics held in Berlin, and an active musical presence in Germany during the entirety of the Second World War.[6] But even so vile a connection could not erase Strauss's importance as a representative of the German culture that was a significant element of Unger's identity. On 31 July 1957, Unger led the CBC Orchestra in a concert at the Stratford Festival of Music that opened with Canadian composer Violet Archer's *Fanfare and Passacaglia*, continued on to Strauss's *Four Last Songs* (with Lois Marshall as soloist) and *Death and Transfiguration*, and closed with Danish composer Carl Nielson's unfamiliar Symphony no. 4 (*The Inextinguishable*).[7] The final work, seldom heard in Canada, had, according to John Kraglund, been heard once before in a broadcast performance by Unger and his forces.[8] Nevertheless, Nielsen's work was sufficiently obscure for Kraglund to feel he needed to help the audience understand how the symphony expressed the composer's belief that

> music was a fundamental part of life and that it was to be found even in the inanimate objects that have a place in life and living. Music was rhythm and tone, to him, and life's basic needs were expressed through movement and sound. In Living Music, his volume of essays, he summed up his feelings in the statement that "Music is life, and, like it, inextinguishable."[9]

Nielsen's vision, so similar to Mahler's own sensibility, helps explain Unger's interest in this particular work and in Nielsen's oeuvre more generally. Unger, like Gustav Mahler and Carl Nielsen, believed that music and nature were connected and suffused with a meaning that transcended humanity's limits.

But most importantly, there remained the matter of Unger's Jewish reawakening and its stimulation of his decades-old dream to conduct in Israel. A brief piece in the *Jerusalem Post* in the summer of 1959 reporting that he had become "the first Canadian conductor to be awarded the Mahler Medal" may have led him to believe that his dream was imminent.[10] Just as promising was the fact that the brief article noted Bruno Walter's

4.1 Members of the Israel Philharmonic Orchestra in Ohel Shem Hall, Tel Aviv, 1954. Source: PriOr Photohouse/Courtesy of the Murray S. Katz Photo Archives of the IPO.

verdict that "Dr. Heinz Unger ... [is] the outstanding exponent of Mahler of our age."[11] The possibility of establishing a relationship with the Israel Philharmonic Orchestra (IPO) was reinforced by Unger's leading role in the performance and dissemination of a music that was beginning to hold a special meaning for Jews around the world, not least in a young Israel seeking to construct a proud artistic tradition.

Lending further support to the possibility of an engagement with the IPO was the fact that Unger was becoming a recognized point on the Israeli cultural compass. In the winter of 1958, he had been personally invited by Israel's ambassador to Canada, Arthur Lourie, to serve as a patron of the Toronto premiere of the Inbal Dance Theatre Group, held as part of Israel's tenth anniversary celebrations at Toronto's Royal Alexandra Theatre.[12] Even at the highest official levels, segments of the Israeli community were beginning to see Unger as a constituent part of their cultural milieu.

None of this, however, seemed to bear on the directorship of the Israel Philharmonic Orchestra. By 1959, even as Unger expectantly looked forward to working with Israel's national orchestra, the fruitless and often turbulent relationship between the conductor and the IPO was nearly at an end. For decades, Unger had been attempting to conduct in "the country to which I have more personal ties than any of you can possibly know."[13] Indeed, he had been attempting to establish a working relationship with the IPO since the 1930s, in the period just after his emigration from Germany to England. As he would recount in a long and bitter letter sent in June 1958 to two of his closest and most trusted friends and supporters, Mark Levy and his wife:

> For order's sake I should like to put on record that since 25 years I have expressed my great interest to conduct in Israel on countless occasions. As a Jewish conductor I need hardly give special reasons for this interest. I have written them several times from England (after our immigration from Germany), I have written to them later from Spain. I have written to them from Canada. I have written to the administration of the old "Palestine Orchestra" (Mr. Levertoff), I have written to the administration of the new "Israel Orchestra" (Mr. Haftel, Mr. C. Salomon, and others whose names I do not remember). I have always written directly (conductors mostly do not act through agents). As replies I have received nothing but excuses, pretexts for indefinite postponement etc. etc.[14]

Since its creation in 1936, Unger had witnessed Polish Jewish violinist Bronisław Huberman's (1882–1947) Palestine Orchestra evolve into a first-rate ensemble renamed the Israel Philharmonic Orchestra. He had, moreover, witnessed many of his colleagues – Jewish and otherwise – receive invitations to conduct and even record with the director-less orchestra.[15] And while some of the conductors invited were certainly world class – Arturo Toscanini (1867–1957) led the orchestra in its inaugural concert on 26 December 1936, while the years that followed saw such musical luminaries as Sergiu Celibidache (1912–1996), Dimitri Mitropolous (1896–1960), Eugene Ormandy (1899–1985), and Leonard Bernstein (1918–1990) do the same – many of the conductors who led the orchestra following its debut – such as Paul Paray (1886–1979), Jean Martinon (1910–1976), Bernardino Molinari (1880–1952), Erich Leinsdorf (1912–1993), and Paul Kletzki (1900–1973), to name but a few – possessed reputations and profiles not dissimilar to Unger's.[16]

Under any normal circumstances, Unger, never the most patient or accommodating of men, would have taken these rejections – and his being passed over while other conductors of similar stature were granted opportunities with the IPO – at face value and looked elsewhere for opportunities. But a chance to conduct the Israel Philharmonic was no normal circumstance. The key to his persistence in trying to obtain an engagement with the Israel Philharmonic lay in his self-identification as a "Jewish conductor," a position that he never abandoned and an element of his identity that was central to his very existence. Indeed, despite the fact that throughout his life he most often only alluded to the reason for his exodus from Germany, the longevity of the affair with the Israel Philharmonic suggests that the Jewish elements of his persona constituted a core value which he had silently borne for many years. Moreover, the centrality of his Jewish identity is underpinned by his rage – expressed in his candid correspondence with the Levys – at being told "that the administration of the [Israel Philharmonic] orchestra believes me to be baptised, a libellous error, which I have rectified straight-away."[17] In this unguarded exchange with his close friends, Unger confessed how his failure to secure an invitation from the IPO felt as though he was being denied entry into the Jewish world in which he felt he belonged:

> With countless non-Jewish conductors having been and being invited to Israel, I consider it almost an insult to Jewish musiclovers [*sic*] in general that a Jewish conductor of my standing should be deliberately and successfully kept out of Israel by some irresponsible and petty intrigue on the part of one or two people whom or whose real motives I do not even know.[18]

In this critical letter, he also elucidated his views on the significance of the Mahler centenary and, indeed, of Mahler as a Jewish composer:

> The year 1960 will bring the 100th Birthday of Gustav Mahler, one of the most important composers of Jewish origin, to whose music as you know I have devoted my whole life. No doubt that the Israel Philharmonic will do something on a grand scale about this Centenary. It would have made me proud to make this the occasion of my belated first appearance in Israel, but if not a miracle happens, I fear this will remain a dream.[19]

In the context in which these words were written, one cannot fail to see the deep significance that Mahler bore for Unger; Mahler had come to represent a summation and a nexus of Jewish identity he felt should be shared with Jewish audiences as an expression of their shared culture and history.

Mystified by the "excuses [and] pretexts for indefinite postponement" that he had received from the Israel Philharmonic, the conductor desperately tried to unravel the mystery of this "entirely unnatural attitude towards a well-known Jewish conductor."[20] Unger and his acquaintances thus began an intense campaign to help him achieve his goal of conducting in Israel. Foremost among those seeking to assist him was the aforementioned Mark Levy, Unger's Toronto-based lawyer and a friend to whom he openly wrote of his concerns. Levy and his wife mixed and socialized with those in the upper echelons of Canada's

Jewish community; they were seated, for instance, at the head table for the 1963 Annual Ambassador's Ball held at Toronto's Conservative Beth Tzedec Synagogue, patronized by the Israeli ambassador to Canada, Yaacov Herzog.[21] Unger, then, by no means isolated, had key allies in his quest to visit Israel in a professional capacity. As early as the winter of 1957–8, Unger's representatives had been in touch with the America-Israel Cultural Foundation – founded in 1939 with the express purpose of helping develop Israel's cultural institutions – and with Reform rabbi Arthur Lelyveld (1913–1996) (who later served as president of the American Jewish Congress between 1966 and 1972) to see whether anything could be arranged. In his polite reply, Mr. Lelyveld lamented that nothing could be done in the short term because "the 1957–58 season had been planned long before our conversation, and the 1958–59 season will be a short one for the Orchestra inasmuch as they will be on tour in the United States and Canada beginning in January 1959."[22] Seemingly, the impasse had nothing to do with animosity and more to do with logistics, a fact borne out by Lelyveld's assurances that he had "written once again to our friends in the Orchestra and I hope that this letter will elicit some expression of interest in bringing Dr. Unger to Israel at some future date."[23] Despite this promised aid, Lelyveld was more circumspect about Unger's prospects, closing his letter by noting that "the Israel Philharmonic, as you know, controls independently its own programming and its own invitations to guest artists."[24] However positively disposed Lelyveld might have been, the final decision would be made not by him but in Israel.

In the months that followed, Mark Levy travelled to Israel. On that occasion, he took the opportunity to meet with Joseph Jacobson, one of the board members of the Israel Philharmonic. In a letter following his visit, Levy thanked Jacobson for receiving him in his home and stressed that he felt Unger's appearance in Israel would be a great success: "I can assure you that Dr. Unger's experience with first-rate orchestras all over the world, and now with the reputation he has made in Toronto, that he would appeal very much to the cultivated tastes of the Israeli music-lovers."[25] Levy, acting as both friend and lobbyist, was doing all in his power to help Unger achieve his dream of conducting the Israel Philharmonic.

The steps that the Levys had taken on behalf of their friend during their trip to Israel, however, proved little comfort to an impatient Unger after the many years of setbacks that he had already faced on this front. A mere three days after Mark Levy had written his letter to Jacobson, Unger himself was writing a letter to Mrs. Levy, noting his frustration at how little had been achieved despite the persistent lobbying on his behalf.[26] On

Unger's insistence, Mark Levy wrote Jacobson another letter – his second in the space of a week – including with it a package of promotional literature and a further note from the conductor about his unhappiness at not having conducted in Israel.[27] The answer to that letter came later in the summer, the IPO declaring once again that no decision could be made at the time because "our program for 1959/60 will be discussed only in January."[28] His hopes again raised by contact with Jacobson, Unger sent him a personal letter at the beginning of September 1958 in which he expressed his "sincere hope that the mentioned correspondence [with Mark Levy] and your kind personal interest in this matter will lead to an entirely new page being turned over in my – so far negative – relations to the Israel Philharmonic Orchestra."[29]

But by 1959 Unger had become utterly despondent. In a penultimate letter to the Israel Philharmonic – its ostensibly supplicatory nature notwithstanding – Unger's tone suggests that his patience was in fact nearing its end. After writing that he "had long ago given up any expectation to visit Israel in my lifetime," he would still end the letter with another overture, declaring, "it is obvious that the next step, if any at all, would have to come from your side, as I do not wish to give the impression, that I am trying to intrude where I am apparently not wanted."[30]

However much Unger hoped for the executive of the Israel Philharmonic Orchestra to invite him to Israel, such a rapprochement never came. And despite being thoroughly disheartened by the entire affair, he tried a final approach that he hoped might lead to the fulfilment of his long-held dream of conducting in Israel. In late summer 1960, he wrote one last letter to the executive of the Israel Philharmonic Orchestra lamenting how he would be absent from the orchestra's visit to Canada:

> I regret my absence, not only because it deprives me again of an opportunity to listen to your orchestra in person, but also because after all these years of artificially created misunderstandings I would have very much welcomed an opportunity for personal contact with you. Meeting personally would probably have gone a long way to confirm a natural understanding as to our mutual outlook, which has been missing so far from our relations in consequence of false informations [*sic*] spread by parties unknown to me.[31]

In other words, he believed that a reconciliation was still possible and that the true reason behind the impasse lay in a misunderstanding of his Jewish "outlook" and that a face-to-face meeting would dispel any such misconceptions. Unger, despite his decades-long attempt to conduct in "the country to which I have more personal ties than any of you can possibly know," failed to achieve this goal. A musician who had suffered immeasurably as a result of being Jewish, Heinz Unger would never walk in the Promised Land.

His frustrations with the Israel Philharmonic notwithstanding, the late 1950s represent a fruitful period in Unger's career. In January 1958, Unger was finally afforded the opportunity to lead one of Mahler's more ambitious symphonic utterances, his Symphony no. 2 (*Resurrection*) with the Toronto Symphony Orchestra. This performance, a Canadian premiere, embodied his growing reputation on the Canadian musical scene and also served to punctuate the mounting interest in Mahler's work as the centenary of the composer's birth approached.

So great was the interest stimulated that many found themselves writing expectantly about the event even before it occurred, Kraglund commenting in the *Globe and Mail* how the much-anticipated performance of the Second Symphony "had renewed our interest in the music of Mahler."[32] The Canadian choral conductor Leslie Bell (1906–1962) also chimed in, comparing Unger's work on behalf of Gustav Mahler to that of Hans von Bülow for Richard Wagner or Thomas Beecham for Frederick Delius. Bell's words about Unger and the challenges that he faced in his devotion to Mahler's cause bear repeating:

> The greatest missionary conductor in Canada is Heinz Unger who has devoted years in championing the music of Gustav Mahler. It has not been an easy task. The length of Mahler's symphonies and the huge orchestral personnel they require have made it difficult to get them heard. Some have said that Mahler's music is not worth the trouble involved in its performance. But Unger affirms that Mahler is one of the ... greats and has suffered shameful neglect.[33]

The CBC, swayed perhaps by this groundswell of support, seemed to agree that the performance of Mahler's music, whatever the complications, was a worthwhile enterprise. On 22 January 1958, after the first half of a program composed of Beethoven's Overture to *The Creatures of Prometheus* and three of Mahler's orchestral *Rückert Songs* ("Ich atmet' einen linden Duft," "Ich bin der Welt abhanden gekommen," and "Um Mitternacht," sung by Mary Simmons), concertgoers were joined by listeners across the entire CBC network to hear Unger and the TSO (its usual complement of 80 players boosted to 102 to meet the requirements of Mahler's soundscape) present the Canadian premiere of Mahler's Second Symphony.

Critical understanding of the vast work varied. George Kidd cast the deeply spiritual work as a showy piece, calling it a "technicolour three-dimensional stereophonic symphony that Hollywood would call colossal,"[34] while John Kraglund questioned "the musical worth of [the symphony's] long last movement."[35] Despite these concerns, the performance was described as a great achievement, unfamiliarity with the score and a questioning of some of the symphony's elements failing to prevent Kraglund from noting the correctness of the symphony's execution under the conductor's baton:

> A measure of Dr. Unger's deep insight into the score was demonstrated in his ability to shape the numerous climaxes with a rightness that made each seem inevitable and yet without a loss of musical detail ... It was Dr. Unger's interpretation of the Resurrection Symphony that made the evening something to be remembered.[36]

If some critics were disoriented by the length and complexity of Mahler's score, few in the audience seemed to echo those concerns. When the last strains of Mahler's music died away, the smaller-than-expected Massey Hall audience – Kraglund noted that "doubtless many were kept away by reports of the length of the symphony" – rose to their feet in response to the work and its moving finale: "the applause and shouts that greeted Dr. Unger [became] a thunder of stamping feet by the time he appeared for his third curtain call."[37] At the last curtain call, the conductor picked up the Mahler score with a flourish and lifted it proudly above his head – this was not only Unger's glory but Mahler's as well.

Unger was quite understandably buoyed by the opportunity to conduct this work and by the reception his leadership received. He also remained convinced, as he had been since his youth, of Mahler's importance and that further performances could win over those who were not yet wholehearted supporters of the composer's art. William Krehm, music critic and commentator for the CBC, was also convinced of the merit of Mahler's work, lamenting at the York Concert Society Women's Committee annual luncheon of 13 February 1958 that far too many "Torontonians chose to sleep through the sounding of the last trumpet" and missed Unger's "memorable" performance of Mahler's Second Symphony.[38] At that same meeting, Women's Committee president Lady Robinson humorously compared the conductor's work to contemporary events: "Ranking with Sputniks and moon travel in importance ... was the fact that last season Toronto audiences seemed suddenly to awake to the fact that we have a great conductor in Dr. Unger."[39]

However hyperbolic Robinson's claims for the conductor's importance, the TSO's directorship quite suddenly realized that in Unger they indeed had a unique talent working in their midst. And while he was overlooked when the orchestra went looking for a new music director to replace the soon-to-retire Ernest Macmillan – the younger and more charismatic Walter Susskind (1913–1980) was selected instead – the directorship still recognized that after a decade of life in Canada, Unger merited the opportunity to conduct works that not only meant a great deal to him but also intrigued concertgoers.[40] Thus, even when contracted to conduct Pops concerts, Unger was allowed to program Mahler's works, as he did on 9 February 1958 when the second movement from Mahler's Second Symphony was included in a concert of lighter fare.[41] Later that same week, he was again at the podium for a TSO concert, this time conducting not Mahler but another set of works that were an integral part of his repertoire: Weber's *Der Freischütz* Overture, Beethoven's Symphony no. 7, and, in between, the Canadian premiere of Walter Braunfels's *Phantastic Apparitions of a Theme by Hector Berlioz*.

Unger's Canadian career continued to develop over the course of the next year. The inaugural York Concert Society concert of 1958, held on 22 April, consisted of three works: Schumann's Piano Concerto (with Patricia Parr as soloist), Hector Berlioz's *Symphonie fantastique*, and three preludes from Hans Pfitzner's opera *Palestrina*.[42] The second concert of the season, meanwhile, included Ralph Vaughan William's Violin Concerto and Arnold Schoenberg's *Transfigured Night*. The third concert of the season, held on 6 May, also included a novelty mixed in among more familiar fare: performances of Tchaikovsky's Piano Concerto no. 1 and Dvořak's Eighth Symphony were preceded by the Canadian composer Harry Somers's *Passacaglia and Fugue*.[43] The final concert of the YCS season – an all-Beethoven program consisting of two of the composer's overtures (*Fidelio* and *Leonore No. 3*) and his First and Fourth Symphonies – found critics unanimous in their disappointment, a surprise given the generally positive reviews that Unger's concerts usually received.[44]

Yet whatever immediate frustration reviewers' comments may have caused Unger was surely blunted by his Mahler-related achievements. In March 1958, Mahler's widow, Alma Mahler-Werfel, invited him to join the honorary board of directors of the newly founded Gustav Mahler Society of America.[45] But this recognition could not rival the next award bestowed upon the German Jewish conductor. In 1959, Unger was honoured with the Mahler Medal, an award granted by the recently formed Mahler society (functioning under the auspices of the Bruckner Society of America) to a select few who had done vital work in the dissemination of Mahler's music and creed. The medal, granted only to those at the summit of the musical world (Bruno Walter, Eugene Ormandy, Dmitri Mitropolous, Otto Klemperer, William Steinberg, Leonard Bernstein, and George Szell among them) was a sculpted piece of bronze work created by the artist Julio Kilenyi (1885–1959) that bore a profile of Mahler's head on one side and, on the other, the prophetic quote "Meine Zeit wird noch kommen" (My time will come) that neatly encapsulated Mahler's posthumous fate as well as the aims of the society founded to help achieve Mahler's popularization. Heinz Unger, for performing Mahler's works and advocating on his behalf the world over, was now to become a member of this elite company of Mahlerians.

The award, and the international prestige that accompanied it, also helped bring to prominence Unger's work within Canada itself. To celebrate this prestigious award, the CBC scheduled the Canadian premiere of Mahler's Fifth Symphony. Indeed, the hype surrounding the granting of the Mahler Medal was fully exploited by a CBC keen to draw attention to their resident artist. In the days leading up to the concert, the *CBC Times* ran a full-page article that told of the conductor's life and also provided space for Unger to share his view that "the fifth symphony is in its final outcome an apotheosis of joy, not of a shallow and meaningless frolic, but of that deep contentment and joy of life obtainable only after severe struggles and the experience of deepest despair."[46]

On 25 February 1959, the CBC devoted extended time to the event so that the nationwide broadcast could include the official presentation of the Mahler Medal to Unger as well as his leadership of Mahler's Symphony no. 5.[47] Unger's comments upon receiving the medal from CBC music director Geoffrey Waddington tell us much about the central role that Mahler's music played in his life:

> It was on a November evening as far back as 1915 when I, as a very young person, heard for the first time the message of the music of Gustav Mahler. The place was Munich. The occasion was a performance of the "Song of the Earth" under Bruno Walter. That evening became decisive for my life because it was this impression which made me a conductor. Since then, I have had the opportunity and the privilege to contribute [to] spreading Mahler's work in many countries, in recent years in an increasing degree here in Canada, my new home country. And it makes me happy that a growing number of music lovers here, too, seem to be opening their hearts to the message of this music. The Mahler Medal, which the directors of the Bruckner Society of America are awarding to me, comes to me as a heart-warming token of appreciation of my efforts. It makes me proud to accept the medal out of the hands of the director of music of the Canadian Broadcasting Corporation. And it gives me very special satisfaction that this, to my knowledge, is the first medal of its kind which has found its way into Canada and which has been won in cooperation with and through the efforts of Canadian orchestras.[48]

But as had been the case with the premiere of Mahler's Second Symphony the previous year, a less-than-full Massey Hall was the backdrop to this event, and as before, the Toronto crowd proved ambivalent about Mahler's music. The critical reception was also mixed: while John Kraglund praised "the power, color and clarity of Mahler's orchestration" and George Kidd heard "a glowing work, strongly melodic, dramatically exciting and often emotionally moving," the *Toronto Daily Star*'s Hugh Thompson declared the piece "excessively long" and filled with "strenuous, excessively busy orchestration."[49] And yet, whatever the critics' opinions of the work itself, all agreed that the conductor's presentation left little to be desired, Kraglund noting that "it was Dr. Unger's ability ... that made last night's interpretation a resounding success."[50] George Kidd, meanwhile, stressed how the evening represented a "moment of deep emotion" for Unger, an astute and touching observation that highlighted the profound musical and extra-musical meaning of the event for the musician who had for decades laboured to increase the reputation of a composer whom he cherished, not only for his oeuvre but also as a conduit through which he had come to express his German Jewish identity.[51]

In other ways, too, the period represented an important moment in Unger's growing Jewish self-awareness. One of his most interesting relationships was with Rabbi Maxwell Dubin, who had served as director of religious education and social activities at the Reform Wilshire Boulevard Temple in Los Angeles since 1926.[52] And while nothing is known about how the two men had met, it is clear that they became close friends; by the late 1950s, their correspondence bore a warm familiarity, indicating that they had known each other for a number of years and had made mutual efforts to keep abreast of each other's activities. Indeed, by the late 1950s Rabbi Dubin had become one of Unger's most fervent supporters, one who lent his weight to helping the conductor obtain wider exposure in the United States. In a letter sent in the spring of 1959, Rabbi Dubin noted how he had "taken the liberty" of forwarding Unger's name as a candidate for the directorship of the Los Angeles Philharmonic, a position that had recently become vacant after its director, the Dutch conductor Eduard van Beinum (1900–1959), had unexpectedly died of a heart attack while rehearsing with the Concertgebouw Orchestra in the Netherlands.[53]

But Dubin's advocacy of Unger for the post of conductor of the Los Angeles Philharmonic was not the only time that the rabbi pledged his support for the conductor. In late summer 1959, Dubin interceded on Unger's behalf to see whether he might help the conductor attain the representation of famous impresario Sol Hurok (1888–1974), the Ukrainian-born Jewish concert agent who had moved to the United

States in 1906 and assumed responsibility for the careers of many of the classical world's musical stars (including Vladimir Ashkenazy, Van Cliburn, Emil Gilels, David Oistrakh, Jan Peerce, Mstislav Rostropovich, Arthur Rubinstein, and Isaac Stern). In a letter sent to Hurok, Dubin spoke of how Unger was "anxious to place himself under your management, provided, you feel, and it must be solely on the basis of his professional ability, justified in handling his affairs."[54] Despite stressing that any future relationship should be built on a foundation of professionalism, Dubin could not help but mention one of the main extra-musical reasons that he bore such affection for Unger:

> Not only is Dr. Unger a distinguished conductor; he is, in addition, one of the few Jewish maestros who refused to compromise with his faith and accept baptism in order to further his career. As a rabbi, this has made him doubly close to me.[55]

Unbeknownst to Dubin, however, the possibility of a relationship between Unger and Hurok had already been poisoned a decade earlier by the conductor's defence of Wilhelm Furtwängler in what has come to be known as "the Chicago Affair." In the winter of 1949, the board of the Chicago Orchestral Association announced that the organization had contracted the renowned German conductor Wilhelm Furtwängler (1886–1954) as principal conductor for a series of concerts in the coming season. While the appointment of so famous a conductor was no doubt a coup for the Chicago Orchestral Association, it had little time to revel in its success, as Furtwängler's appointment immediately set off a series of protests by musicians and members of the public suspicious of his conduct during the Second World War, when he had chosen to stay in Nazi Germany instead of emigrating in protest. And despite having been cleared of any wrongdoing by American authorities in 1947, rumours swirled about Furtwängler's support of the Nazi regime. Even Furtwängler's conviction that he had done no wrong, that he had remained in Germany because of his allegiance to the nation and that he had resigned his official posts and avoided as much as possible any involvement with the regime, did little to dispel the suspicions many held. In their eyes, Furtwängler was a Nazi and deserved to be punished for supporting the criminal government.[56]

During January 1949, the battle raged over Furtwängler's appointment to the Chicago post, the pages of the *New York Times* becoming a key battleground as notable musicians and members of the Jewish community voiced their positions. The opening salvo was launched on 6 January 1949, with numerous well-known musicians – including Vladimir Horowitz, Artur Rubinstein, Lily Pons, and Andre Kostelanetz – warning "the Chicago Symphony Orchestra that they would not appear as soloists or guest leaders with that ensemble if Wilhelm Furtwaengler [*sic*] became principal conductor." The article even quoted the very clear and curt telegram sent by Artur Rubinstein from his home in Beverly Hills: "I will not collaborate, musically or otherwise, with anyone who collaborated with Hitler, Goering and Goebbels."[57]

But not all musicians saw the matter in such a stark light. Most significant among Furtwängler's defenders was the Jewish violinist Yehudi Menuhin, who had performed with the conductor in a fabled 1947 recording of Beethoven's Violin Concerto. Another ally was Unger. On 13 January 1949, the *Times* ran a lengthy letter that Unger wrote in defence of Furtwängler. In it, he articulated his understanding of Furtwängler's decision to remain in Nazi Germany:

> True, he could have left Germany as did many of his colleagues, and the world would have been open to him. But ... he felt so strongly connected with German music and musical life that the idea of possibly shutting the door behind them forever was more intolerable for him than to put up with circumstances as they were. Weakness? Perhaps; certainly not more.[58]

Unger, who had not easily reached his own decision to abandon Germany, understood the paradox in which his colleague had found himself, at once resistant to Nazi policies but also bound by a love of his homeland.

But the resistance to Furtwängler could not be surmounted. In this tension-laden post-Holocaust atmosphere, and concurrent with the young State of Israel's struggle for survival, the presence in America of a German conductor who had chosen to remain in Germany during the dark years of Nazi rule was bound to divide. Soon, prominent members of the Jewish community weighed in on the affair. On 14 January, the *New York Times* noted that "Rabbi Morton M. Berman, president of the Chicago division, American Jewish Congress, today joined the forces opposing the proposed engagement of Wilhelm Furtwaengler [*sic*], German conductor, as conductor of the Chicago Symphony Orchestra."[59] And so it was that by the third week of January 1949 the affair had come to an end, Furtwängler issuing a public statement in which he signalled the end of his candidacy.[60]

While the Chicago Affair ended abruptly for Furtwängler, the aftershocks were felt by those who had supported him. Yehudi Menuhin, concertizing in Italy, was appalled to hear that Jewish leaders in Rome had urged the members of the local community to boycott his final two concerts in the city.[61] Unger's support of Furtwängler in 1949 had, meanwhile, caused a deep and permanent rift between himself and many Jews in the United States. Thus, while Rabbi Dubin had approached Hurok in good faith in 1959, the events of ten years earlier had already compromised the possibility of Hurok showing any affection or sympathy – personal or professional – for Unger. Not surprisingly, then, nothing came of Dubin's initiative and the matter of Hurok's representation of Unger, a representation that could have borne great fruit for the conductor in the twilight of his career, faded away. The negative conclusion to the affair notwithstanding, Unger must have been touched by Dubin's reference to his being a "Jewish maestro." In light of Unger's frustrating dealings with the Israel Philharmonic and his fury at being called anything other than Jewish, the rabbi's words must have moved him deeply.

But by this point Unger was becoming increasingly assured in his devotion to his German Jewish identity, at least insofar as it was expressed by way of his allegiance to Mahler. Thus, whatever his disappointment at being rejected by the Israel Philharmonic Orchestra or by Sol Hurok, he could take comfort in the knowledge that during the 1960 centenary of Mahler's birth he would have the rest of the world with which to share the composer's vision. But the Mahler centenary was vital to Unger not only because of his deep devotion to the composer's music but because of his understanding of Mahler – both the man and his music – as an expression and reflection of his own German Jewish identity. The centenary's arrival allowed Unger to fervently realize that Mahler represented a nexus of overlapping German *and* Jewish meanings. Reflecting on *Das Lied von der Erde*, Unger would observe that Mahler's music had led him back across the little bridge to the pavilion where he could once again join "a host of young friends enjoying life, chatting, playing, writing verses."[62] By way of Mahler, Unger – after years of wandering – reconnected with his roots, with his youth, and with the world he thought he had lost as the Nazis rose to power.

And so Mahler's music reawakened the German Jewish soul that Unger had in fact carried deep within him all along. But Unger's Jewish revival represented more than a self-understanding, translating also into philanthropic activity. So, informed by his German Jewish identity and impelled to reconnect with the German Jewish community from which he had stemmed, his activities in this sphere centred not on the Canadian or American Jewish communities, but rather on the difficulties faced by a post-Holocaust German Jewish community. In late summer 1960, Unger proudly donated 720 deutsche marks – the full sum of an honorarium he had received from the Westdeutschen Rundfunks in Köln (Cologne) for a concert conducted the previous year – to the Zentralrat der Juden in Deutschland to finance the training and education of a Jewish teacher for the local community.[63]

The Mahler centenary served, moreover, as a means by which the German Jewish conductor could negotiate his sense of displacement in a period when, in Frank Bialystock's words, "the Holocaust was not a defining element in Canadian Jewish identity."[64] The Mahler centenary thus became Unger's way of expressing his identity in a period – this was before the Adolf Eichmann trial, when Jews around the world finally recognized the true magnitude of the Holocaust and began to see it as an existential experience rather than a more abstract historical event – during which Canada's Jews had yet to confront the Holocaust and the trauma that survivors, both those who had been in the camps as well as those who had managed to escape such a fate, had undergone.[65]

For all these reasons, Unger was desperate to mark the significant milestone of Mahler's centenary with as many concerts of the composer's music as possible. In point of fact, Unger's preparations had begun at the very time that he was ensnared in the imbroglio with the Israel Philharmonic, the conductor devoting much of the summer of 1958 to feverishly writing to orchestras around the world in the hopes of securing concerts through which he could celebrate the centenary in grand fashion. In that summer and in the year that followed, Unger wrote letters to many of the world's leading orchestras and organizations – such as the BBC, the Concertgebouw in Amsterdam, the Radio-Symfonie Orchester of Berlin, and the Vienna Philharmonic – in the hopes of sharing Mahler's music with as many as possible.[66] Far too many of those letters – to such Mahlerian musical meccas as Vienna and Amsterdam no less – failed to lead to concert engagements in this, one of the most important years in the entirety of Unger's artistic life.

Still, the year brought Unger many opportunities to share Mahler's music with fellow musicians and audiences. The first of these concerts had been a taping of *Das Lied von der Erde* for the BBC, recorded in January 1959 and aired the following year as part of the BBC's celebration of Mahler's centenary. In late 1959, Unger was supposed to have returned to England to record a performance of *Das Klagende Lied*, Mahler's first official composition and still a relative rarity in the concert hall, as well as a selection of Mahler songs. But while the songs – the five comprising the song group *Lieder nach Gedichten von Friedrich Rückert* ("Ich atmet' einen linden Duft," "Liebst du um Schönheit," "Um Mitternacht," "Blicke mir nicht in die Lieder," and "Ich bin der Welt abhanden gekommen") and two further songs from *Des Knaben Wunderhorn* ("Revelge" and "Der Tamboursg'sell"), sung by Kerstin Meyer and Richard Lewis – were indeed recorded and grafted onto the following year's broadcast of *Das Lied von der Erde*, it is unclear whether *Das Klagende Lied* was in fact broadcast or even recorded.[67] Nonetheless, in being selected as one of the

4.2 Despite some important engagements to celebrate the milestone of Mahler's centenary, Unger's celebration in part proved to be a private idyll. Artist unknown. Source: Library and Archives Canada, MUS 56, Box 4, File 73.

conductors to lead the BBC's Mahler centenary concerts, Unger was in elite company, the only other conductors being the much-admired and respected Jascha Horenstein (1898–1973), Sir John Barbirolli (1899–1970), William Steinberg (1899–1978), and Antal Dorati (1906–1988).

In the winter of 1960, the Canadian leg of Unger's year-long celebration of Mahler well and truly began. On 24 February 1960, the Toronto Symphony Orchestra, working on that occasion under the auspices of the York Concert Society, assembled to give the YCS's Mahler Centenary Concert at Massey Hall, with a performance of Mahler's *Das Lied von der Erde* (the guest soloists for the occasion were Elena Nikoloidi and, replacing the indisposed Richard Lewis, David Lloyd).[68] Given the commemorative nature of the concert, it should come as no surprise that the reviews were unanimous in their praise of the conductor's directorship of the orchestra and of his advocacy of Mahler's idiom: the *Toronto Daily Star*'s Blaik Kirby called Unger's conducting "eloquent" and "graceful," while George Kidd was even more effusive in his praise, noting that

"Dr. Unger seized the work with his usual authority for Mahler and produced it with care and affection."[69] Underlining the fact that the evening was an event rather than just a concert, the music was followed with reception held in honour of Unger and the performers at the Royal York Hotel and hosted by the consul general of the Federal Republic of Germany, Gottfried von Waldheim.

In the spring of 1960, CBC listeners were treated to a further helping of Mahler, this time selections from the Mahler completion and orchestration of Carl Maria von Weber's uncompleted opera *Die Drei Pintos*, this rare music accompanied by a performance of Mahler's more familiar First Symphony.[70] In the fall of 1960, Unger returned yet again to his familiar place on the conductor's podium with the Orquesta Municipal de Valencia, repeating his performance of Mahler's First Symphony on two consecutive November nights, this time as a part of the Valencian commemoration of the centenary.[71]

And with these last concerts of the 1960 calendar year, Heinz Unger's contribution to the Mahler centenary came to a close. For Unger, the centenary was supposed to have been a great celebration of the composer's art. It was to be the moment in the life of the conductor during which, after the honours bestowed upon him by the Bruckner Society of America, his status as a leading conductor of Mahler's music was recognized the world over. It was also to be the moment at which he revelled in his German Jewish identity. And yet, Unger's involvement in the Mahler centenary was less than what he would have hoped for. His contributions to the commemoration of his beloved composer were limited to places (Toronto, Valencia, London) where he had already helped bring about a Mahler revival; and moreover, there was little if any recognition at these events of the shared German Jewish identity that united composer and conductor beyond whatever Unger carried within him throughout the year. And with the passage of time, Unger's contributions to the Mahler centenary – much like his other achievements – have been forgotten. Unger had once written that the conclusion of Mahler's Fourth Symphony is a heavenly music "so beautiful that nothing on earth can stand comparison with it."[72] Unger's observance of the composer's 1960 centenary was also intended as a depiction of heaven, for both himself and for others. But as in that eloquent passage, nothing on earth could compare to his imagining of a Mahlerian heaven, leaving the musician alone in his visions of having achieved apotheosis.

*Chapter Five*

# The Final Years and a Farewell to the World (1961–1965)

On 4 January 1961, John Kraglund penned a lengthy laudatory piece that shared with *Globe and Mail* readers the details of Heinz Unger's most recent tour. On this journey, Unger had conducted in Geneva, Stuttgart, Madrid, and Valencia, capping things off with a stop in London, where he marked his sixty-fifth birthday conducting Mozart with his friend Harry Newstone's chamber-sized Haydn Orchestra, an engagement broadcast on the BBC.[1] In the same article, the often dour Kraglund also voiced his enthusiasm for the upcoming York Concert Society season, declaring that "the York's ninth season promises to be one of the most impressive in programming and soloists."[2]

Just one week later, though, any expectations for the upcoming YCS season – and indeed for the society's future – lay in ruins as the society's chairman, Malcolm A. Moysey, announced that "a review of the organization's financial situation and the outlook for a major concert series had prompted the decision to cancel [the season]."[3] In exposing the sad fate of the York Concert Society, Kraglund noted that the Canada Council – the Crown corporation created as recently as 1957 to oversee the development of the arts in Canada – "had decided to withdraw its support ($3000 last season)."[4]

Come the spring of 1961, however, strong support for the York Concert Society and its musical leader led to a reconsideration of the society's future, Kraglund reporting that "the most recent [musical phoenix] to rise from what seemed a fairly conclusive funeral pyre is the York Concert Society, which has just announced plans for a 1962 season under the direction of Heinz Unger."[5] This new course was undertaken in the wake of a barrage of letters of support that "expressed the dismay of part of Toronto's concert public" and made clear the sentiments of "many of those that had supported the organization through nine troubled years [who] were not prepared to accept complete failure."[6] As a consequence, a new executive board was formed and plans for the 1962 season quickly got underway.

In the weeks and months that followed, the circumstances that had compelled the YCS to cancel its 1961 concert season would emerge. The Canada Council's motivation for withholding YCS funding was not an isolated phenomenon but had come as a consequence of a study by the Australian musician Bernard Heinze (1894–1982) meant to report "on the present state of development of Canadian symphony orchestras."[7] For the purposes of the report, the Canada Council requested Heinze – not only an accomplished musician but also an experienced music administrator who had served as music advisor to the Australian Broadcasting Corporation since 1929 and had been knighted in 1949 for his work in advancing musical culture – travel across Canada and survey the artistic level of almost two dozen orchestras spread out across the land. Asking Heinze to examine the situation from a national perspective and keeping in mind the conditions (that is, the limited funds available) that had stimulated the report, the Canada Council in essence obliged the Australian to recommend the continued funding of one orchestra per established region (Toronto, Montreal, and Vancouver), along with the funding of "young" orchestras to serve the needs of smaller Canadian cities and regions (Victoria, Halifax, and Calgary/Edmonton, for example).

Once the details of the Canada Council's initiative came to light, the ever-opinionated and often outspoken Unger could not keep his disappointment at the council's directives to himself. In the summer of 1961, he wrote a lengthy article for the *Globe Magazine* in which he aired his views on the matter in detail. Unger ranged far and wide in his criticisms, ultimately condemning the Canada Council for the damage that he felt it was causing to the development of the performing arts in Canada with its inconsistent policies ("by way of abrupt changes of its policy ... the responsible organization increases insecurity and instability instead of doing the opposite") and by supporting only one orchestra in each major city as well as in smaller urban centres, a policy that could only lead to "monopolies" and "stagnation."[8] And though one can argue that Unger's motivation for writing this piece lay in his frustration at seeing the YCS season cancelled, he still defended the Canada Council's important role in cultivating Canadian culture, arguing that the institution needed to be better managed if it was to prove effective:

> We need the Canada Council badly in the realm of the performing arts, in order not to be entirely dependent on private support and its inevitable fluctuations. May these experimental years lead to greater wisdom, greater responsibility and greater consistency in all quarters for the benefit of

> culture in Canada, so that we can confidently attack greater heights from the high plateau reached without fear that we must descend.[9]

But the difficulties Unger faced with the York Concert Society's cancelled 1961 season serves as a leitmotif of the conductor's last years. Thus, while the first half of the 1960s should have been an autumn period during which Unger attracted ever more listeners to Mahler's music on account of his own growing reputation and a global upsurge in the composer's popularity, many of his happiest moments were eroded by dissenting voices and negative turns.

Indeed, the new decade – the tense episode with the Canada Council notwithstanding – had begun with great promise. In late summer 1961, Unger was notified by the Gustav Mahler Society of Vienna (with the esteemed Mahlerian Bruno Walter as its president) that he had been named an honorary member of that society.[10] And as noted above, he was shortly thereafter once again in Europe, conducting his regular series of concerts in Valencia as well as extending his tour to include concerts in Barcelona, Geneva, Zurich, Stuttgart, and London.[11]

The following season also began well. As so many times before, Unger's 1962–3 season began with a trip to Europe during which he passed a lengthy spell in Valencia before proceeding on to Germany, Norway, and England.[12] But without doubt the highlight of the season lay in his leading of the Canadian premiere of Gustav Mahler's final completed symphonic work, his Ninth Symphony. Convinced of its importance and desperate to persuade Canadians of its worth, Unger used every opportunity to rehearse the symphony with the Toronto Symphony Orchestra so that they would be attuned to all the nuances of this complex work. As a complement to the usual rehearsal time, the conductor even exploited a TSO student concert to perform the Scherzo and Burlesque third and fourth movements of the Ninth Symphony as a "trial run" for the premiere proper, scheduled for the following evening.[13]

The reactions of the two thousand audience members assembled at Massey Hall on that late-January evening and of the countless thousands who listened to the first Canadian performance of Mahler's final completed symphony on the CBC have been lost to posterity. An assessment of the evening is thus limited to the reactions of a Toronto critical community that recognized the conductor's achievement and the importance of the work. John Kraglund, by now one of Unger's most sympathetic allies, not only called the concert an "exceedingly engrossing performance" but also paused to reflect upon how "last night's opening concert in the York Concert Society series was a towering climax to [Unger's] more than four decades of devoted service to the music of Gustav Mahler."[14]

Not all of the critical press, however, considered the event a success. In the *Toronto Daily Star*, the Estonian-born Canadian composer Udo Kasemets (1919–2014) wrote a scathing review of the concert that focussed on the failures of Gustav Mahler's music. An avant-garde musician who, despite founding the Toronto Bach Society in 1957, was heavily influenced by the American John Cage and employed elements such as "chance operations" in his own compositions, Kasemets[15] damned Mahler's music as lacking both universal appeal ("Agonies and frustrations of a particular generation, living in a confined locality, are expressed through Mahler's music, rather than matters meaning something to all humanity") and compositional skill ("The music loses even more interest since the composer's treatment of ideas and forms is heavy-handed and unskilled").[16]

So critical was Kasemets's review that Unger felt compelled to write a letter to the *Toronto Daily Star*'s editor that same day in defence of Mahler:

> I have to state with utter frankness that never in my life has any concert of mine in any country been exposed to the amount of malicious falsehood and ignorance evident in Mr. Udo Kasemets' attack on Gustav Mahler and his Ninth Symphony in your edition of January 24th. His way of thinking would perhaps have done honour to some of those critics of the early century – poor souls – who were faced with Mahler's music when it was new and not yet readily understood or understandable. However, I am far from stooping to try to defend the truly all-embracing message of Mahler's music against Mr. Kasemets, or to explain it to his apparently stone-deaf soul ... Let Mr. Kasemets say about my conductorial work what he pleases, but if he attempts with derogatory insolence to attack the work of Gustav Mahler, and to soil it with his outpourings, he will find me on my place and ready to retaliate in any way, not only by conducting.[17]

The conductor's deeply personal and angry reply – complete with threat of force – surely indicates the depth of feeling that Unger reserved for Mahler's music, as well as the fact that he viewed the composer as a personal spiritual guide, each performance of his work representing a ritualized manifestation of his very identity. To attack Mahler, therefore, was to attack his own German Jewish essence, or what Unger called the "truly all-embracing message of Mahler's music." In a sense, then, Kasemets's critique of Mahler's work – however crude its formulation – was correct, for the composer's music did in fact possess a strain that limited the universality of its appeal; this is, after all, the precise reason that Unger had been so moved by Mahler's music for all those many years.

Unger's belligerent response to Kasemets, however, belies the weakness that the conductor was beginning to display. Indeed, he had become sufficiently concerned about his deteriorating health to contact both Leonard Bernstein and John Barbirolli to ask whether they might lead this most important performance were he unable to do so.[18] And while he ultimately proved well enough to premiere the work, Unger had been obliged to conduct seated, a fact that surely indicates the conductor's declining health as well as the lengths to which he would go to present the Canadian performance of a work that meant so much to him. Indeed, Unger's awareness of his growing ill health provided a further poignancy to the work's already visceral gravity. According to Kraglund:

> Mahler's last completed work, his Ninth, can be considered a symphonic continuation of his "Song of the Earth." "The Farewell," as the last part of the "Song of the Earth" is called, would be an appropriate inscription for the Ninth Symphony as a whole, a farewell, however, raised far above any individual human fate, and therefore not requiring human song or words as a medium of expression, but using orchestral language in its most absolute form. This music represents contemplation of life from a tremendous distance, almost from a point beyond.[19]

The fears over his health that Unger had faced in the lead-up to the premiere of the Mahler Ninth, however, were more than but a passing problem. Rather, they were the early warnings that a heart problem would soon end both his career and his life. In fact, the conductor had for years been warned by doctors that he needed to work a less rigorous schedule to avoid the requisite strains of his conducting and that it would only be possible for Unger, in the words of his wife, "to continue his work on a reduced scale."[20]

As his wife was careful to point out, Unger did not intend to retire completely but merely to "allow a little more space for rest between his demanding professional activities."[21] Yet perhaps aware of the little time that remained to him, Unger redoubled his efforts to present as many of Mahler's unknown symphonies to the Canadian public as possible. The first in this sequence of anticipated premieres was the Toronto premiere of Mahler's Third Symphony, a concert that took place at Massey Hall on 4 February 1964 and was broadcast on *CBC Sunday Night* on 9 February 1964.[22] Performance of the ninety-minute-long symphony required not only an enhanced TSO but also three choirs and a soprano soloist in the shape of Mary Simmons, a logistical complexity that underlined the composer's ambition in creating a work that was meant to describe "the world, nature as a whole, which ... is bursting into song and music out of an unfathomable silence."[23] Even then, Unger's desire to present so complex a work still required considerable compromise: the use of a score for reduced orchestra – "published by Universal Edition for business reasons (4 horns instead of 8 etc.)" – that he conceded "would never have found the approval of the composer for whom the color of the orchestra was all-important."[24]

Perhaps unsurprisingly, Unger was not entirely satisfied with the results of the performance or, especially, in the lack of interest that it generated. However engrossed he may have been in the work, he could not fail to notice "the rows of empty seats" in Massey Hall that evening or the performance's shortcomings.[25] In a rueful mood, he could not even feel pleased by the plaudits directed his way when the work itself remained so misunderstood. For while George Kidd noted that Unger had "conducted with depth, sincerity and belief," his remaining unconvinced by a symphony he described as filled with "too many moments of complete boredom ... and cluttered with the use of solo voice and chorus" would have been anathema to a man who saw the success of Mahler's work as paramount.[26] Even Kraglund, the Toronto critic with perhaps the greatest interest in Mahler's work, praised the conductor's achievement but alluded to his frustrations with the work itself:

> Unger's ability to draw delicately shaded musical contrasts from an orchestra was superbly demonstrated in the final Adagio – what love is telling me. This is the sort of movement that can seem endless and formless. Last night it was neither. Rather, it was completely engrossing, from the string section's most breathless pianissimos to the transparent, resonant climaxes.[27]

Unger was not satisfied with having presented the Canadian premieres of Mahler's Second, Fifth, and Ninth Symphonies as well as the Toronto premiere of the Third Symphony. In the time that remained, he hoped to introduce to Canada those Mahler works that had not yet been heard, including the Eighth Symphony, colloquially known as the "Symphony of a Thousand" due to the large number of performers required for its presentation. Indeed, he had originally presented his plans to the Canada Council in June 1963, proposing to premiere the work during the Canadian centenary in 1967 as a showcase for "what Canada has to offer."[28]

But Unger's hopes to lead this vastest of Mahler's symphonies in Canada were ultimately stymied by the verdict of the Centenary Council. In the fall of 1964, Unger received a letter stating that "the Centennial Commission will not be able to extend financial assistance to this project [because] it is a matter of Canadian Commission policy to consider only projects that are national in scope," a precondition that could never be met by a project in which "a performance could only take place in one city and could not possibly be toured to make it a project of wider significance."[29] The conductor's myopic and misguided attempt to link Mahler's grandest symphonic statement to the Canadian Centennial had failed miserably, revealing how Unger, despite contributing to the Canadian cultural landscape, possessed a perspective distinct from his surroundings.

Unger's inability to see matters clearly had resulted in more than just his wasted efforts to lead Mahler's Eighth Symphony. In the final years of his life, the musician was plagued by a lack of representation that foretold his career's end. For many years, the famous English management agency of Ibbs and Tillett had represented him in the English-speaking world. On numerous occasions, Unger felt that the agency had failed to effectively promote him, prompting in him the desire to obtain the support that someone like Sol Hurok might have provided. In the Spanish-speaking world, meanwhile, Unger had worked with Daniel Attractions, a Spanish-based agency that had effectively represented him in Spain and also arranged for his many successful trips to Latin America. When Daniel Attractions opened a branch office in Canada, Unger leapt at the opportunity, signing a contract in the spring of 1964 that made the Hungarian-born Aladar Ecsedy his agent the world over.[30]

In the first few months of the Unger-Ecsedy relationship, the musician's decision seemed to bear fruit. In contrast to his rather infrequent correspondence with Ibbs and Tillet, communication between Unger and Ecsedy as well as between Ecsedy and parties interested in securing the conductor's services came frequently. In September 1964, the agent updated Unger on his recent promotional work, noting that he had received "a number of good responses" and that the conductor's prospects for the coming seasons looked extremely good.[31] Compared to the Ibbs and Tillet era, in which Unger was obliged to make many of his own concert arrangements, the conductor must have been delighted to find an agent who was willing to do some of this work for him. Seemingly, Unger had made a wise decision in choosing Ecsedy and Daniel Attractions as his representatives.

But as fall turned to winter, the Unger-Ecsedy relationship came to an abrupt end. On 21 December 1964, the *Globe and Mail* ran a brief article reporting that Aladar Ecsedy had "been charged under Section 50 of the Immigration Act ... in connection with the admission to Canada of three immigrants."[32] The circumstances of the charge could have come straight out of a spy movie:

> Three Hungarian immigrants told RCMP officers they were told by a man in Buenos Aires that he could get them into Canada for $300 each. They paid the money, they said, but they never heard from the man.[33]

THE TELEGRAM, Toronto, Wed., Feb. 5, 1964

**Enthusiastic Reception For Unger With TSO**

The applause was long and loud; many stood and others stomped their feet in applauding Dr. Unger.

And with good reason.

Both the Mahler and the Schubert "Rosamunde" were first-rate.

His interpretation of the Mahler was a profound and moving experience. A long work (90 minutes), in Unger's hands it was charged with electric excitement. In the third and sixth movements especially, he showed the genius that won him the Mahler medal.

THE GLOBE AND MAIL, WEDNESDAY, FEB. 5, 1964

**Mahler's 3rd Symphony Engrossing**

**During the 12 years** since the beginning of the York Concerts Unger has offered us most of Mahler's major works, consistently providing evidence that he ranks among the very few outstanding interpreters of this composer's music.

**As for Mahler's** Third, if one survives the opening movement the rest offers a rewarding example of the composer's songful style. But it is not easy to equate Mahler's suggestion that the first 30 minutes depicts the awakening of everything, including life from inert matter.

**There my reservations** ceased. Mahler's flowers received my full attention in the second movement, a graceful minuet, in which both the music and Unger's choreography communicated the delicate message of natural beauty. And the Scherzo, depicting, according to Mahler, what the animals in the woods are telling me, convinced me that one of the reasons today's audiences have difficulty understanding him is that they are not making woods like that any more. What woods do you know where so many animals scurry and chatter in a most unhibited and melodic fashion and which boasts a coach with an apparently very longwinded postillion?

And Unger's ability to draw delicately shaded musical contrasts from an orchestra was superbly demonstrated in the final Adagio—what love is telling me. This is the sort of movement that can seem endless and formless. Last night it was neither. Rather, it was consistently engrossing, from the string section's most breathless pianissimos to the transparent, resonant climaxes.

TORONTO DAILY STAR

WEDNESDAY, FEBRUARY 5, 1964

***Unger's Mahler electric***

SUPERLATIVE

There is no question about the superlative work of Dr. Unger and his orchestra. He conducted with depth, sincerity and belief and his performance on the podium was one of dignity and musical intelligence. It seems a pity he only appears for such a short time each year.

Dr. Heinz Unger and the Toronto Symphony Orchestra were faced with a rousing ovation at the conclusion of the over-long, gigantic, and sometimes ponderous work, which opened what promises to be a rewarding season for the York Concert Society.

EXCLUSIVE MANAGEMENT: DANIEL ATTRACTIONS, INC.

96 Mayfair Crescent, Hamilton, Ontario, Canada

*Tel: 527-0054* *Cable: DANIEL*

5.1 Near the end of his life Heinz Unger was represented for a short time by Aladar Ecsedy of Daniel Attractions. This publicity advert dates to fall 1964. Source: Library and Archives Canada, MUS 56, Box 2, File 29.

Ecsedy appeared in the city magistrate's court on 29 December 1964 and, facing his own problems, silently disappeared from Unger's life.

But Unger had little time left to reflect upon this professional setback. Instead, his final months were filled with a number of important events. In January 1965 he was honoured by the West German government with the Commander's Cross of the Order of Merit of the Federal Republic of Germany on the occasion of his golden jubilee as a conductor and – as he put it – "in recognition for what I have done in the course of my career for the music of the country of my birth."[34] The award was more than a professional honour for the conductor – on a more personal level it also served a curative purpose, granted as it was, in Unger's words, "in an effort to mend what the years of darkness [the Nazi period] have done to me and so many others."[35]

Heinz Unger received the award at a ceremony in Toronto hosted by the West German consul general to Canada on 28 January 1965.[36] On this occasion, he made a speech that, coming so close to the end of his life and being one of his last public utterances, serves as a summation of his life and views and helps us understand the values that he had long borne and, now honoured, felt he could finally express. Here, at last, lay Unger's opportunity to publicly expound and reflect upon his fate.

Unger's speech began shaded with anger. Having so long carried the burden of being a Jewish refugee, he shared his views concerning what the period of Nazi domination represented and what he experienced in those "years of darkness":

> Our generation has experienced things unfathomable. None of us will or must ever forget the years of darkness we have witnessed or of which we have been victims. It was a sinister day indeed when those who held power temporarily in the country which I, like generations of my ancestors, had considered home, deprived me on account of my race of the right to continue in my profession, and when I, to escape worse, left the country with my family. Every tie broke in those evil years.[37]

But however final the breaking of ties in that period had seemed, Unger made clear that a permanent rift with German culture, whatever his experience, could never have occurred:

> Would I not have had to sacrifice my very own and truest nature, if I had not continued also on foreign soil and also during the years of darkness, to remain faithful to that art which meant everything to me, and which was, so to say, my self-expression?[38]

While the formal ties with Germany had indeed been severed, Unger could not but maintain his allegiance to the values that underpinned German culture and had existed prior to the Nazi seizure of power. In his formulation, Nazi values were not German values but were instead an artificial imposition that had subsumed the true Germany, if only for a short, desperate time.

But what was this true Germany? And just as importantly, how did Unger view the role of Germans Jews in this Germany? In addressing the matter, he made a definitive statement that clearly demonstrated his conviction that German Jews had played an integral role in the development of German culture:

> Germany always was for me not only the country of Beethoven, of Brahms, the country of Goethe, Lessing, Hans Sachs and Walter von der Vogelweide. It was and will always remain also the country of Felix von Mendelssohn, of Heinrich Heine, of Albert Einstein, the country of the "Magic Horn" romanticism and of Faustian poetry, which inspired Gustav Mahler to his greatest creations.[39]

While acknowledging the German cultural essence borne by the greatest lights in the German cultural firmament, Unger was careful to point out that German Jews had also played a central role in the development and evolution of German culture. Moreover, he unmistakably articulated that Mahler's art had been inspired by these same sources of German culture and had continued its development. In a life devoted to Gustav Mahler's symphonic utterances, Unger had clearly arrived at a point where he saw himself as an integral part of a rich German tradition that had more than just accepted its Jewish countrymen – indeed, according to Unger, its very fabric was interwoven with Jewish achievement.

Unger then ended his speech with a final reflection on the Germany that had re-emerged from the cataclysms of the first half of the twentieth century:

> Are we really capable of changing in things essential to us? I do not quite believe it. Only the times are changing, and I do not hesitate to say that I was very happy indeed to be able to return to Germany, a different Germany, for very enjoyable musical activities on various occasions after the nightmare years had passed.[40]

Germany had not changed substantively after the period of Nazi rule. Instead, it had awoken as if from a bad dream and the values that it had borne within itself before the nightmare had once again risen to the

5.2 Heinz Unger celebrates receiving the West German government's Order of Merit for Cultural Achievements at a ceremony hosted by the West German Consul General in Toronto on 28 January 1965. Source: Library and Archives Canada, MUS 56, Box 14.

surface. Unger, on the occasion that marked his being awarded the highest civilian honour that the West German government could bestow, was exalted that the Germany he had known, the Germany where Germans both Jewish and Christian were recognized as equal and perhaps even inseparable, had once more arisen.

~

Heinz Unger had for many years struggled with health problems. In the final years of his life, however, he bore one particular ailment that pursued him relentlessly. This ailment, a heart condition that required him to avoid undue stress, only worsened with time. By the winter of 1965, he had to accept that he could no longer continue as director of the York Concert Society in any major capacity. As he put it in a letter to his friend Leon Weinstein dated 12 February, "my medical advisors are trying to convince me in ever more urgent terms that it is not advisable for me to continue beyond my seventieth year with any kind of permanent activity such as organizing a whole concert series, however short, with its inevitable excitements, [as it is] damaging to my health."[41] Unger, however, could not imagine retiring from the conductor's podium and so reconciled himself "to a very limited number of guest engagements here and abroad, where the enjoyable experience of making music and fulfilling tasks of special interest to me, is the only excitement."[42]

Yet Unger did not have the opportunity to put into motion his plans for retirement. In the final month of his life, the conductor continued to work as he had always done, concentrating on disseminating Mahler's music. On 2 February 1965, in celebration of his fiftieth year as a conductor, he led a final performance of Mahler's *Das Lied von der Erde* with the Toronto Symphony Orchestra. This concert was then broadcast on CBC Radio on 7 February, the first of what was intended as a trio of performances of Mahler's music to be followed by the Canadian premieres of Symphony no. 6 on 28 February and Symphony no. 7 scheduled for 25 April – a fitting honour bestowed upon a conductor who had done so much to familiarize Canadians with Mahler's oeuvre.[43]

Shortly after the performance of *Das Lied*, Unger turned to preparing the Canadian premiere of Symphony no. 6 (*Tragic*) – in the end, the last of his Canadian Mahler premieres. Indeed, the conductor's last act was to record the first three movements of this work, a symphony that bore in its final movement three hammer blows that the composer's wife said – perhaps apocryphally – signified the three tragedies in Mahler's life: the death of his daughter Maria Anna; his forced departure from the directorship of the Vienna Opera and his beloved Viennese home; and the diagnosis of a heart condition that would prove fatal and "fell him like a tree." But Unger did not survive long enough to perform this tragic conclusion to the symphony, suffering on 25 February 1965 a life-ending heart attack upon returning home from the CBC studios after the day's recording session.

On 28 February 1965, the CBC broadcast Unger's performance of Mahler's Sixth Symphony, the final movement led by Unger's now forgotten protégé Hans Bauer. Writing in the wake of this broadcast, the doyen of Toronto music criticism, John Kraglund, reflected on Unger's life as well as his relationship with the conductor:

> After years of close affiliation with Heinz Unger, as a friend – albeit on the armed basis that must exist between performer and critic – as a sounding-board for hopes, frustrations, and program plans and, consequently, sometimes in an advisory capacity, it is difficult to view objectively his final contribution to our musical life.[44]

Kraglund then looked to Unger's final moments and their meaning:

> But it can safely be said that Dr. Unger would have been happy, although not entirely satisfied with the results. Perhaps I am giving way too much to romanticism when I suggest that the CBC's broadcast of the work ... gave the impression that everyone from conductor to recording technician had done everything within his power to make this a fitting memorial to Dr. Unger.[45]

Finally, Kraglund weighed in on the matter of whether the final movement of Mahler's Sixth Symphony, left unrecorded at Unger's death, should have been completed by Hans Bauer:

> It was suggested by a friend that the tribute might have been more fitting if only the three movements recorded by Dr. Unger had been broadcast. Such is not, I believe the case. The fact that he died virtually in the middle of a performance, after repeated warnings from doctors, seems ample evidence that he deemed music, especially the music of Mahler, more important than his own life. He would doubtless have felt neither Mahler nor the public had been properly served if the work had not been completed.[46]

Kraglund fittingly concluded that Mahler's music represented for the German Jewish musician a spiritual essence that transcended life itself. And if Kraglund was right, then Unger would have surely been pleased to have seen the work's completion, even as it cost him his life.

Years before his death, Heinz Unger had reflected on the meaning of Gustav Mahler's *Das Lied von der Erde.* Commenting on the work's final movement, entitled "Der Abschied" (The Farewell), he wrote that it bore neither resignation nor pessimism but an acceptance of the end in a continual reawakening:

> After an orchestral interlude depicting tragedy and disappointment, the real "Farewell" part begins. The singer ... meets his closest friend to bid him the last farewell. He tells him that it has to be, and that he is going away into the mountains (a Buddhist expression for going to another incarnation). Fate has not been kind to him in this world, he says, and he is longing for home and rest. And then follow, replacing completely the resigned and tired words of the original poem, those incomparable words of Mahler's own: "Quiet is my heart and waiting for its hour. This beloved earth always will blossom up in spring and green anew. Always and everywhere will shine a blue light in the distance. Ever ... Ever ..."[47]

In bidding his own farewell to the world, one can only hope that Unger somehow learned of the light that came to shine on Mahler's once-neglected music. A richer and more fitting fate the conductor could surely not have imagined.

# Conclusion

Heinz Unger died on 25 February 1965. Discounting his long and arduous time in the Soviet Union (of which we know little more than what he himself tells us in his memoir), by the time of his passing he had managed to construct a life three times over, first in his native Germany, again during his residence in wartime England, and once more following the Second World War as he succeeded in becoming a key cultural player in his adopted Canadian home and a frequent traveller who won many admirers, not least in Spain. And while Unger's name continues to circulate in one very meaningful albeit limited context – by 1968, a scholarship had been created in his name that to this day continues to help young Canadian conductors build their careers – today very few know of his achievements, regardless of whether we are speaking in a Canadian or European context.[1] Even among Mahlerites, Unger is a mysterious figure, perhaps a name alone, an obscure footnote in musical history. In short order, he disappeared from the cultural scene after his death in 1965, forgotten by most despite his many accomplishments around the world.

The neglect from which Unger's legacy has suffered is difficult to comprehend. At the time of his death, the loss that the musical world had suffered was widely recognized; the Heinz Unger Fonds at Library and Archives Canada is filled not only with expressions of sadness at the conductor's passing from friends but also with enough notes sent by musicians to assure us that the loss of a major musical talent was widely recognized by Unger's contemporaries. Of course, close friends and family also wrote to his widow Hella Unger to soften the grief of her husband's passing. But as news of his death circulated through the Canadian cultural community, Hella Unger was inundated with a barrage of condolence letters from such distinguished Canadian musicians as Greta Kraus, Oskar Morawetz, and Harry Somers. In sum, musicians and music lovers decried the fate of a conductor who throughout his life had laboured to introduce audiences to fine music and who had worked tirelessly to help develop Canadian culture in his two decades resident in the country.

Most of the expressions of grief at the time commented on Unger's love of Gustav Mahler and correctly noted that the composer had lost one of his most important followers who had for decades expressed an almost missionary zeal in attempting to convince the concert-going public and the world at large of the composer's significance. Yet today, Heinz Unger's name is lost, few people knowing his name at all and even fewer knowing the extent of his contribution to the acceptance of Mahler's music.

In a letter to Unger's recently widowed wife, the Czech Canadian composer Oskar Morawetz would note:

> I couldn't help but think, during these last few days, of Mahler's "Abschied" from the "Lied von der Erde." I feel that Dr. Unger's life had many things in common with Mahler's life as a composer, including the fact that, although he had many great admirers, his real greatness was never appreciated to the full extent. But I am glad that he at least lived in an age when great conductors can always be remembered through their tapes.[2]

Yet Morawetz's hope has not come to pass. In a Canada dominated by the towering genius of Glenn Gould, many others seem lost on the fringes of history. Instead of serving as a means for Canadians to better understand their cultural history, Gould's legacy has eclipsed that of many other Canadian artists. Most people interested in Canadian culture, instead of looking beyond the cult of the eccentric and mercurial Canadian pianist, seem content to begin and end their explorations there, just beyond the reach of a vast universe of stars, like Unger, who shone just as brightly in their time yet have not received the posthumous attention they so merit. The CBC, all too aware of the bottom line in today's precarious economic climate, helped spawn this Glenn Gould industry, satisfied if Canadian high culture can earn a mention or generate revenue for the often economically beleaguered Crown corporation.

Heinz Unger, then, has been relegated to the fringes of Canadian cultural history. Why this is also the case in the European, Mahlerian, and Jewish contexts is a question that in part must go begging. That said, a few guesses can still be wagered. First, we must remind ourselves that the twentieth century was tremendously turbulent, fraught as it was with displacement and destruction on an unprecedented scale. Due to the seismic historical events of the period and the need to avoid them in order to stay alive, Unger died in Canada, where, as we have seen, he has been all but forgotten. Moreover, any chance that researchers from around the world might happen upon material relating to the musician has been largely compromised by this very devastation, with some documentary evidence pertaining to Unger's life destroyed during the war.[3] As a result, the entirety of Unger's known archive (amounting to a little more than two metres of textual records and consisting of an extensive collection of letters, documents, and numerous recordings) is in Canada; all the material Unger had kept was deposited by his family at Library and Archives Canada after his passing. And because no one, until now, has explored this rich collection, Unger's achievements have, with the passage of time, been forgotten both in Canada and elsewhere.

But there are other possible reasons for the neglect that Unger has suffered. As has been made abundantly clear in the course of this book, the conductor looked upon Gustav Mahler's oeuvre with an almost holy reverence, devoting the majority of his life to trying to see that the composer's work was better understood and appreciated. I would here like to suggest that Unger's single-minded devotion to Mahler may have in fact come at the wrong time. As noted earlier, the composer was for many decades forgotten, his fortunes rising again only in the 1960s, when charismatic and talented young conductors – such as the American Leonard Bernstein – helped re-popularize his admittedly difficult works. In the rush to rediscover Mahler's importance, the musical world embraced a new breed of conductors to inject new life into a flagging art music culture being assaulted by the more visceral (and better selling) genre of rock and roll. Older conductors such as Unger – with their *Kapellmeister*-like ways – simply would not "sell." And so as new recordings of Mahler's works were made – most in stereo and thus better able to convey the complexity of the scores – there seemed little reason to rely on older recordings made in Canada to introduce a new generation of listeners to the work of this master.[4] Unger, so vital in sustaining Mahler at the edges of the repertoire for decades, was cast aside and forgotten just as the composer was rediscovered and transformed into a cultural icon.

In overlooking Unger's role as a Mahler disciple, the musical world has been deprived of the knowledge of a musician whose recordings of Mahler's music represent an important example of mid-century understandings of Mahler performance. Yet as we have already noted, Unger's widow was at the time of her husband's death bombarded with a barrage of letters of condolence, letters written by friends, colleagues, associates, and fans who had followed the conductor's career from his earliest days and fondly remembered his intensity and devotion to composer's music. However quickly he may have disappeared from the public consciousness, Unger did not die alone and defeated – rather, he died doing what he loved most: conducting Gustav Mahler's music, secure in the knowledge that he had made the composer many new supporters.

But even in death, Unger's crusade for Mahler did not cease. At his funeral, the music that accompanied the mourners was the famous Adagietto from Mahler's Fifth Symphony, surely sign of a devotion that transcended the temporal and was more than just a singular dedication to a composer and his oeuvre. As we have seen in the course of this book, Gustav Mahler represented for Unger an affiliation with his German Jewish identity, an identity that could not be lost whatever the circumstances or events of his life and that grew ever clearer through the years. For Unger, the Mahlerian cause became an act of devotion that transcended the purely artistic; it was a delicate string connecting Unger to a Jewish world, transforming his performance of Mahler's music into a performative Jewish ritual. Historians of Jewry, deprived of a critical example of the importance that Gustav Mahler bore for a generation of German Jews whose two-fold identity privileged neither "Germanness" nor "Jewishness," have only recently and belatedly begun to dismantle the long-dominant narrative of the failure of German Jewish integration.

Alongside the composer's affection and enthusiasm for Mahler's music, another significant theme appeared repeatedly at the time of Unger's death, and it bears noting here. For one who was often excluded from or who failed to make a deep impression on the Jewish world (and especially within the confines of the Canadian Jewish community), the many outpourings of grief, expressed as they were within a fabric of Jewish communal sentiment, reveal a surprisingly marked Jewish component to the conductor's public persona. Mr. and Mrs. Mark Levy, among Unger's closest friends in Canada, immediately made a donation to the Toronto-based organization Canadian Friends of the Hebrew University in his name.[5] Others, too, would make gifts on Unger's behalf to notable Jewish institutions in the Toronto area.[6] Rabbi Gunther Plaut, of Toronto's Holy Blossom Temple and himself a refugee from Nazi Germany, would write to Unger's widow that "all of us were the richer for his presence and all of us the poorer for his absence," while Unger's long-time friend and supporter Rabbi Maxwell Dubin of Los Angeles's Wilshire Boulevard Temple wrote that he had been "shocked beyond words this morning when I looked through a copy of the London Jewish Chronicle and noted an obituary that my good friend Heinz Unger had passed away."[7] And while in isolation these sentiments might possess limited significance, taken as a whole – and in tandem with the tremendous importance with which Unger endowed his admittedly sporadic activities at the Jewish community level – they present us with a far fuller understanding of Unger's affiliation with segments of the Jewish community within Canada and beyond. Having come to better understand that broad swathes of the Canadian Jewish community bore little meaning for Unger, his marginalization on the Canadian Jewish scene is not difficult to understand. This book, however, demonstrates that the study of only the mainstream segments of the Canadian Jewish community fails to show its plurality; members of the Jewish Diaspora that did not find a place within the Canadian Jewish community have gone unrecognized as an important, albeit numerically small, part of the story of Canadian Jewry.[8]

In the final sequence of Paul Wegener's 1921 film *Der Golem*, Rabbi Loew's Golem strays outside the gates of the Jewish ghetto. Happening upon a fair-haired child, he lifts her up and takes her in his arms. The child, drawn to the Star of David affixed to the Golem's neck, grabs at it and pulls it from the well-formed clay body in which it is embedded. The creature immediately falls to the ground lifeless, only to be discovered soon after by the Jews coming to find the creature's whereabouts. Relieved that no harm has been done, the Jews carry off the Golem's motionless form, returning it to the ghetto from whence it had sprung while praising God and closing the gates behind them. The Jews, at least in this particular interpretation of Jewish history, are seemingly only secure in their separate sphere behind the safety of the ghetto's walls.

In some respects, the life of the Jewish musician Heinz Unger echoes this very scenario, albeit perhaps in less stark black-and-white imagery. Unger was, like the Golem, a child of the Jewish people. He was also created as a consequence of the circumstances that swept the Jewish people into and through modernity. Like the Golem, he, too, broke through the bounds of the Jewish community, emancipated and set loose upon a world that did not understand him or his intentions. The great difference is that Unger was not taken back by the Jewish people (neither in Canada nor beyond). He was cast adrift, his legacy left to grow ever dimmer and his achievements all but forgotten. My hope is that with this work I have helped illuminate his legacy, a legacy that deserves to be rehabilitated. Unger's life not only teaches us about the perseverance and single-mindedness of an individual artist, but also helps us better understand modern Jewish history across the Diaspora.

*Appendix*

# Known Concerts and Performances by Heinz Unger

1915
Berlin, Germany
Unknown amateur orchestra
Beethoven: Symphony no. 5 (excerpts)

13 September 1919
Berlin, Germany
Berlin Philharmonic
Wagner: *Faust Overture*; Mahler: Symphony no. 1

19 September 1919
Berlin, Germany
Berlin Philharmonic
Gluck: Overture to *Iphigenia in Aulis*; Mahler: *Das Lied von der Erde*
Soloists: Waldemar Henke (tenor), Ida Harth zur Nieden (alto)

7 January 1920
Berlin, Germany
Blüthner Orchester
Beethoven: *Coriolan Overture*; Bach: Violin Concerto (E-Dur); Mendelssohn: Violin Concerto (E minor, Op. 64); Paganini: Violin Concerto (D-Dur)
Soloist: Carola Zellenka (violin)

20 March 1920
Berlin, Germany
Berlin Philharmonic
Mozart: Symphony no. 36, Arias from *Il Re Pastore* and *Die Entführung aus dem Serail*
Soloist: Maria Ivogün (soprano)

29 April 1920
Berlin, Germany
Berlin Philharmonic
Mahler: *Lieder eines fahrenden Gesellen*, Symphony no. 5
Soloist: Josef Mann (tenor)

9 September 1920
Berlin, Germany
Berlin Philharmonic
Mahler: *Kindertotenlieder*, Symphony no. 5
Soloist: Olga Schaeffer

27 October 1920
Berlin, Germany
Blüthner Orchester
Mozart: Overture to *The Marriage of Figaro*; Beethoven: Symphony no. 1; Liszt: *Hungarian Rhapsody* no. 1; Wagner: Vorspiel III Akt and Brantchor (?) from *Lohengrin*; Beethoven: *Leonore No. 3* Overture

27 November 1920
Berlin, Germany
Blüthner Orchester
Beethoven: Piano Concerto no. 5; Brahms: Violin Concerto; Liszt: Piano Concerto no. 2
Soloists: Elisabeth Lesser-Cohn (violin), Irene Freimann (piano)

17 December 1920
Oranienburg, Germany
Blüthner Orchester
Beethoven: *Coriolan Overture*, 2nd and 3rd Movements from Violin Concerto, Overture to *The Creatures of Prometheus*, Symphony no. 2
Concertmaster and Soloist: Lambinon (violin)

18 December 1920
Oranienburg, Germany
Blüthner Orchester
Beethoven: *Coriolan Overture*, 2nd and 3rd Movements from Violin Concerto, Overture to *The Creatures of Prometheus*, Symphony no. 2
Concertmaster and Soloist: Lambinon (violin)

28 December 1920
Berlin, Germany

Blüthner Orchester
Beethoven: Overture to *Egmont*, Symphony no. 6 (*Pastorale*), Symphony no. 5

10 January 1921
Berlin, Germany (Glaubenskirche)
Blüthner Orchester
Haydn: *Die Schöpfung*
Soloists: Rose Walter (soprano), Paul Bauer

16 January 1921
Berlin, Germany
Blüthner Orchester
Liszt: *Les Préludes*, Piano Concerto no. 2; Wagner: Overture to *Rienzi*, *Siegfried Idyll*, Vorspiel (Prelude) to *Die Meistersinger von Nürnberg*

26 January 1921
Berlin, Germany
Berlin Philharmonic
Mozart: *Eine Kleine Nachtmusik*; Handel: Aria sequence from *L'Allegro, il Pensieroso ed il moderato*; Gluck: Larissa's Aria from *Il trionfo di Clelia*; D. Scarlatti: Andante from Ballet-Suite *Les femmes de bonne humeur*; Mozart: Aria from *Il Re Pastore* and Sandrina's Aria from *Die Gärtnerin aus Liebe*, Serenade no. 7 (*Haffner Serenade*) (selections)
Soloist: Rose Walter (soprano)

11 February 1921
Berlin, Germany
Berlin Philharmonic
Mahler: Symphony no. 7

17 March 1921
Berlin, Germany
Orchester aus 46 ersten Berliner Künstlern
Handel: Concerto Grosso no. 17; Mozart: Piano Concerto no. 24 (K. 491); Beethoven: Piano Concerto no. 1, Symphony no. 8
Soloist: Felix Dyck (piano)

1 November 1922
Berlin, Germany
Blüthner Orchester

Internationale Componisten Gilde, Berlin, Erstes Konzert (founded by Varese and Salzedo, 1921)
Hindemith: String Quartet Op. 16; Arthur Lourie: *Volga Pastorale*; Busoni: *Gesang vom Reigen der Geister*; Varese: unknown work; Bernard van Dieren (1887–1936): Overture Op. 7
Note: Unger appears only on select (orchestral?) parts of program

19 March 1924
Magdeburg, Germany
Städtisches Orchester zu Magdeburg
Bruckner: Overture in G minor; Beethoven: Violin Concerto, Symphony no. 5
Soloist: Otto Kobin (violin)

9 April 1924
Magdeburg, Germany
Städtisches Orchester zu Magdeburg
Works by Mozart and Dittersdorf (unknown)
Soloist: Gertrud Žurek (soprano)

26 March 1925
Berlin, Germany
Berlin Philharmonic
Beethoven: *Grosse-Fugue* (for String Orchestra), Op. 133; Brahms: Piano Concerto no. 2; Beethoven: Symphony no. 5
Soloist: Artur Schnabel (piano)

15 October 1925
Berlin, Germany
Berlin Philharmonic
Mahler: Drei Lieder mit Orchester, Symphony no. 9
Soloist: Maria von Basilides (vocalist)

12 November 1925
Berlin, Germany
Berlin Philharmonic
Handel: *Samson*
Soloists: Lotte Leonard, Maria von Basilides, Gunner Graarud, Otto Helgers Choir: Berliner Caecilienchor

10 December 1925
Berlin, Germany

Berlin Philharmonic
Ravel: *La Valse*; Prokofiev: Piano Concerto no. 3 (BPO premiere); Beethoven: Symphony no. 7
Soloist: Heinz Jolles (piano)

21 January 1926
Berlin, Germany
Berlin Philharmonic
Mendelssohn: Overture to *A Midsummer Night's Dream*; Chopin: Piano Concerto no. 1; Brahms: Symphony no. 1
Soloist: Artur Schnabel (piano)

18 February 1926
Berlin, Germany
Berlin Philharmonic
Mozart: Serenade no. 7 (*Haffner Serenade*); Hindemith: Kammermusik no. 4 (Violinkonzert) (Erstaufführung); R. Strauss: *Till Eulenspiegels lustige Streiche*

18 March 1926
Berlin, Germany
Berlin Philharmonic
Bruckner: Symphony no. 3; Verdi: *Quattro pezzi sacri*
Soloists: Rose Walter, Lilli Dreyfus, Meta Glass-Villaret, Alfred Wilde, Martin Abendroth, and Berliner Caecilienchor

14 October 1926
Berlin, Germany
Berlin Philharmonic
Mahler: Symphony no. 3
Soloists: Maria Olszewska (alto), Berliner Caecilienchor, Knabenchor der XII Realschule

11 November 1926
Berlin, Germany
Berlin Philharmonic
Respighi: Piano Concerto in the Mixolydian mode, *La Primavera* (symphonic tone poem for solo, choir, and orchestra)
Soloists: Ottorino Respighi (piano); *La Primavera*: Mitwurkung: Elma von Haynal, Marianne Hoeglauer, Marga Burlin, Gerrit Visser, Hans Herm. Nissen, Kurt Weiler; Berliner Caecilienchor (with Antonie Sternschen Frauenchor)

9 December 1926
Berlin, Germany
Berlin Philharmonic
Beethoven: *Choral Fantasia*, Symphony no. 9
Soloists: *Choral Fantasia*: Artur Schnabel (piano), Kate Ravoth, Hede Turk, Lilli Dreyfus, Gerrit Visser, Georg Muller, Albert Fischer; Symphony no. 9: Kate Ravoth, Lilli Dreyfus, Gerrit Visser, Albert Fischer, and Berliner Caecilienchor (with Antonie Sternschen Frauenchors)

20 January 1927
Berlin, Germany
Berlin Philharmonic
Weber: Overture to *Euryanthe*, Zwischenaktsmusik a.d. Oper *Die Drei Pintos* (orchestrated Mahler); Brahms: Violin Concerto; Mendelssohn: Symphony no. 3 (*Scottish*)
Soloist: Bronislaw Huberman (violin)

24 February 1927
Berlin, Germany
Berlin Philharmonic
Mozart: Serenade no. 12; Violin Concerto no. 5; Mahler: Symphony no. 4
Soloists: Mozart: Adila Fachiri (violin); Mahler: Lotte Schöne (soprano)

10 November 1927
Berlin, Germany
Berlin Philharmonic
Prokofiev: *Ala und Lolly* (*Scythian Suite*); Mussorgsky: Gesang der Parassja aus *Der Jahrmarkt von Soroschintzi*; Rimsky-Korsakov: Szene und Aria der Martha aus *Die Zarenbraut* (aria); Tchaikovsky: Symphony no. 6 (*Pathetique*)
Soloists: Meta Seinmeyer (singer); Fritz Fischer (piano); Hugo Strelitzer (celesta)

16 February 1928
Berlin, Germany
Berlin Philharmonic
Wagner: *Siegfried-Idyll* (chamber version); Weill: Violin Concerto (premiere); Schreker: Kammersymphonie
Soloist: Stefan Frenkel (violin)

3 March 1928
Berlin, Germany
Berlin Philharmonic
Mahler: Symphony no. 8
Soloists: Lotte Leonard (soprano), Anna-Marie Lenzburg (soprano), Elma von Heymal (alto), Julia-Lotte Stern (alto), Paul Stieber-Walter (tenor), Hermann Schey (baritone), Albert Fischer (bass)
Choirs: Berliner Caecilienchor, Clara Krause'scher Frauenchor, Neuer Berliner Frauenchor, Das verstarkte Philharmonischen Orchester, Antonie Stern'scher Frauenchor, Berliner Lehrer-Gesangverein, Knabenchor der XII Realschule
Others: Walter Fischer (organ), Fritz Gahlenback (piano), Hugo Strelitzer (celesta), Otto Ackermann (harmonium)

13 November 1928
Berlin, Germany
Berlin Philharmonic
Schubert: Overture in the Italian Style (D. 591); Schumann: Piano Concerto; Mahler: Symphony no. 1
Soloist: Moritz Rosenthal (piano)

6 December 1928
Berlin, Germany
Berlin Philharmonic
Krenek: *Potpourri* (erstaufführung); Mozart: Symphonie concertante fur Violine und Bratsche; H. Wolf: *Italian Serenade* (arr. Max Reger); R. Strauss: *Don Juan*
Soloist: Zlatko Balokovic, Josef Wolfsthal

14 February 1929
Berlin, Germany
Berlin Philharmonic
Haydn: *Der Jahreszeiten*
Soloists: Hanne: Anna Maria Lenzberg; Lukas: Hans Hoefflin; Simon: Hermann Schey; Landvolk, Jager: Berliner Cacilienchor; Am Flugel: Hugo Strelitzer

10 October 1929
Berlin, Germany
Berlin Philharmonic
Graener: *Comedietta* (Erstaufführung); Dvořak: Violin Concerto; Bruckner: Symphony no. 3
Soloist: Carl Flesch (violin)

21 November 1929
Berlin, Germany
Berlin Philharmonic
Haydn: Cello Concerto; Mahler: Symphony no. 5
Soloist: Judith Bokor (cello)

19 December 1929
Berlin, Germany
Berlin Philharmonic
Beethoven: Symphony no. 1; Brahms: Piano Concerto no. 1; Atterberg: Symphony no. 5 (*Sinfonia Funebre*) (Erstaufführung)
Soloist: Wilhelm Backhaus (piano)

20 February 1930
Berlin, Germany
Berlin Philharmonic
Bach: Orchestersuite (arr. Gustav Mahler); Beethoven: Piano Concerto no. 4; Brahms: Symphony no. 1
Soloist: Walter Gieseking (piano)

20 March 1930
Berlin, Germany
Berlin Philharmonic
R. Strauss: *Tod und Verklärung*; Bach: Violin Concerto E-Dur; Verdi: *Quattro pezzi sacri*
Soloist: Bach: Vecsey (violin); Verdi: Hede Turk, Albert Peters, Lilly Dreyfus, Fritz Lechner, Berliner Cacilienchor, Klara Krauseschen Frauenchors

23 April 1931
Berlin, Germany
Berlin Philharmonic
Beethoven: *Leonore No. 3* Overture, Violin Concerto, Symphony no. 3 (*Eroica*)
Soloist: Adolf Busch (violin)

15 October 1931
Berlin, Germany
Berlin Philharmonic
J.C. Bach: Sinfonia in B-flat major; Beethoven: Piano Concerto no. 1; Bruckner: Symphony no. 8
Soloist: Georg Bertram (piano)

10 December 1931
Berlin, Germany
Berlin Philharmonic
Prokofiev: Les Ridicules und Marsch from *The Love of Three Oranges*; Franck: *Les Djinns* (Symphonic Poem for Piano and Orchestra) (Erstaufführung); Saint-Saens: Piano Concerto no. 2; Bruch: Andromache's Aria from *Achilleus*; Verdi: Eboliaus's Aria from *Don Carlos*; Tchaikovsky: Symphony no. 6 (*Pathetique*)
Soloists: Sigrid Onegin (contralto); Paul Loyonnet (piano)

3 March 1932
Berlin, Germany
Berlin Philharmonic
Mozart: *Maurerische Trauermusik*; Brahms: Violin Concerto; Toch: *Bunte Suite für Orchester* (am Flugel: Irina Westermann); Beethoven: Symphony no. 5
Soloist: Carl Flesch (violin)

13 October 1932
Berlin, Germany
Berlin Philharmonic
Mahler: Drei Orchesterlieder, Symphony no. 9
Soloist: Alexander Kipnis (bass)

17 November 1932
Berlin, Germany
Berlin Philharmonic
Wunsch: *Kleine Lustspielsuite*; Dvořak: Cello Concerto; Tchaikovsky: Symphony no. 5
Soloist: Joseph Schuster (cello)

12 January 1933
Berlin, Germany
Berlin Philharmonic
Beethoven: *Grosse Fugue*; Vivaldi: Concerto for 4 Violins (transcribed by J.S. Bach as Concerto for Four Pianos); Bruckner: Symphony no. 9
Soloists: Goldberg, Hanke, Rostal, Totenberg, Bertram, Eisner, Kreutzer, Osborn

2 March 1933
Berlin, Germany
Berlin Philharmonic

Schoenberg: *Pelleas und Mélisande*; Weber: Konzertstück no. 1; R. Strauss: *Burleske*, *Till Eulenspiegels lustige Streiche*

16 April 1934
London, England
London Philharmonic Orchestra
Mahler: Symphony no. 1; Beethoven: Piano Concerto no. 4; R. Strauss: *Till Eulenspiegels lustige Streiche*
Soloist: Franz Osborn (piano)

23 June 1935
Valencia, Spain
Orquesta Sinfónica de Valencia
Unknown program

2 July 1935
Valencia, Spain
Orquesta Sinfónica de Valencia
Beethoven: Overture to *Egmont*, *Leonore No. 3* Overture, Symphony no. 9 (Valencia premiere)
Soloists: Carmen Andujar (soprano), Vicente Palop (tenor), Vicenta Bordes (contralto), Emilio Cortés (baritone)

21 November 1936
Leeds, England
Northern Philharmonic Orchestra
Mozart: Symphony in D (K. 385); Lalo: *Symphonie Espagnole* for Violin and Orchestra; Weinberger: Polka and Fugue from *Schwanda the Bagpiper*; Tchaikovsky: Symphony no. 4
Soloist: Samuel Dushkin (violin)

9 November 1937
Toronto, Canada
Toronto Symphony Orchestra
Mozart: Overture to *The Marriage of Figaro*, Symphony no. 35 (*Haffner*); Tchaikovsky: Violin Concerto (conducted by Ernest MacMillan); Berlioz: *Symphonie fantastique*
Soloist: Mishel Piastro (violin)

22 January 1938
Leeds, England
Northern Philharmonic Orchestra

Schubert: Overture in the Italian Style in C major (D. 591); Liszt: Piano Concerto no. 1; Beethoven: Symphony no. 7; Weber-Mahler: Entr'acte from *Die Drei Pintos*; Piano Solos (Dohnanyi: Rhapsody in C; Albeniz: Triana; Holst: Toccata); Bizet: *l'Arlésienne Suite No. 2*
Soloist: Cyril Smith (piano)

29 November 1938
Toronto, Canada
Toronto Symphony Orchestra
Brahms: Symphony no. 4; Liszt: *Les Préludes*; Wagner: "Siegfried's Rhine Journey" from *Götterdämmerung*; Tchaikovsky: *Romeo and Juliet* Fantasy Overture

7 January 1939
Leeds, England
Northern Philharmonic Orchestra
Mendelssohn: Overture to *Athalie*; Brahms: *Haydn Variations*; Beethoven: Violin Concerto; Tchaikovsky: Symphony no. 6 (*Pathetique*)
Soloist: Albert Sammons (violin)

18 March 1939
Leeds, England
Northern Philharmonic Orchestra
Rossini: Overture to *La Scala di Seta*; Mozart: Violin Concerto no. 5 (K. 219); Franck: *Les Éolides*; Vaughan Williams: *The Lark Ascending*; Dvořak: Symphony no. 9 (*From the New World*)
Soloist: Orrea Pernel (violin)

28 January 1940
London, England
West London Amateur Orchestra
Schubert: Overture in the Italian Style in C major (D. 591); Mozart: Serenade no. 7 (*Haffner Serenade*), Unknown Serenade; Brahms: *Zigeuner Lieder*, Beethoven: Symphony no. 1
Soloists: Erika Storm (soprano)

4 February 1940
London, England
West London Amateur Orchestra
Schubert: Overture in the Italian Style in C major (D. 591); Beethoven: Symphony no. 1; Brahms: *Zigeuner Lieder*, Mozart: Serenade no. 7 (*Haffner Serenade*); Sibelius: *Finlandia*
Soloists: Erika Storm (soprano), Mosco Carner (piano)

10 February 1940
Leeds, England
Northern Philharmonic Orchestra
Schubert: Symphony no. 6; Mozart: Piano Concerto no. 20 (K. 466); Smetana: "Blaník" from *Má Vlast*; Chopin: Scherzo in B flat; J. Strauss: *Roses from the South* Waltz
Soloist: Irene Kohler (piano)

24 February 1940
Leeds, England
Northern Philharmonic Orchestra
Sibelius: *Finlandia*; Franck: *Symphonic Variations for Piano and Orchestra*; Tchaikovsky: *Romeo and Juliet* Fantasy Overture; Piano Solos (Bizet-Rachmaninov: Minuet from *L'Arlésienne*; Dohnanyi: Rhapsody no. 3); Beethoven: Symphony no. 3 (*Eroica*)
Soloist: Lance Dossor (piano)

27 July 1940
London, England
West London Amateur Orchestra
Schubert: Overture in the Italian Style in C major (D. 591); Mozart: Serenade no. 7 (*Haffner Serenade*); *Eine Kleine Nachtmusik*; Dittersdorf: Sinfonia no. 3 (*Actaeon*)

9 November 1940
Leeds, England
Northern Philharmonic Orchestra
Weber: Overture to *Euryanthe*; Brahms: Symphony no. 1; Mendelssohn: Violin Concerto in E minor, Op. 64; Borodin: "Polovtsian Dances" from *Prince Igor*
Soloist: Eda Kersey (violin)

7 December 1940
Leeds, England
Northern Philharmonic Orchestra
Bizet: *Carmen* Suite; Mozart: Arias from the *Marriage of Figaro* ("Deh Vieni," "Voi che Sapete"); Holst: *Somerset Rhapsody*; Songs by Eric Fogg ("Peace"), Ivor Gurney ("Spring") and Hamilton Harty ("A Lullaby," "Grace for Light"); Tchaikovsky: Symphony no. 5
Soloist: Isobel Baillie (soprano); accompanist: Melville Cook

25 October 1941
Leeds, England
Northern Philharmonic Orchestra
Glinka: Overture to *Ruslan and Ludmilla*; Tchaikovsky: Piano Concerto no. 1; Verdi: Introduction to Act III from *La Traviata*; Piano Solo (Brahms: *Variations on a Theme of Paganini*); Brahms: Symphony no. 4
Soloist: Moiseiwitch (piano)

9 November 1941
Wakefield, England
Northern Philharmonic Orchestra
Glinka: Overture to *Ruslan and Ludmilla*; Tchaikovsky: Piano Concerto no. 1; Beethoven: Symphony no. 5; Piano Solos (Chopin: Waltz in A flat, Scherzo in C sharp minor); Wagner: Overture to *Tannhäuser*
Soloist: Phyllis Sellick (piano)

23 November 1941
Harrogate, England
Northern Philharmonic Orchestra
Glinka: Overture to *Ruslan and Ludmilla*; Tchaikovsky: Piano Concerto no. 1; Beethoven: Symphony no. 7; Wagner: Overture to *Tannhäuser*
Soloist: Phyllis Sellick (piano)

6 December 1941
Leeds, England
Northern Philharmonic Orchestra
Scarlatti: *The Good Humoured Ladies* Suite; Haydn: Piano Concerto in D, Op. 21; Beethoven: Symphony no. 8; Mussorgsky: *Night on Bald Mountain*; Piano Solos (Debusssy: "Reflet dans l'eau"; Holst: Toccata); Chabrier: *Joyeuse*
Soloist: Phyllis Sellick (piano)

(19?) January 1941
Harrogate, England
Northern Philharmonic Orchestra
Wagner: Overture to *The Mastersingers*; Liszt-Busoni: *Rhapsodie Espagnol* for Piano and Orchestra; Beethoven: Symphony no. 5; Massenet: *Scenes Pittoresques* Suite; Piano Solos (Brahms: Ballade in D minor, Op. 10; Chopin: Polonaise in A flat, Op. 53); Rossini: Overture to *William Tell*
Soloist: Daphne Coburn (piano)

29 January 1942
Doncaster, England
Northern Philharmonic Orchestra
Wagner: Overture to *Die Meistersinger*; Mendelssohn: Violin Concerto, Op. 64; Dvořak: Symphony no. 8
Soloist: Daniel Melsa (violin)

21 February 1942
Leeds, England
Northern Philharmonic Orchestra
Weber: Overture to *Oberon*; Schumann: Piano Concerto; Dvořak: Symphony no. 8
Soloist: Myra Hess (piano)

28 February 1942
Wakefield, England
Northern Philharmonic Orchestra
Smetana: Overture to *The Bartered Bride*; Mendelssohn: Violin Concerto, Op. 64; Brahms: Symphony no. 4
Soloist: Daniel Melsa (violin)

21 March 1942
Leeds, England
Northern Philharmonic Orchestra
Mozart: Overture to *Il Seraglio*; Liszt: Piano Concerto no. 1; Schubert: Symphony no. 9
Soloist: Cyril Smith (piano)

6 September 1942
London, England
London Symphony Orchestra
Mendelssohn: Overture to *Athalie*; Mahler: *Songs of a Wayfarer*; Tchaikovsky: *Romeo and Juliet* Fantasy Overture; Brahms: Symphony no. 3; Glinka: Overture to *Ruslan and Ludmilla*
Soloist: Sabine Kalter (vocalist)

26 September 1942
Wakefield, England
Northern Philharmonic Orchestra
Beethoven: Overture to *Fidelio*; Grieg: Piano Concerto; Mendelssohn: Symphony no. 4 (*Italian*); Tchaikovsky: *Romeo and Juliet* Fantasy Overture
Soloist: Phyllis Sellick (piano)

10 October 1942
Leeds, England
Northern Philharmonic Orchestra
Beethoven: Overture to *Fidelio*; Brahms: Piano Concerto no. 2; Mendelssohn: Symphony no. 4 (*Italian*)
Soloist: Louis Kentner (piano)

11 October 1942
Birmingham, England
City of Birmingham Orchestra
Smetana: Overture to *The Bartered Bride*; Bruch: Violin Concerto no. 1; Brahms: Symphony no. 1
Soloist: Norris Stanley (violin)

28 November 1942
Leeds, England
Northern Philharmonic Orchestra
Mozart: Overture to *The Marriage of Figaro*; Mendelssohn: Violin Concerto in E minor; Tchaikovsky: *Romeo and Juliet* Fantasy Overture; Brahms: Symphony no. 3
Soloist: Ida Haendel (violin)

27 December 1942
Leeds, England
Northern Philharmonic Orchestra
Mendelssohn: Overture to *A Midsummer Night's Dream*; Mozart: Piano Concerto no. 27 (K. 595); Tchaikovsky: Symphony no. 4
Soloist: Clifford Curzon (piano)

10 January 1943
Birmingham, England
City of Birmingham Orchestra
A. Benjamin: *Overture to an Italian Comedy*; Beethoven: Symphony no. 2; Rachmaninov: Piano Concerto no. 3
Soloist: Cyril Smith (piano)

2 October 1943
Wakefield, England
Northern Philharmonic Orchestra
Berlioz: *Le Carnaval Romain* Overture; Franck: *Symphonic Variations for Piano and Orchestra*; Dvořak: Symphony no. 8; Brahms: *Hungarian Dances* (in G minor and D major only)
Soloist: Kendall Taylor (piano)

3 October 1943
Barnsley, England
Northern Philharmonic Orchestra
Berlioz: *Le Carnaval Romain* Overture; Sibelius: *Valse Triste*; Massenet: Suite no. 4 (*Scenes Pittoresques*); Dvořak: Symphony no. 8; Brahms: *Hungarian Dances* (in G minor and D major only)

9 October 1943
Leeds, England
Northern Philharmonic Orchestra
Berlioz: *Le Carnaval Romain* Overture; Chopin: Piano Concerto no. 1 in E minor; Cesar Franck: Symphony in D minor
Soloist: Louis Kentner (piano)

25 October 1943
Watford, England
London Philharmonic Orchestra
Mendelssohn: *Calm Sea and Prosperous Voyage* Overture; Schumann: Piano Concerto; Brahms: Symphony no. 4
Soloist: Eileen Joyce (piano)

31 October 1943
London, England
London Philharmonic Orchestra
Gluck: Overture to *Iphigenia in Aulis*; J.S. Bach: *Brandenburg Concerto* no. 3; Brahms: Symphony no. 4; Beethoven: Symphony no. 2

7 November 1943
Birmingham, England
City of Birmingham Orchestra
Mendelssohn: Overture to *Athalie*; Elgar: Violin Concerto; Beethoven: Symphony no. 6 (*Pastorale*)
Soloist: Henry Holst (violin)

27 November 1943
Leeds, England
Northern Philharmonic Orchestra
Mozart: Symphony no. 41 (*Jupiter*); Dvořak: Cello Concerto; Wagner: Arias ("Spring Song" from *The Valkyrie* and "Lohengrin's Narration" from *Lohengrin*); Tchaikovsky: *Romeo and Juliet* Fantasy Overture
Soloists: Thelma Reiss (cello), Walter Widdop (vocalist)

18 December 1943
Leeds, England
Northern Philharmonic Orchestra
Weber: Overture to *Der Freischütz*; J.S. Bach: Keyboard Concerto no. 1 in D minor; Beethoven: Symphony no. 6 (*Pastorale*); Mussorgsky: *Pictures from an Exhibition*
Soloist: Harriet Cohen (piano)

11 January 1944
Coventry, England
London Philharmonic Orchestra
Mendelssohn: *Calm Sea and Prosperous Voyage* Overture; Beethoven: Symphony no. 2; Brahms: Symphony no. 4

12 January 1944
Nottingham, England
London Philharmonic Orchestra
Mendelssohn: *Calm Sea and Prosperous Voyage* Overture; Schumann: Piano Concerto; Brahms: Symphony no. 4
Soloist: Eileen Joyce (piano)

13 January 1944
Leicester, England
London Philharmonic Orchestra
Mendelssohn: *Calm Sea and Prosperous Voyage* Overture; Grieg: Piano Concerto; Brahms: Symphony no. 4
Soloist: Eileen Joyce (piano)

16 January 1944
London, England
London Philharmonic Orchestra
Mozart: Symphony no. 41 (*Jupiter*); H. Wolf: *Italian Serenade*; Bruckner: Symphony no. 4 (*Romantic*)

20 January 1944
Swindon, England
London Philharmonic Orchestra
Mendelssohn: *Calm Sea and Prosperous Voyage* Overture; H. Wolf: *Italian Serenade*; Dohnanyi: *Variations on a Nursery Theme* for Piano and Orchestra; Brahms: Symphony no. 4
Soloist: Joan Baker (piano)

24 January 1944
Hanley, England
London Philharmonic Orchestra
Mendelssohn: *Calm Sea and Prosperous Voyage* Overture; Elgar: Violin Concerto; H. Wolf: *Italian Serenade*; Beethoven: Symphony no. 2
Soloist: Jean Pougnet (violin)

25 January 1944
Walsall, England
London Philharmonic Orchestra
Program unknown

26 January 1944 (Lunch-Hour Concert)
Bristol, England
London Philharmonic Orchestra
Schubert: Overture and Ballet Music from *Rosamunde*; Mozart: Ballet Music to the Pantomime from *Les Petits Riens*; H. Wolf: *Italian Serenade*; J. Strauss: *Roses from the South* Waltz

26 January 1944 (Evening)
Bristol, England
London Philharmonic Orchestra
Mendelssohn: *Calm Sea and Prosperous Voyage* Overture; Grieg: Piano Concerto; Brahms: Symphony no. 4
Soloist: Eileen Joyce (piano)

5 February 1944
Chatham, England
London Philharmonic Orchestra
Mendelssohn: *Calm Sea and Prosperous Voyage* Overture; Schumann: Piano Concerto; Brahms: Symphony no. 4
Soloist: Eileen Joyce (piano)

12 February 1944
Leeds, England
Northern Philharmonic Orchestra
A. Benjamin; *Overture to an Italian Comedy*; Beethoven: Violin Concerto; Mendelssohn: Symphony no. 3 (*Scottish*)
Soloist: Eda Kersey (violin)

13 February 1944
Harrogate, England

Northern Philharmonic Orchestra
A. Benjamin: *Overture to an Italian Comedy*; Brahms: Piano Concerto no. 2; Mendelssohn: Symphony no. 3 (*Scottish*)
Soloist: Kendall Taylor (piano)

26 February 1944
Leeds, England
Northern Philharmonic Orchestra
Bach-Mahler: Suite; Beethoven: Piano Concerto no. 1; Tchaikovsky: Symphony no. 6 (*Pathetique*)
Soloist: Kendall Taylor (piano)

5 March 1944
London, England
London Philharmonic Orchestra
Wagner: Overture to *The Flying Dutchman*; Elgar: Violin Concerto; Brahms: *Variations on a Theme of Haydn* (St. Anthony Chorale); Berlioz: three pieces from *The Damnation of Faust*
Soloist: Jean Pougnet (violin)

14 March 1944
Newcastle, England
London Philharmonic Orchestra
Schubert: Overture to *Rosamunde*; Berlioz: two pieces from *The Damnation of Faust* ("Menuet des Follets," "Ballet des Sylphes"); Schumann: Piano Concerto; Brahms: Symphony no. 4
Soloist: Eileen Joyce (piano)

15 March 1944
Darlington, England
London Philharmonic Orchestra
Wagner: Overture to *The Flying Dutchman*; Berlioz: two pieces from *The Damnation of Faust* ("Menuet des Follets," "Ballet des Sylphes"); Beethoven: Symphony no. 2; Brahms: Symphony no. 4

19 March 1944
Dewsbury, England
Northern Philharmonic Orchestra
Haydn: *The Creation*

22 March 1944
Dewsbury, England

Northern Philharmonic Orchestra
Mendelssohn: Overture to *A Midsummer Night's Dream*; Tchaikovsky: Symphony no. 6 (*Pathetique*); Schumann: Piano Concerto; Glinka: Overture to *Ruslan and Ludmilla*
Soloist: Irene Kohler (piano)

1 April 1944
Leeds, England
Northern Philharmonic Orchestra
Mendelssohn: *Calm Sea and Prosperous Voyage* Overture; Mozart: Piano Concerto no. 27 (K. 595); Brahms: Symphony no. 1
Soloist: Eileen Joyce (piano)

4 April 1944
Birmingham, England
London Philharmonic Orchestra
Tchaikovsky: *Serenade for Strings*; Beethoven: Symphony no. 2; Brahms: Symphony no. 4

14 April 1944
Bristol, England
London Philharmonic Orchestra
Wagner: Overture to *The Flying Dutchman*; Brahms: *Variations on a Theme of Haydn*; Berlioz: three pieces from *The Damnation of Faust*; Beethoven: Symphony no. 3 (*Eroica*)

27 April 1944
Manchester, England
London Philharmonic Orchestra
Wagner: Overture to *The Flying Dutchman*; Berlioz: two pieces from *The Damnation of Faust*; Grieg: Piano Concerto; Beethoven: Symphony no. 3 (*Eroica*)
Soloist: Cyril Smith (piano)

18 May 1944
Newcastle, England
London Philharmonic Orchestra
Wagner: Overture to *The Flying Dutchman*; Berlioz: two pieces from *The Damnation of Faust*; Grieg: Piano Concerto; Beethoven: Symphony no. 3 (*Eroica*)
Soloist: Eileen Joyce (piano)

26 July 1944
Peterborough, England
London Philharmonic Orchestra
Mendelssohn: *Fingal's Cave Overture*; H. Wolf: *Italian Serenade*; Schumann: Symphony no. 4; Dvořak: Symphony no. 8

27 July 1944
Leicester, England
London Philharmonic Orchestra
Program unknown

28 July 1944
Nottingham, England
London Philharmonic Orchestra
Mendelssohn: *Fingal's Cave Overture*; H. Wolf: *Italian Serenade*; Schumann: Symphony no. 4; Dvořak: Symphony no. 8

9 September 1944
Leeds, England
Northern Philharmonic Orchestra
Haydn: *The Creation*
Soloists: Isobel Baillie (soprano), Parry Jones (tenor), Norman Walker (bass), Arthur Haywood (piano), Edward Allam (organ)

30 September 1944
Leeds, England
Northern Philharmonic Orchestra
Gluck: Overture to *Iphigenia in Aulis*; Haydn-Brahms: *St. Anthony Variations*, Op. 65a; Chopin: Piano Concerto no. 2; Schubert: Symphony no. 6; J. Strauss: *The Blue Danube* Waltz
Soloist: Louis Kentner (piano)

14 October 1944
Leeds, England
Northern Philharmonic Orchestra
Rossini: Overture to *La Gazza Ladra*; Dvořak: Violin Concerto; Beethoven: Symphony no. 7
Soloist: Max Rostal (violin)

8 October 1944
Doncaster, England

Northern Philharmonic Orchestra
Rossini: Overture to *La Gazza Ladra*; Tchaikovsky: Piano Concerto no. 1; Wagner: *Siegfried Idyll*; Schubert: Symphony no. 6
Soloist: Julius Isserlis (piano)

11 October 1944
Dewsbury, England
Northern Philharmonic Orchestra
Rossini: Overture to *La Gazza Ladra*; Rachmaninov: Piano Concerto no. 3; Wagner: *Siegfried Idyll*; Schubert: Symphony no. 6
Soloist: Irene Kohler (piano)

22 October 1944
Leeds, England
The Northern Philharmonic Orchestra
Dvořak: *Carnival* Overture; Tchaikovsky: Piano Concerto no. 1; Wagner: *Siegfried Idyll*; Borodin: Symphony no. 2
Soloist: Julius Isserlis (piano)

28 October 1944
Leeds, England
Northern Philharmonic Orchestra
Mozart: Symphony no. 39 (K. 543); Edward German: "Valse Gracieuse" from Symphonic Suite in D minor; Rachmaninov: Piano Concerto no. 3; Berlioz: three pieces from *The Damnation of Faust*
Soloist: Irene Kohler (piano)

11 November 1944
Leeds, England
Northern Philharmonic Orchestra
Bloch: Concerto Grosso for Strings and Piano; Beethoven: Piano Concerto no. 4; Brahms: Symphony no. 4
Soloist: Franz Osborn (piano)

19 November 1944
Leeds, England
Northern Philharmonic Orchestra
Rimsky-Korsakov: Introduction and Cortege from *Le Coq d'Or*; Grieg: Piano Concerto in A minor; Delius: "La Calinda" from *Koanga*; Tchaikovsky: Symphony no. 4
Soloist: Phyllis Sellick (piano)

23 November 1944
Doncaster, England
Northern Philharmonic Orchestra
Wagner: Overture to *Rienzi*; Grieg: Piano Concerto; Dvořak: Symphony no. 9 (*From the New World*); Bizet: *L'Arlésienne Suite*
Soloist: Phyllis Sellick (piano)

25 November 1944
Leeds, England
Northern Philharmonic Orchestra
John Milanes (orch. J. Turina): *Suite Espagnole*, Op. 3; Brahms: Violin Concerto; Dvořak: Symphony no. 9 (*From the New World*)
Soloist: Maurice Raskin (violin)

9 December 1944
Leeds, England
Northern Philharmonic Orchestra
Nicolai: Overture to *The Merry Wives of Windsor*; Mozart: Concerto in E flat for Two Pianos (K. 365); Elgar: *Severn Suite*; Schumann: Symphony no. 4
Soloists: Cyril Smith and Phyllis Sellick (pianos)

30 December 1944
Bristol, England
London Philharmonic Orchestra
Gluck: Overture to *Iphigenia in Aulis*; Schumann: Symphony no. 4; Mahler: Adagietto from Symphony no. 5; Dvořak: Symphony no. 8

4 January 1945
Guildford, England
London Philharmonic Orchestra
Schumann: Symphony no. 4; Mendelssohn: Violin Concerto in E minor; Dvořak: Symphony no. 8
Soloist: Jean Pougnet (violin)

5 January 1945
Wembley, England
London Philharmonic Orchestra
Schumann: Symphony no. 4; Dvořak: Symphony no. 8

9 January 1945
Birmingham, England

London Philharmonic Orchestra
Schumann: Symphony no. 4; Tchaikovsky: Symphony no. 4

10 January 1945
Leicester, England
London Philharmonic Orchestra
Tchaikovsky: Symphony no. 4; Schumann: Symphony no. 4

13 January 1945
Leeds, England
Northern Philharmonic Orchestra
Cherubini: Overture to *Ali Baba*; Mahler: Symphony no. 2 (Third Movement); Lalo: Cello Concerto in D minor; Mozart: "The Catalogue Song" from *Don Giovanni*; Verdi: "O tu Palermo" from *Sicilian Vespers*; Beethoven: Symphony no. 8
Soloists: Anthony Pini (cello), Ronald Stear (vocalist)

14 January 1945
Northern Philharmonic Orchestra
Nicolai: Overture to *The Merry Wives of Windsor*; Liszt: Piano Concerto no. 1; Bizet: Movements from *L'Arlésienne* (Adagietto, Farandole); Tchaikovsky: Symphony no. 4
Soloist: Julius Isserlis (piano)

21 January 1945
Leeds, England
Northern Philharmonic Orchestra
Gluck: Overture to *Iphigenia in Aulis*; Mendelssohn: Violin Concerto in E minor; Bizet: Movements from *L'Arlésienne* (Adagietto, Farandole); Delius: *On Hearing the First Cuckoo in Spring*; Elgar: *Enigma Variations*
Soloist: Frederick Grinke (violin)

27 January 1945
Leeds, England
Northern Philharmonic Orchestra
Mendelssohn: Overture to *Ruy Blas*; Wagner: *Siegfried Idyll*; Schumann: Piano Concerto in A minor; Dvořak: Symphony no. 8
Soloist: Eric Hope (piano)

28 January 1945
London, England
London Philharmonic Orchestra

Gluck: Overture to *Iphigenia in Aulis*; Beethoven: Piano Concerto no. 3; Mahler: Adagietto from Symphony no. 5; Brahms: Symphony no. 4
Soloist: Iso Elinson (piano)

1 February 1945
Oxford, England
London Philharmonic Orchestra
Gluck: Overture to *Iphigenia in Aulis*; Mahler: Adagietto from Symphony no. 5; Dvořak: Symphony no. 8; Brahms: Symphony no. 4

10 February 1945
Leeds, England
Northern Philharmonic Orchestra
Mozart: Overture to *The Magic Flute*; Delius: Piano Concerto; Sibelius: *Karelia* Suite; Tchaikovsky: Symphony no. 5
Soloist: Moura Lympany (piano)

14 February 1945
Huddersfield, England
Northern Philharmonic Orchestra
Nicolai: Overture to *The Merry Wives of Windsor*; Liszt: Piano Concerto no. 1; Bizet: movements from *L'Arlésienne*; Dvořak: Symphony no. 9 (*From the New World*)
Soloist: Julius Isserlis (piano)

18 February 1945
Leeds, England
Northern Philharmonic Orchestra
Wagner: Overture to *Rienzi*; Prokofiev: Piano Concerto no. 3; Dvořak: Symphony no. 9 (*From the New World*); Eric Coates: "London Suite" (two movements only)

21 February 1945
Leeds, England
Northern Philharmonic Orchestra
Beethoven: Symphony no. 9, *Choral Fantasia*
Soloists: Elena Danieli (soprano), Parry Jones (tenor), Freda Townson (contralto), Ronald Stear (baritone), Edward Allam (pianist)

24 February 1945
Leeds, England
Northern Philharmonic Orchestra

Shostakovich: Symphony no. 1; Mozart: Piano Concerto no. 22 (K. 482); Rimsky-Korsakov: Prelude and Cortege from *Le Coq d'Or*; Borodin: Dances from *Prince Igor*
Soloist: Kendall Taylor (piano)

3 March 1945
Liverpool, England
Liverpool Philharmonic Orchestra
Schubert: Overture to *Rosamunde*; Schubert: Symphony no. 5; Mahler: *Das Lied von der Erde*
Soloists: Mary Jarred, Paul Jones (vocalists)

10 March 1945
Leeds, England
Northern Philharmonic Orchestra
Tchaikovsky: *Serenade for Strings*, Op. 48; Elgar: Violin Concerto; Bizet: Symphony no. 1
Soloist: Albert Sammons (violin)

11 March 1945
Doncaster, England
Northern Philharmonic Orchestra
Dvořak: *Carnival* Overture; Liszt: Piano Concerto no. 1; Wagner: Prelude and Isolde's Death from *Tristan und Isolde*; Elgar: *Enigma Variations*; Glinka: Overture to *Ruslan and Ludmilla*
Soloist: Kendall Taylor (piano)

18 March 1945
Leeds, England
Northern Philharmonic Orchestra
Rossini: Overture to *William Tell*; Saint-Saens: Piano Concerto no. 2; Haydn: Symphony no. 100 (*Military*); Tchaikovsky: *Romeo and Juliet* Fantasy Overture
Soloist: Leslie England (piano)

21 March 1945
York, England
London Philharmonic Orchestra
Dvořak: *Carnival* Overture; Mahler: Adagietto from Symphony no. 5; Tchaikovsky: *Romeo and Juliet* Fantasy Overture; Beethoven: Symphony no. 3 (*Eroica*)

24 March 1945
Leeds, England
Northern Philharmonic Orchestra
Beethoven: *Coriolan Overture*; Liszt: Piano Concerto no. 2; Elgar: *Enigma Variations*; Wagner: Prelude and Isolde's Death from *Tristan und Isolde*, Overture to *The Mastersingers*
Soloist: Clifford Curzon (piano)

4 April 1945
Bristol, England
London Philharmonic Orchestra
Dvořak: *Carnival* Overture; Mahler: Adagietto from Symphony no. 5; Tchaikovsky: *Romeo and Juliet* Fantasy Overture; Beethoven: Symphony no. 3 (*Eroica*)

12 April 1945
London, England
London Philharmonic Orchestra
Dvořak: *Carnival* Overture; Mahler: Adagietto from Symphony no. 5; Tchaikovsky: *Romeo and Juliet* Fantasy Overture; Beethoven: Symphony no. 3 (*Eroica*)

16 May 1945
Manchester, England
London Philharmonic Orchestra
Weber: Overture *Oberon*; Mahler: Adagietto from Symphony no. 5; Tchaikovsky: *Romeo and Juliet* Fantasy Overture; Dvořak: *Carnival* Overture, Symphony no. 8

1 June 1945
Nottingham, England
London Philharmonic Orchestra
Mendelssohn: Overture to *Athalie*; Mahler: Adagietto from Symphony no. 5; Grieg: Piano Concerto in A minor; Weber: Overture to *Oberon*; Schubert: Symphony no. 5; J. Strauss: *Roses from the South* Waltz
Soloist: Eileen Joyce (piano)

2 June 1945
Boston, England
London Philharmonic Orchestra

Weber: Overture to *Oberon*; Schubert: Symphony no. 5; Mahler: Adagietto from Symphony no. 5; Tchaikovsky: Fantasy Overture *Romeo and Juliet*; Dvořak: Symphony no. 8

4 June 1945
Watford, England
London Philharmonic Orchestra
Weber: Overture to *Oberon*; Schubert: Symphony no. 5; Grieg: Piano Concerto in A minor; Mahler: Adagietto from Symphony no. 5; Dvořak: *Carnival* Overture; J. Strauss: *Roses from the South* Waltz
Soloist: Eileen Joyce (piano)

13 October 1945
Chatham, England
London Philharmonic Orchestra
R. Strauss: *Don Juan*; Tchaikovsky: *Serenade for Strings*; Dvořak: Symphony no. 8

21 October 1945
London, England
London Philharmonic Orchestra
Mahler: Symphony no. 5 (English premiere)

10 December 1945
Valencia, Spain
Orquesta Municipal de Valencia
Dvořak: *Carnival* Overture; Smetana: "Vltava"; Beethoven: Symphony no. 3 (*Eroica*); A. Benjamin: *Overture to an Italian Comedy* (Valencia premiere); Liszt: *Les Préludes*

16 December 1945
Valencia, Spain
Orquesta Municipal de Valencia
R. Strauss: *Till Eulenspiegels lustige Streiche*; Berlioz: three pieces from *The Damnation of Faust*; Tchaikovsky: Symphony no. 5

17 December 1945
Valencia, Spain
Orquesta Municipal de Valencia
R. Strauss: *Till Eulenspiegels lustige Streiche*; Tchaikovsky: Symphony no. 5; Gordon Jacob: Passacaglia; Berlioz: three pieces from *The Damnation of Faust*

30 December 1945
Madrid, Spain
Orquesta Sinfónica de Madrid
Brahms: Symphony no. 1; Gordon Jacob: Passacaglia; Wagner: *Siegfried Idyll*; Dvořak: *Carnival* Overture

11 January 1946
Madrid, Spain
Orquesta Nacional
Weber: Overture to *Oberon*; Smetana: "Vltava"; John Milanes (orch. J. Turina): *Suite Espagnole*, Op. 3; Tchaikovsky: Symphony no. 5

25 January 1946
Madrid, Spain
Orquesta Nacional
Gluck: Overture to *Iphigenia in Aulis*; Brahms: Symphony no. 4; R. Strauss: *Don Juan*; Berlioz: three pieces from *The Damnation of Faust*

9 February 1946
Sheffield, England
Hallé Orchestra
Rossini: Overture to *Semiramide*; Debussy: *Prélude à l'Après-midi d'un Faune*; Beethoven: Piano Concerto no. 4; Dvořak: Symphony no. 9 (*From the New World*)
Soloist: Noel Mewton-Wood (piano)

10 February 1946
Manchester, England
Hallé Orchestra
Dvořak: *Carnival* Overture; Tchaikovsky: Piano Concerto no. 1; Bruckner: Symphony no. 4 (*Romantic*) (First Movement); Mendelssohn: Symphony no. 3 (*Scottish*)
Soloist: Benno Moiseiwitch (piano)

29 March 1946
Madrid, Spain
Orquesta Nacional
Schubert: Overture to *Rosamunde*; Schumann: Piano Concerto; Mahler: Symphony no. 1
Soloist: Jose Cubilés (piano)

5 April 1946
Madrid, Spain
Orquesta Nacional
Mozart: Serenade no. 7; Holst: *The Perfect Fool* Ballet Suite; Berlioz: *Symphonie fantastique*

1 May 1946
Valencia, Spain
Orquesta Municipal de Valencia
Gluck: Overture to *Iphigenia in Aulis*; Mozart: Serenade no. 7; Mahler: Symphony no. 1

5 May 1946
Valencia, Spain
Orquesta Municipal de Valencia
Weber: Overture to *Oberon*; Schubert: Symphony no. 8 (*Unfinished*); Mahler: Symphony no. 1

September 1946
BBC Symphony Orchestra (broadcast only)
Wagner: *Siegfried Idyll*; Beethoven (unknown); Tchaikovsky: Symphony no. 4

4 October 1946
Madrid, Spain
Orquesta Nacional
Bloch: Concerto Grosso; De Falla: *Nights in the Gardens of Spain*; Tchaikovsky: Symphony no. 4
Soloist: José Cubiles (piano)

5 October 1946
Madrid, Spain
Orquesta Nacional
Bloch: Concerto Grosso; De Falla: *Nights in the Gardens of Spain*; Tchaikovsky: Symphony no. 4
Soloist: José Cubiles (piano)

11 October 1946
Madrid, Spain
Orquesta Nacional
Bruckner: Symphony no. 4 (*Romantic*); Wagner: "Siegfried's Rhine Journey" from *Götterdämmerung*, "Good Friday Spell" from *Parsifal*, Overture to *Die Meistersinger*

12 October 1946
Madrid, Spain
Orquesta Nacional
Bruckner: Symphony no. 4 (*Romantic*); Wagner: "Siegfried's Rhine Journey" from *Götterdämmerung*, "Good Friday Spell" from *Parsifal*, Overture to *Die Meistersinger*

18 October 1946
Madrid, Spain
Orquesta Nacional
Weber: Overture to *Der Freischütz*; Schumann: Symphony no. 4; E.J. Moeran: *Overture for a Masque*; Mendelssohn: Symphony no. 4 (*Italian*)

19 October 1946
Madrid, Spain
Orquesta Nacional
Weber: Overture to *Der Freischütz*; Schumann: Symphony no. 4; E.J. Moeran: *Overture for a Masque*; Mendelssohn: Symphony no. 4 (*Italian*)

24 October 1946
Valencia, Spain
Orquesta Municipal de Valencia
Schubert: Overture to *Rosamunde*; Tchaikovsky: Symphony no. 4; Britten: Passacaglia from the Opera *Peter Grimes* (Valencia premiere); Wagner: "Good Friday Spell" from *Parsifal*, Overture to *Rienzi*

25 October 1946
Madrid, Spain
Orquesta Nacional
Beethoven: Symphony no. 6 (*Pastorale*); Brahms: *Variations on a Theme by Haydn*; Britten: Passacaglia from *Peter Grimes*; Liszt: *Les Préludes*

26 October 1946
Madrid, Spain
Orquesta Nacional
Beethoven: Symphony no. 6 (*Pastorale*); Brahms: *Variations on a Theme by Haydn*; Britten: Passacaglia from *Peter Grimes*; Liszt: *Les Préludes*

1 November 1946
Barcelona, Spain

Orquesta Municipal de Barcelona
Weber: Overture to *Der Freischütz*; Britten: Passacaglia from *Peter Grimes* (Barcelona premiere); Liszt: *Les Préludes*; Brahms: Symphony no. 1; Wagner: "Siegfried's Rhine Journey" from *Götterdämmerung*, Overture to *Die Meistersinger*

3 November 1946
Barcelona, Spain
Orquesta Municipal de Barcelona
Brahms: Symphony no. 1; Liszt: *Les Préludes*; Wagner: "Siegfried's Rhine Journey" from *Götterdämmerung*, Overture to *Die Meistersinger*

15 November 1946
Concert for the fourth centenary of Miguel Cervantes
Valencia, Spain
Orquesta Municipal de Valencia
R. Strauss: *Don Quixote*
Soloist: Juan Ruiz Casaux (cello)

17 November 1946
Valencia, Spain
Orquesta Municipal de Valencia
Dvořak: Symphony no. 8; R. Strauss: *Don Quixote*; Liszt: *Les Préludes*
Soloist: Juan Ruiz Casaux (cello)

29 November 1946
Valencia, Spain
With the collaboration of a hundred Valencia musicians
Concert for the Spanish Red Cross
Weber: Overture to *Der Freischütz*; Dvořak: Symphony no. 8; Tchaikovsky: Symphony no. 4

1 December 1946
Valencia, Spain
Orquesta Municipal de Valencia
Weber: Overture *Der Freischütz*; Mendelssohn: Symphony no. 4 (*Italian*); Brahms: Symphony no. 1

2 December 1946
Valencia, Spain
Orquesta Municipal de Valencia

Schubert: Overture to *Rosamunde*; Britten: Passacaglia from *Peter Grimes*; Brahms: Symphony no. 1; Wagner: "Good Friday Spell" from *Parsifal*, Overture to *Rienzi*

8 December 1946
Birmingham, England
City of Birmingham Orchestra
Stanford: *Irish Rhapsody*; Borodin: *In the Steppes of Central Asia*; Chopin: Piano Concerto no. 1; Beethoven: Symphony no. 6 (*Pastorale*)
Soloist: Weingarten (piano)

9 February 1947 or 1948 (broadcast date)
BBC Symphony Orchestra
Mozart: Serenade no. 7 (*Haffner Serenade*); Wagner: *Siegfried Idyll*; Mendelssohn: Piano Concerto no. 1; Schubert: Symphony no. 5
Soloist: Leslie England (piano)

14 March 1947
Madrid, Spain
Orquesta Nacional
Berlioz: *Le Carnaval Romain* Overture; Tchaikovsky: Symphony no. 6 (*Pathetique*); Mendelssohn: Scherzo from *A Midsummer Night's Dream*; R. Strauss: *Till Eulenspiegels lustige Streiche*

21 March 1947
Madrid, Spain
Orquesta Nacional
Beethoven: Overture to *Egmont*; Liszt: *Tasso*; Wagner: *Wesendonck Lieder*, Dvořak: Symphony no. 9 (*From the New World*)
Soloist: Carlota Dahmen (soprano)

28 March 1947
Madrid, Spain
Orquesta Nacional
Schubert: Symphony no. 5; Beethoven: Symphony no. 9
Soloists: Angelita Calvo (soprano), Maria Teresa Estremera (contralto), Enrique de la Vara (tenor), Chano Gonzalo (baritone)

11 April 1947
Madrid, Spain
Orquesta Nacional

J.S. Bach: *Brandenburg Concerto* no. 4; Mozart: Symphony no. 41 (*Jupiter*); Tchaikovsky: Fantasy Overture *Romeo and Juliet*; Turina: *Fantastic Dances*

20 April 1947
Valencia, Spain
Orquesta Municipal de Valencia
Schubert: Symphony no. 5; Tchaikovsky: Fantasy Overture *Romeo and Juliet*; Beethoven: Symphony no. 7

27 April 1947
Valencia, Spain
Orquesta Municipal de Valencia
Tchaikovsky: Symphony no. 6 (*Pathetique*); Turina: *Fantastic Dances*; Liszt: *Hungarian Rhapsody* no. 2; J. Strauss: *Roses from the South* Waltz

1 May 1947
Valencia, Spain
Orquesta Municipal de Valencia
Schubert: Symphony no. 5; Mozart: Symphony no. 41 (*Jupiter*); Beethoven: Symphony no. 5

2 May 1947
Valencia, Spain
Orquesta Municipal de Valencia
Tchaikovsky: Symphony no. 6 (*Pathetique*); Turina: *Fantastic Dances*; Liszt: *Hungarian Rhapsody* no. 2; J. Strauss: *Roses from the South* Waltz

4 May 1947
Valencia, Spain
Orquesta Municipal de Valencia
Mendelssohn: Overture and Scherzo from *A Midsummer Night's Dream*; Mendelssohn: Symphony no. 4 (*Italian*); Beethoven: Symphony no. 5

21 October 1947 or 1948
London, England
Philharmonia Orchestra
Gluck: Overture to *Iphigenia in Aulis*; Mozart: Piano Concerto no. 23 (K. 488); Tchaikovsky: Symphony no. 5
Soloist: Clara Haskil (piano)

6 February 1948
Valencia, Spain

Orquesta Municipal de Valencia
Mozart: Overture to *The Marriage of Figaro*; Mendelssohn: Symphony no. 4 (*Italian*); Tchaikovsky: Symphony no. 5; Borodin: *In the Steppes of Central Asia*; Berlioz: three pieces from *The Damnation of Faust*

13 February 1948
Valencia, Spain
Orquesta Municipal de Valencia
Smetana: Overture to *The Bartered Bride*; Mozart: Serenade no. 13 for Strings (*Eine Kleine Nachtmusik*); Brahms: Symphony no. 4; R. Strauss: *Don Juan*; J. Strauss: Waltz *Roses from the South*

20 February 1948
Valencia, Spain
Orquesta Municipal de Valencia
Smetana: Overture to *The Bartered Bride*; Mozart: Serenade no. 13 for Strings (*Eine Kleine Nachtmusik*); Mendelssohn: Symphony no. 4 (*Italian*); Brahms: Symphony no. 4 (Valencia premiere)

22 February 1948
Valencia, Spain
Orquesta Municipal de Valencia
Mendelssohn: *Calm Sea and Prosperous Voyage* Overture; Haydn: Symphony no. 100 (*Military*); Mahler: Symphony no. 4 (Orquesta Municipal de Valencia premiere)
Soloist: Emilia Muñoz (soprano)

27 February 1948
Valencia, Spain
Orquesta Municipal de Valencia
Mendelssohn: *Calm Sea and Prosperous Voyage* Overture; Haydn: Symphony no. 100 (*Military*); Beethoven: Symphony no. 9
Soloists: Emilia Muñoz (soprano), Esperanza Pérez de Durán (contralto), Enrique de la Vara (tenor), Enrique Dominguez (baritone)

5 March 1948
Madrid, Spain
Orquesta Nacional
Mendelssohn: *Calm Sea and Prosperous Voyage* Overture; Beethoven: Symphony no. 8; Grieg: Piano Concerto; R. Strauss: *Death and Transfiguration*
Soloist: Martin Imaz (piano)

12 March 1948
Madrid, Spain
Orquesta Nacional
Smetana: Overture to *The Bartered Bride*; Mendelssohn: Symphony no. 3 (*Scottish*); Brahms: Symphony no. 3; Sibelius: *Finlandia*

23 March 1948
Valencia, Spain
Orquesta Municipal de Valencia
Schubert: Symphony no. 5; Beethoven: Symphony no. 3 (*Eroica*); Wagner: "Good Friday Spell" from *Parsifal*, "Funeral March" from *Götterdämmerung*

16 April 1948
Madrid, Spain
Orquesta Nacional
Muñoz Moleda: *Introduction and Fugue*; Mozart: Serenade no. 13 for Strings (*Eine Kleine Nachtmusik*); Berlioz: *Symphonie fantastique*

23 April 1948
Madrid, Spain
Orquesta Nacional
Mozart: Overture to *The Marriage of Figaro*; Haydn: Symphony no. 100 (*Military*); Mahler: Symphony no. 4
Soloist: Emilia Muñoz (soprano)

30 April 1948
Madrid, Spain
Orquesta Nacional
Schubert: Overture in the Italian Style; Beethoven: Symphony no. 3 (*Eroica*); Joaquín Rodrigo: *El Lirio Azul*; J. Strauss: Waltz *Roses from the South*

7 May 1948
Madrid, Spain
Orquesta Nacional
Rossini: Overture to *La Gazza Ladra*; Dvořak: Symphony no. 8; Beethoven: Symphony no. 5

21 May 1948
Barcelona, Spain
Orquesta Municipal de Barcelona

Rossini: Overture to *La Gazza Ladra*; Mozart: Serenade no. 13 for Strings (*Eine Kleine Nachtmusik*); Dvořak: *Carnival* Overture; Berlioz: *Symphonie fantastique*

23 May 1948
Barcelona, Spain
Orquesta Municipal de Barcelona
Berlioz: *Le Carnaval Romain* Overture; Beethoven: Symphony no. 5; Smetana: "Vltava"; R. Strauss: *Till Eulenspiegels lustige Streiche*

27 June 1948
Havana, Cuba
Orquesta Filharmónica de la Habana
Rossini: Overture to *La Gazza Ladra*; Chopin: Piano Concerto no. 1; Tchaikovsky: Symphony no. 5
Soloist: Ivette Hernandez (piano)

28 June 1948
Havana, Cuba
Orquesta Filharmónica de la Habana
Rossini: Overture to *La Gazza Ladra*; Chopin: Piano Concerto no. 1; Tchaikovsky: Symphony no. 5
Soloist: Ivette Hernandez (piano)

11 July 1948
Havana, Cuba
Orquesta Filharmónica de la Habana
Beethoven: *Leonore No. 3* Overture, Piano Concerto no. 3, Symphony no. 3 (*Eroica*)
Soloist: Ivette Hernandez (piano)

15 July 1948
Toronto, Canada
Toronto Philharmonic Orchestra
Beethoven: *Coriolan Overture*; Bizet: Agnus Dei (Orchestral Aria); Arias with piano accompaniment (Brahms: "Lullaby"; Horsman: "The Bird of the Wilderness"); Borodin: Dances from *Prince Igor*; Rossini: Overture to *La Gazza Ladra*; Orchestral Arias (Gluck: "Che faro senza Euridice" from *Orfeo*; Mozart: "Non piu di fiori" from *Titus*); Schubert: Symphony no. 5; J. Strauss: Waltz *Roses from the South*
Soloists: Carol Brice (contralto), Jonathon Brice (piano)

26 November 1948
Mexico City, Mexico
Sinfónica Mexicana
Gluck: Overture to *Iphigenia in Aulis*; Brahms: Piano Concerto no. 2; Tchaikovsky: Symphony no. 5
Soloist: Rosita Renard (piano)

28 November 1948
Mexico City, Mexico
Sinfónica Mexicana
Gluck: Overture to *Iphigenia in Aulis*; Brahms: Piano Concerto no. 2; Tchaikovsky: Symphony no. 5
Soloist: Rosita Renard (piano)

13 August 1950
Mexico City, Mexico
Orquesta Sinfónica de la Universidad
Beethoven: Overture to *Egmont*, Symphony no. 8, Symphony no. 3 (*Eroica*)

20 August 1950
Mexico City, Mexico
Orquesta Sinfónica de la Universidad
Rachmaninov: Piano Concerto no. 2; Berlioz: *Symphonie fantastique*
Soloist: Stella Contreras (piano)

14 November 1950
Toronto, Canada
Forest Hill Community Ensemble
Weber: Overture to *Oberon*; Schubert: Symphony no. 8 (*Unfinished*); Mozart: Serenade no. 12 for Eight Wind Instruments; Beethoven: Overture to *Egmont*

14 January 1951
Madrid, Spain
Orquesta Sinfónica de Madrid
Berlioz: *Le Carnaval Romain* Overture; Turina: *Fantastic Dances*; Beethoven: Symphony no. 3 (*Eroica*)

21 January 1951
Madrid, Spain
Orquesta Sinfónica de Madrid

Brahms: Symphony no. 1; J. Guridi: *Ten Basque Melodies*; R. Strauss: *Till Eulenspiegels lustige Streiches*

28 January 1951
Madrid, Spain
Orquesta Sinfónica de Madrid
Mendelssohn: Overture to *A Midsummer Night's Dream*; Mozart: Serenade no. 13 (*Eine Kleine Nachtmusik*); Tchaikovsky: Symphony no. 5

4 February 1951
Valencia, Spain
Orquesta Municipal de Valencia
Beethoven: Symphony no. 3 (*Eroica*); Turina: *Fantastic Dances*; Berlioz: *Le Carnaval Romain* Overture

9 February 1951
Valencia, Spain
Orquesta Municipal de Valencia
Mozart: Serenade no. 13 (*Eine Kleine Nachtmusik*); Beethoven: Symphony no. 3 (*Eroica*); Turina: *Fantastic Dances*; Berlioz: *Le Carnaval Romain* Overture

11 February 1951
Valencia, Spain
Orquesta Municipal de Valencia
Mendelssohn: Overture to *A Midsummer Night's Dream*; Mozart: Serenade no. 13 (*Eine Kleine Nachtmusik*); Tchaikovsky: Symphony no. 5

18 February 1951
Valencia, Spain
Orquesta Municipal de Valencia
Dvořak: Symphony no. 9 (*From the New World*); Guridi: *Ten Basque Melodies*; Liszt: *Les Préludes*

21 February 1951
Valencia, Spain
Orquesta Municipal de Valencia/Coral Polifónico Valentina and Orfeón de Godella (dir. Agustin Alamán)
Mendelssohn: Overture to *A Midsummer Night's Dream*; Mahler: Symphony no. 2 (*Resurrection*) (Spanish premiere)
Soloists: Fuensanta Sola (contralto), Emilia Muñoz (soprano)

22 February 1951
Valencia, Spain
Orquesta Municipal de Valencia/Coral Polifónico Valentina and Orfeón de Godella (dir. Agustin Alamán)
Mendelssohn: Overture to *A Midsummer Night's Dream*; Mahler: Symphony no. 2 (*Resurrection*)
Soloists: Fuensanta Sola (contralto), Emilia Muñoz (soprano)

25 February 1951
Valencia, Spain
Orquesta Municipal de Valencia/Coral Polifónico Valentina and Orfeón de Godella (dir. Agustin Alamán)
Mendelssohn: Overture to *A Midsummer Night's Dream*; Mahler: Symphony no. 2 (*Resurrection*)
Soloists: Fuensanta Sola (contralto), Emilia Muñoz (soprano)

1 March 1951
Barcelona, Spain
Orquesta Sinfónica del Gran Teatro del Liceo
Mendelssohn: Overture to *A Midsummer Night's Dream*; Brahms: *Variations on a Theme by Haydn*; Dvořak: Symphony no. 9 (*From the New World*); Wagner: "Funeral March" from *Götterdämmerung*, Prelude from *Die Meistersinger*

3 March 1951
Castellón, Spain
Orquesta Municipal de Valencia
Mendelssohn: Overture to *A Midsummer Night's Dream*; Mozart: Serenade no. 13 (*Eine Kleine Nachtmusik*); Tchaikovsky: Symphony no. 5

4 March 1951
Valencia, Spain
Orquesta Municipal de Valencia
Mozart: Serenade no. 13 (*Eine Kleine Nachtmusik*); Turina: *Fantastic Dances*; J. Strauss: Waltz *Roses from the South*

18 March 1951
Valencia, Spain
Orquesta Municipal de Valencia
Beethoven: Overture to *Egmont*; Mendelssohn: Symphony no. 4 (*Italian*); Brahms: *Variations on a Theme by Haydn*; Smetana: "Vltava"

21 March 1951
Valencia, Spain
Orquesta Municipal de Valencia
Beethoven: Symphony no. 5; Wagner: "Funeral March" from *Götterdämmerung*, "Good Friday Spell" from *Parsifal*, Overture to *Die Meistersinger*

1 April 1951
Valencia, Spain
Orquesta Municipal de Valencia
Mendelssohn: *Calm Sea and Prosperous Voyage* Overture; Schubert: Symphony no. 8 (*Unfinished*); Dvořak: Symphony no. 9 (*From the New World*); Ruperto Chapí: Prelude to *La Reveltosa*

8 April 1951
Madrid, Spain
Orquesta Sinfónica de Madrid
Beethoven: Overture to *Egmont*, Symphony no. 5; Wagner: Prelude and Death of Isolde from *Tristan und Isolde*, Overture to *Die Meistersinger*

15 April 1951
Leeds, England
Yorkshire Symphony Orchestra
Wagner: Overture to *Die Meistersinger*; Brahms: *Variations on a Theme by Haydn*; R. Strauss: *Don Juan*; Schubert: Symphony no. 9

31 May 1951
Toronto, Canada
Toronto Philharmonic Orchestra
Tchaikovsky: Fantasy Overture *Romeo and Juliet*; piano-accompanied songs (Mussorgsky: "to the Little Star"; Revutzki: "The Merry Fiddler"; Del Riego: "Homing"; Villa Lobos: "Xango [Brazilian Ritual Chant]"; Goehl: "For you Alone"); Arias with orchestra (Leoncavallo: Prologue from "I Pagliacci"; Mattei: "Non e Ver"); Dvořak: Symphony no. 9 (*From the New World*)
Soloists: Igor Gorin (baritone), Simeon Joyce (piano)

7 June 1951
Toronto, Canada
Toronto Philharmonic Orchestra
Mendelssohn: *Calm Sea and Prosperous Voyage* Overture; violin-piano works (Foster-Heifetz: "Jeanie with the Light Brown Hair"; Kreisler:

"Leibeslied"; Sarasate: Introduction et Tarantelle); Mozart: Violin Concerto no. 4; Beethoven: Symphony no. 5
Soloists: Donna Grescoe (violin), Simeon Joyce (piano)

11 June 1951
Toronto, Canada
Beaches Orchestra
Rossini: *The Barber of Seville* Overture; Haydn: Symphony no. 100 (*Military*); Mozart: Symphony no. 35 (*Haffner*)

23 August 1951
Buenos Aires, Argentina
Orquesta Sinfónica de la Radio del Estado
Berlioz: *Le Carnaval Romain* Overture; Brahms: *Variations on a Theme by Haydn*; Turina: *Fantastic Dances*; Tchaikovsky: Symphony no. 5

30 August 1951
Buenos Aires, Argentina
Orquesta Sinfónica de la Radio del Estado
Mozart: Symphony no. 41 (*Jupiter*); Ginastera: "Canto de Estío" and "Marcha fúnebre" from *Palambo*; Troiani-Bandini: *Cueca*; Berlioz: *Symphonie fantastique*

6 September 1951
Buenos Aires, Argentina
Orquesta Sinfónica de la Radio del Estado
E. Drangosch: *Obertura Criolla*, Op. 29; Mendelssohn: Symphony no. 4 (*Italian*); Mahler: Symphony no. 1

20 September 1951
Buenos Aires, Argentina
Orquesta Sinfónica de la Radio del Estado
Beethoven: Overture to *Egmont*, Symphony no. 6 (*Pastorale*), Symphony no. 5

22 September 1951
Buenos Aires, Argentina
Orquesta Sinfónica de la Radio del Estado
Beethoven: Overture to *Egmont*, Symphony no. 6 (*Pastorale*), Symphony no. 5

12 November 1951
Toronto, Canada
Forest Hill String Chamber Orchestra
Bloch: Concerto Grosso; Leo Smith: *Occasion for Strings* (premiere); Tchaikovsky: *Serenade for Strings*, Op. 48

23 January 1952 (CBC broadcast)
Toronto, Canada
CBC Symphony Orchestra
Schoenberg: *Transfigured Night*

29 January 1952
Toronto, Canada
Department of Parks and Recreation Community Centre Orchestra
Mozart: Ballet-Suite from *Les Petits Riens*, Concerto for Violin no. 4, Serenade no. 12 for Wind Instruments, Serenade no. 7 (*Haffner Serenade*)
Soloist: David Wulkan (violin)

26 February 1952
Toronto, Canada
Toronto Symphony Orchestra
Berlioz: *Le Carnaval Romain* Overture; Tchaikovsky: Fantasy-Overture *Romeo and Juliet*; Wagner: Overture to *Rienzi*; Liszt: *Les Préludes*

20 March 1952
London, Canada
London Chamber Orchestra
Handel: Concerto Grosso, Op. 6, no. 1; Franck: *Symphonic Variations*; Mozart: Piano Concerto no. 23 (K. 488), Overture to *The Marriage of Figaro*
Soloist: Helen Ingram (piano)

18 April 1952
London, Canada
London Chamber Orchestra
J.S. Bach: Cantata no. 51 (*Jauchzeit Gott in alle Landen*), Air in D from Suite no. 3, *Brandenburg Concerto* no. 3, Overture in G minor
Soloists: Eunice MacDonald (soprano), Gerald Knipfel (trumpet)

19 April 1952
London, Canada

London Chamber Orchestra
J.S. Bach: *Brandenburg Concerto* no. 4, Trio in C major, Concerto for Harpsichord (BWV 1056), Suite no. 2

6 October 1952 (CBC broadcast)
Toronto, Canada
CBC Symphony Orchestra
Mahler: Symphony no. 3 (Second Movement); R. Strauss: *Till Eulenspiegels lustige Streiche*; Mahler: *Songs of a Wayfarer*
Soloist: James Milligan (baritone)

13 October 1952 (CBC broadcast)
Toronto, Canada
CBC Symphony Orchestra
Scarlatti: Ballet-Suite from *The Good Humoured Ladies*; Brahms: Symphony no. 4

20 October 1952
London, Canada
London Chamber Orchestra
J.S. Bach: Overture in G minor; Schubert: Symphony no. 5; Beethoven: Piano Concerto no. 2
Soloist: Helen Ingram (piano)

22 October 1952
Toronto, Canada
Department of Parks and Recreation Community Centre Orchestra
Schubert: Overture in the Italian Style, Symphony no. 8 (*Unfinished*); Beethoven: Overture to *Egmont*, Symphony no. 2

2 November 1952
Valencia, Spain
Orquesta Municipal de Valencia
J.S. Bach: Overture no. 6 (?); Dittersdorf: Sinfonia no. 3 (*Actaeon*); Brahms: Symphony no. 4

9 November 1952
Valencia, Spain
Orquesta Municipal de Valencia
Beethoven: Symphony no. 7; Mahler: Adagietto from Symphony no. 5; Alexander Brott: "Quebec" and "British Columbia" (Two Movements from the *Canadian Suite* [*From Sea to Sea*?]); Chabrier: *España*

16 November 1952
Valencia, Spain
Orquesta Municipal de Valencia
Weber: Overture to *Oberon*; Tchaikovsky: Serenade, Op. 48; A. Brott: *Fancy and Folly* (Valencia premiere); Mendelssohn: Symphony no. 4 (*Italian*)

21 November 1952
Valencia, Spain
Orquesta Municipal de Valencia
Beethoven: Symphony no. 7; Weber: Overture to *Oberon*; Mahler: Adagietto from Symphony no. 5; Tárrega: *Two Brief Pieces*; Chabrier: *España*

23 November 1952
Valencia, Spain
Orquesta Municipal de Valencia
Schubert: Symphony no. 8 (*Unfinished*); Mahler: *Das Lied von der Erde* (Spain premiere)
Soloists: Fuensanta Sola (contralto), Jesus Aguirre (tenor)

24 November 1952
Valencia Spain
Orquesta Municipal de Valencia
Dittersdorf: Sinfonia no. 3 (*Actaeon*); Mahler: *Das Lied von der Erde*
Soloists: Fuensanta Sola (contralto), Jesus Aguirre (Tenor)

30 November 1952
Valencia Spain
Orquesta Municipal de Valencia
Mendelssohn: *Fingal's Cave Overture*; Ravel: *Ma Mère L'Oye*; Smetana: "Vltava"; Dvořak: Symphony no. 9 (*From the New World*)

7 December 1952
Valencia, Spain
Orquesta Municipal de Valencia
Schubert: Overture to *Rosamunde*; E. Lopez Chavarri: *Acuarela Valencianas*; Paul Creston: *Chant of 1942* (Spain premiere); Tchaikovsky: Symphony no. 5

14 December 1952
Valencia Spain

Orquesta Municipal de Valencia
Beethoven: Symphony no. 5; Wagner: Prelude from *Lohengrin*, Prelude and Death from *Tristan und Isolde*, Overture to *Rienzi*

7 January 1953
Hull, England
Yorkshire Symphony Orchestra
Borodin: Overture to *Prince Igor*; Handel-Harty: *Water Music Suite*; Smetana: "Vltava"; Beethoven: Symphony no. 7

9 January 1953
Huddersfield, England
Yorkshire Symphony Orchestra
Borodin: Overture to *Prince Igor*; Handel-Harty: *Water Music Suite*; Smetana: "Vltava"; Beethoven: Symphony no. 7

10 January 1953
Leeds, England
Yorkshire Symphony Orchestra
Borodin: Overture "Prince Igor"; Handel-Harty: *Water Music Suite*; Smetana: "Vltava"; Beethoven: Symphony no. 7

11 January 1953
Wakefield, England
Yorkshire Symphony Orchestra
Borodin: Overture to *Prince Igor*; Handel-Harty: *Water Music Suite*; Smetana: "Vltava"; Beethoven: Symphony no. 7

21 January 1953
Valencia, Spain
Orquesta Municipal de Valencia
Beethoven: Overture to *Egmont*, Symphony no. 2, Symphony no. 3 (*Eroica*)

25 January 1953
Valencia, Spain
Orquesta Municipal de Valencia
J.S. Bach: *Brandenburg Concerto* no. 4 (Valencia premiere); Paul Creston: *Chant of 1942*; Beethoven: Symphony no. 3 (*Eroica*)

1 February 1953
Valencia, Spain
Orquesta Municipal de Valencia

Tchaikovsky: Symphony no. 6 (*Pathetique*); Turina: *Fantastic Dances*; Berlioz: three pieces from *The Damnation of Faust*; J. Strauss: Waltz *Roses from the South*

8 February 1953
Madrid, Spain
Orquesta Sinfónica de Madrid
Tchaikovsky: Symphony no. 5; de Falla: *The Three-Cornered Hat*; R. Strauss: *Till Eulenspiegels lustige Streiche*

15 February 1953
Valencia, Spain
Orquesta Municipal de Valencia
Nicolai: Overture to *The Merry Wives of Windsor*, de Falla: *The Three-Cornered Hat*; Berlioz: *Symphonie fantastique*

22 February 1953
Madrid, Spain
Orquesta Sinfónica de Madrid
Beethoven: Symphony no. 3 (*Eroica*); Wagner: Prelude from *Lohengrin*, Prelude and Death from *Tristan und Isolde*, Overture to *Rienzi*

1 March 1953
Valencia, Spain
Orquesta Municipal de Valencia
Beethoven: Symphony no. 2; Dvořak: Symphony no. 8; R. Strauss: *Till Eulenspiegels lustige Streiches*

2 March 1953
Valencia, Spain
Orquesta Municipal de Valencia
J.S. Bach: *Brandenburg Concerto* no. 4; Dvořak: Symphony no. 8; de Falla: *The Three-Cornered Hat*; R. Strauss: *Till Eulenspiegels lustige Streiches*

23 April 1953
Toronto, Canada
York Concert Society
Beethoven: *Coriolan Overture*, Piano Concerto no. 3, Symphony no. 7
Soloist: Lubka Kolessa (piano)

6 May 1953
Toronto, Canada
York Concert Society

J.S. Bach: Overture in G minor, Harpsichord Concerto in F minor, *Brandenburg Concerto* no. 3, Air from Suite no. 3 in D, Suite no. 2 in B minor
Soloist: Greta Kraus (harpsichord)

14 May 1953
Toronto, Canada
York Concert Society
Mozart: Serenade no. 7 (*Haffner Serenade*); H. Wolf: *Italian Serenade*; Berlioz: Serenade from *Harold in Italy*; Tchaikovsky: *Serenade for Strings*, Op. 48
Soloist: Robert Warburton (viola)

26 May 1953
Toronto, Canada
York Concert Society
Mozart: Symphony no. 35 (*Haffner*), Aria from *Il Re Pastore*; Mahler: Adagietto from Symphony no. 5, two songs from the *Des Knaben Wunderhorn* ("Wo die schönen Trompeten Blasen," "Wer hat dies Liedlein erdacht?"); Schubert: Symphony no. 6
Soloist: Lois Marshall (soprano)

17 September 1953
Toronto, Canada
Toronto Philharmonic Orchestra
Creston: *Chant of 1942* (Canada premiere); songs (Handel: "Lascia Chio Pianga," "Un Cenno Leggiadretto"; Canteloube: three songs from *Songs of the Auvergne*; Rossini: Overture "La Scala de Seta"; Bizet: three Arias from *Carmen* ("Habanera," Sequidilla," "Gypsy Song"); Dvořak: Symphony no. 8
Soloist: Gladys Swarthout (mezzo-soprano)

19 October 1953 (CBC broadcast)
Toronto, Canada
CBC Symphony Orchestra
Handel-Elgar: Overture in D minor; Nielsen: Symphony no. 4 (*The Inextinguishable*) (Canada premiere)

6 November 1953
Guildford, England
London Philharmonic Orchestra
Borodin: Overture to *Prince Igor*; Tchaikovsky: Symphony no. 6 (*Pathetique*); Smetana: "Vltava"; Berlioz: three pieces from *The Damnation of Faust*

16 November 1953
Acton, England
London Philharmonic Orchestra
Borodin: Overture to *Prince Igor*; Tchaikovsky: Symphony no. 6 (*Pathetique*); Smetana: "Vltava"; Berlioz: three pieces from *The Damnation of Faust*

23 November 1953
High Wycombe, England
London Philharmonic Orchestra
Borodin: Overture to *Prince Igor*; Tchaikovsky: Symphony no. 6 (*Pathetique*); Smetana: "Vltava"; Berlioz: three pieces from *The Damnation of Faust*

6 December 1953 (broadcast?)
England (city unknown)
BBC Symphony Orchestra
Mozart: Symphony no. 38 (*Prague*); Schumann: Concert Piece for Four Horns and Orchestra, Symphony no. 3 (*Rhenish*) (edited by Mahler)

23 February 1954
Toronto, Canada
Toronto Symphony Orchestra (35th Annual Concert for the Toronto Police Association)
Auber: Overture to *Fra Diavolo*; Massenet: Aria "Il est doux, il est bon" from *Herodiade*; Verdi: Aria "Pace, pace, mio Dio" from *La Forza del Destino*; Beethoven: Symphony no. 5; Liszt: Piano Concerto no. 2; songs (Speaks: "Morning"; Rachmaninov: "Floods of Spring"; Charles: "Let My Song Fill Your Heart"); A. Brott: "British Columbia"
Soloists: Eileen Farrell (soprano), Freda Terpel (piano)

2 March 1954
Toronto, Canada
The Community Centre Orchestra
Schubert: Overture to *Rosamunde*; Handel: "Return, return oh God of Hosts" from *Samson*, "Oh thou, that tallest glad tidings to Zion" from *Messiah*; Mendelssohn: Third Movement from Symphony no. 3 (*Scottish*); Gluck: "Que faro" from *Orpheus and Eurydice*; Verdi: "O don Fatale" from *Don Carlos*; Beethoven: Symphony no. 4
Soloist: Catherine Howard (contralto)

20 April 1954
Toronto, Canada

York Concert Society
Beethoven: Overture to *The Creatures of Prometheus*, Violin Concerto, Symphony no. 8
Soloist: Betty-Jean Hagen (violin)

4 May 1954
Toronto, Canada
York Concert Society
Rossini: Overture to *La Scala di Seta*; Schumann: Piano Concerto; Harry Freedman: *Tableau*; Mendelssohn: Symphony no. 4 (*Italian*)
Soloist: Emil Debusman (piano)

18 May 1954
Toronto, Canada
York Concert Society
J.S. Bach: *Brandenburg Concerto* no. 4, Harpsichord Concerto in D minor; Handel: Concerto Grosso no. 16; Scarlatti: Andante; Vivaldi: *Concerto alla Rustica*
Soloist: Greta Kraus (harpsichord)

27 May 1954
Toronto, Canada
York Concert Society
Brahms: *Variations on a Theme by Haydn*; Mahler: *Kindertotenlieder*, Frederick Karam: *Poem for String Orchestra*; Schumann: Symphony no. 3 (*Rhenish*)
Soloist: James Milligan (baritone)

17 June 1954
Toronto, Canada
Toronto Philharmonic Orchestra
Auber: Overture to *Fra Diavolo*; Tchaikovsky: Fantasy Overture *Romeo and Juliet*; Grieg: Piano Concerto (First Movement only); J. Strauss: Waltz *Roses from the South*; piano solos (Chopin: Impromptu no. 2; Schumann: Intermezzo; Paganini-Liszt: Etude in A minor); Liszt: *Les Préludes*
Soloist: Patricia Parr (piano)

29 July 1954
Toronto, Canada
Toronto Philharmonic Orchestra
Weber: Overture *Abu Hassan*; Mendelssohn: Piano Concerto no. 1; Smetana: "Vltava"; Wagner: Overture to *Reinzi*; Flotow: Overture to *Alessandro Stradella*; piano solos (Smetana: Polka in F major; Chopin:

Etude, Op. 25, no. 1, Scherzo in C minor, Op. 39); Tchaikovsky: Waltz from *Sleeping Beauty*; Liszt: *Hungarian Rhapsody* no. 1
Soloist: Mary Syme (piano)

6 August 1954 (CBC broadcast)
Vancouver, Canada
CBC Vancouver String Orchestra
Harry Freedman: *Tableau*; J.S. Bach: Suite

8 August 1954
Vancouver, Canada
BC Electric Orchestra
Schubert: Overture to *Rosamunde*; Lalo: "Vainement, ma Bien Aimee" from *Le Roi D'ys*; Tchaikovsky: Fantasy Overture *Romeo and Juliet*; Berlioz: three pieces from *The Damnation of Faust*; songs (S. Donaudy: "O del Mio Amato Ben," "When I have sung my songs for you"); Liszt: *Les Préludes*; J. Strauss: *Roses from the South* Waltz
Soloist: Bruce Holman (tenor)

13 August 1954
Vancouver, Canada
CBC Vancouver String Orchestra
Bloch: Concerto Grosso no. 1; D. Scarlatti (arr. Tommasini): Five Sonatas

15–21 August 1954 (precise date unknown)
Winnipeg, Canada
CBC Winnipeg Concert Orchestra
Mozart: Suite from *Les Petits Riens*; Dittersdorf: Sinfonia no. 3 (*Actaeon*); Mendelssohn: Symphony no. 4 (*Italian*)

16 September 1954
Buenos Aires, Argentina
Orquesta Sinfónica de Radio del Estado
Beethoven: Symphony no. 2, no. 3 (*Eroica*)

19 September 1954
Buenos Aires, Argentina
Orquesta Sinfónica de Radio del Estado
Beethoven: Symphony no. 2, no. 3 (*Eroica*)

23 September 1954
Buenos Aires, Argentina

Orquesta Sinfónica de Radio del Estado
Beethoven: Symphony no. 1, no. 4, no. 5

26 September 1954
Buenos Aires, Argentina
Orquesta Sinfónica de Radio del Estado
Beethoven: Symphony no. 1, no. 4, no. 5

30 September 1954
Buenos Aires, Argentina
Orquesta Sinfónica de Radio del Estado
Beethoven: Symphony no. 6 (*Pastorale*), no. 7

3 October 1954
Buenos Aires, Argentina
Orquesta Sinfónica de Radio del Estado
Beethoven: Symphony no. 6 (*Pastorale*), no. 7

7 October 1954
Buenos Aires, Argentina
Orquesta Sinfónica de Radio del Estado
Beethoven: Symphony no. 8, no. 9
Soloists: Angel Mattielo (baritone), Maria Kallay (soprano), Sante Borolen (tenor), Franca Golob (contralto)

9 October 1954
Buenos Aires, Argentina
Orquesta Sinfónica de Radio del Estado
Beethoven: Symphony no. 8, no. 9
Soloists: Angel Mattiello (baritone), Maria Kallay (soprano), Sante Rosolen (tenor), Franca Golob (contralto)

10 October 1954
Buenos Aires, Argentina
Orquesta Sinfónica de Radio del Estado
Beethoven: Symphony no. 8, no. 9
Soloists: Angel Mattiello (baritone), Maria Kallay (soprano), Sante Rosolen (tenor), Franca Golob (contralto)

6 December 1954 (CBC broadcast)
Toronto, Canada
CBC Symphony Orchestra
Wagner: *Siegfried Idyll*; Beethoven: Symphony no. 6 (*Pastorale*)

13 December 1954 (CBC broadcast)
Toronto, Canada
CBC Symphony Orchestra
Mahler: Symphony no. 4 (CBC premiere)
Soloist: Elizabeth Benson-Guy (soprano)

5 January 1955 (CBC broadcast)
Toronto, Canada
Unknown orchestra
J.S. Bach: Keyboard Concerto in D minor
Soloist: Beatrice Bennett (piano)

21 February 1955 (CBC broadcast)
Toronto, Canada
CBC Symphony Orchestra
Schumann: *Genoveva* Overture; Beethoven: Piano Concerto no. 3; Brahms: *Variations on a Theme by Haydn*
Soloist: Glenn Gould (piano)

3 March 1955
Toronto, Canada
The Community Centre Orchestra
Gluck: Overture to *Iphigenia in Aulis*; Haydn: Symphony no. 103; Schubert: Symphony no. 6; J. Strauss: Waltz *Roses from the South*

24 March 1955
Toronto, Canada
York Concert Society
Vivaldi: Concerto Grosso in G minor, Op. 3, no. 2, Concerto Grosso Op. 3, no. 10; Corelli: Concerto Grosso Op. 6, no. 8; J.S. Bach: Adagio from Cantata no. 156; Bloch: Concerto Grosso no. 2; Bizet: Adagietto from *L'Arlésienne*; Rossini: Sonata
Soloists: Hyman Goodman, Isidore Dresser, Beauna Somerville, Steven Staryk

30 March 1955 (broadcast – radio documentary)
Toronto, Canada
CBC Symphony Orchestra
Mahler: *Songs of a Wayfarer*, *Kindertotenlieder*, First Movement from Symphony no. 3, First Two Movements from *Das Lied von der Erde*
Soloists: Trudi Carlyle (mezzo-soprano), Andre Turp (tenor), James Milligan (baritone)

26 April 1955
Toronto, Canada
York Concert Society
Schumann: *Genoveva* Overture; Brahms: Violin Concerto; Brahms: Symphony no. 4
Soloist: Betty-Jean Hagen (violin)

5 May 1955
Toronto, Canada
York Concert Society
Handel-Harty: *Water Music Suite*; Handel: Harapha's Aria from *Samson*; Haydn: Simon's Aria from *The Seasons*; Dittersdorf: Sinfonia no. 3 (*Actaeon*); Mozart: Concert Aria "Mentre ti lascio o figlia," Sarastro's Aria from *The Magic Flute*, Symphony no. 41 (*Jupiter*)
Soloist: Jan Rubes (bass)

19 May 1955
Toronto, Canada
York Concert Society
Beethoven: Symphony no. 6 (*Pastorale*), Piano Concerto no. 2, *Leonore No. 3* Overture
Soloist: Patricia Parr (piano)

16 June 1955
Toronto, Canada
Toronto Philharmonic Orchestra
Smetana: Overture to *The Bartered Bride*; Tartini: Violin Concerto no. 1; Scarlatti-Tommasini: Andante from *The Good Humoured Ladies* Suite; R. Strauss: *Don Juan*; violin solos (Rachmaninov: Romance; Vieuxtemps: Rondino); Mendelssohn: Symphony no. 3 (*Scottish*)
Soloist: Pearl Palmason (violin)

23 June 1955
Toronto, Canada
Toronto Philharmonic Orchestra
Wagner: Overture to *Tannhäuser*; Donizetti: Aria "Una furtiva lagrima" from *L'Elisir D'Amore*; Bizet: *L'Arlésienne Suite No. 2*; Aria "Flower Song" from *Carmen*; Liszt: *Tasso*; songs (arr. B. Britten: "The Sally Gardens [Irish Folk Song]," "The Bonny Earl O'Moray [Scots Folk Song]"; L. Lehmann: "Ah, Moon of My Delight"; Lehar: "Yours is My Heart Alone"); Dvořak: Symphony no. 8
Soloists: James Lamond (tenor)

9 July 1955 (CBC TV broadcast)
Canada (city unknown)
Auber: Overture to *Fra Diavolo*; Verdi: Act II and Scene I, Act III from *Aida*; Wagner: Overture to *Rienzi*
Soloists: Camilla Williams (soprano), Jon Crain (tenor), Colette Merola (mezzo-soprano), Napoleon Bisson (baritone), Joseph Rouleau (bass)

10 July 1955 (CBC broadcast date)
Winnipeg, Canada
Mozart: Serenade no. 7; Schubert: Symphony no. 5

15 July 1955 (CBC broadcast date)
Vancouver, Canada
Vancouver Chamber Orchestra
Mozart: Symphony no. 38 (*Prague*); Wolf: *Italian Serenade*

17 July 1955
Vancouver, Canada
BC Electric Orchestra
Auber: Overture to *Fra Diavolo*; Bizet: *L'Arlésienne Suite No. 2*; Grieg: "In the Hall of the Mountain King" from *Peer Gynt*; Smetana: "Vltava" from *Má Vlast*; Dvořak: Symphony no. 8

29 July 1955
Vancouver, Canada
BC Electric Orchestra
Dvořak: Symphony no. 9 (*From the New World*); Unknown

28 August 1955
Mexico City, Mexico
Orquesta Sinfónica de la Universidad
Beethoven: *Leonore No. 3* Overture; Chopin: Piano Concerto no. 2; Tchaikovsky: Symphony no. 4
Soloist: Walter Hautzig (piano)

4 November 1955
Toronto, Canada
Toronto Symphony Orchestra
Auber: Overture to *Fra Diavolo*; Mendelssohn: Nocturne and Scherzo from *A Midsummer Night's Dream*; Mozart: Aria "Parto, parto, ma tu ben mio" from *La Clemenza di Tito*; Mahler: Adagietto from Symphony no. 5; Puccini: Aria "In questa reggia" from *Turandot*; J. Strauss: Waltz

*Roses from the South*; songs and arias (Handel: "So shall the lute and harp awake" from *Judas Maccabeus*; Duparc: "Chanson Triste"; J.J. Niles: "Go way from my window"); Tchaikovsky: Fantasy Overture *Romeo and Juliet*
Soloist: Lois Marshall (soprano)

9 November 1955
Toronto, Canada
Toronto Symphony Orchestra
Berlioz: *Le Carnaval Romain* Overture; Mahler: Adagietto from Symphony no. 5; Beethoven: Symphony no. 8; Tchaikovsky: Symphony no. 5

19 December 1955
Toronto, Canada
CBC Symphony Orchestra
Ginastera: *Variaciones Concertantes*; Berlioz: *Les Nuits d'Été*
Soloist: Elizabeth Benson-Guy (soprano)

26 December 1955
Toronto, Canada
CBC Symphony Orchestra
Bruckner: Symphony no. 4 (*Romantic*)

8 February 1956
Oslo, Norway
Filharmonisk Selskaps Orchester
Dittersdorf: Sinfonia no. 3 (*Actaeon*); R. Skrede: *Den kvite fuglen*; Mahler: Symphony no. 4
Soloist: Randi Helseth (soprano)
February 1956 (precise date unknown)
Oslo, Norway
Oslo Philharmonic Society
Mahler: Symphony no. 2

22 February 1956
Berlin, Germany
Berlin Philharmonic
Smetana: Overture to *The Bartered Bride*, "Maria's Aria" from *The Bartered Bride*; Dvořak: "Song to the Moon" from *Rusalka*; Smetana: "Vltava"; Dvořak: Symphony no. 9 (*From the New World*)
Soloist: Anny Schlemm (soprano)

23 February 1956
Smetana: Overture to *The Bartered Bride*, "Maria's Aria" from *The Bartered Bride*; Dvořak: "Song to the Moon" from *Rusalka*; Smetana: "Vltava"; Dvořak: Symphony no. 9 (*From the New World*)
Soloist: Anny Schlemm (soprano)

12 March 1956
Valencia, Spain
Orquesta Municipal de Valencia
Mozart: Overture to *The Marriage of Figaro*; Smetana: "Vltava"; Beethoven: Symphony no. 6 (*Pastorale*); Ginastera: *Variaciones Concertantes* (Valencia premiere)

22 March 1956
Valencia, Spain
Orquesta Municipal de Valencia
Weber: Overture to *Oberon*; Mendelssohn: Scherzo from *A Midsummer Night's Dream*; Smetana: "Vltava"; Brahms: Symphony no. 1

25 March 1956
Valencia, Spain
Orquesta Municipal de Valencia
Mendelssohn: Overture to *Ruy Blas*; Ginastera: *Variaciones Concertantes*; Tchaikovsky: Symphony no. 5

27 March 1956
Valencia, Spain
Orquesta Municipal de Valencia
Beethoven: Overture to *Egmont*, Symphony no. 6 (*Pastorale*); Wagner: Prelude and Death from *Tristan und Isolde*, Overture to *Tannhäuser*

17 April 1956
Toronto, Canada
York Concert Society
J.S. Bach: *Brandenburg Concerto* no. 3; Handel: Aria "As when the dove" from *Acis and Galatea*; Dittersdorf: Symphony in C major (*The Four Ages*); Haydn: Aria "Oh how pleasing to the senses" from *The Seasons*; Mozart: Serenade no. 12 for Winds, Symphony no. 38 (*Prague*)
Soloist: Elizabeth Benson-Guy (soprano)

24 April 1956
Toronto, Canada

York Concert Society
Mendelssohn: Overture to *Ruy Blas*; Beethoven: Piano Concerto no. 1; Brahms: Symphony no. 1
Soloist: Beatrice Bennett (piano)

8 May 1956
Toronto, Canada
York Concert Society
Beethoven: *Grosse Fugue*, Op. 133, Triple Concerto for Piano, Violin and Cello, Symphony no. 2
Soloists: Pierre Souverain (piano), Hyman Goodman (violin), Rowland Pack (cello)

15 May 1956
Toronto, Canada
York Concert Society
Weber: Overture to *Oberon*; Catalani-Zandonai: *In Sogno* (Canada premiere); Mahler: *Songs of a Wayfarer*, Weber (arr. Mahler): Entr'acte Music from *The Three Pintos*; Schubert: Symphony no. 9
Soloist: Maureen Forrester (contralto)

31 May 1956
Toronto, Canada
Toronto Philharmonic Orchestra
Mendelssohn: Overture to *Ruy Blas*; Weber: Aria "Schweig! damit dich Niemand Warnt" from *Der Freischütz*; Dittersdorf: Symphony in C major (*The Four Ages*); Mozart: Aria "Madamina! il catalogo e questo" from *Don Giovanni*, *Eine Kleine Nachtmusik*; songs (Tosti: "Ideale," "Marechiare"; Quilter: "Fair House of Joy," "fill a Glass of Golden Wine"); Mendelssohn: Symphony no. 4 (*Italian*)
Soloist: Vaclovas Verikaitis (baritone)

14 June 1956
Toronto, Canada
Toronto Philharmonic Orchestra
J.C. Bach: Sinfonia in B major; Arias (Handel: "Care Selve" from *Atalanta*; Bellini: "Qui la Voce" from *I Puritani*); Beethoven: Symphony no. 2; songs (Puccini: "O Mio Babbino Caro" from *Gianni Schicchi*; R. Strauss: "Zueignung"; Bizet: "Ouvre ton Coeur"; Bridge: "O That it Were So"; J. Strauss: "I'm in Love with Vienna"); Catalani-Zandonai: *In Sogno*; Liszt: *Hungarian Rhapsody* no. 1
Soloist: Selma Jetmundson (soprano)

14 July 1956
Stratford, Canada
Festival Orchestra
Beethoven: Overture to *The Creatures of Prometheus*, Piano Concerto no. 1, Symphony no. 7, Piano Concerto no. 5 (*Emperor*)
Soloist: Claudio Arrau (piano)

29 July 1956
Vancouver, Canada
BC Electric Orchestra
Mendelssohn: Overture to *Ruy Blas*; P. Mercure: *Pantomime* (premiere); Meyerbeer: "O Paradiso"; Dittersdorf: Symphony *The Four Ages*; songs (Strauss: With all my Heart"; Geehl: "For You Alone"); Dvořak: Symphony no. 9 (*From the New World*)
Soloist: Karl Norman (tenor)

12 August 1956
Vancouver, Canada
BC Electric Orchestra
O. Morawetz: *Carnival Overture*; vocal works (Saint-Saens: "My Heart at Thy Sweet Voice" from *Samson and Delilah*, "Drink to Me Only with Thine Eyes"); Mendelssohn: Symphony no. 4 (*Italian*); Tchaikovsky: *Nutcracker Suite*; vocal works (Rachmaninov: "In the Silence of the Night"; Tchaikovsky: "None but the Lonely Heart"); Liszt: *Hungarian Rhapsody* no. 1
Soloist: Irene Byatt (vocalist)

8 October 1956 (CBC broadcast)
Toronto, Canada
CBC Symphony Orchestra
Sammartini-Martucci: *Pastorale*; Mahler: Symphony no. 4
Soloist: Elizabeth Benson-Guy (soprano)

15 October 1956 (CBC broadcast)
Toronto, Canada
CBC Symphony Orchestra
F. Valen: *The Silent Island*; Schumann: Symphony no. 3 (*Rhenish*); Turina: *Fantastic Dances*

4 November 1956
Valencia, Spain
Orquesta Municipal de Valencia

Mendelssohn: Overture to *A Midsummer Night's Dream*, Symphony no. 4 (*Italian*); Beethoven: Symphony no. 6 (*Pastorale*)

November 1956 (precise date unknown)
Valencia, Spain
Orquesta Municipal de Valencia
Beethoven: Symphony no. 6 (*Pastorale*); Turina: *Fantastic Dances*; Liszt: *Les Préludes*

November 1956 (precise date unknown)
Valencia, Spain
Orquesta Municipal de Valencia
R. Strauss: *Till Eulenspiegels lustige Streiche*; Tchaikovsky: *Serenade for Strings*, Op. 48; Schumann: Symphony no. 3 (*Rhenish*)

25 November 1956
Valencia, Spain
Orquesta Municipal de Valencia
Mendelssohn: Overture to *A Midsummer Night's Dream*; Symphony no. 4 (*Italian*); Rimsky-Korsakov: *Scheherazade*

2 December 1956
Valencia, Spain
Orquesta Municipal de Valencia
Mozart: *Serenade for Strings* (?); Rossini: *Sonata for Strings* (Valencia premiere); Mahler: Symphony no. 1

3 December 1956
Valencia, Spain
Orquesta Municipal de Valencia
Schumann: Symphony no. 3 (*Rhenish*); Mahler: Symphony no. 1

9 December 1956
Valencia, Spain
Orquesta Municipal de Valencia
Beethoven: Overture to *Egmont*, Symphony no. 7; Pino Donatti: *Tre Acquarelli Paesani* (Valencia premiere); Catalani-Zandonai: *In Sogno* (Valencia premiere); J. Strauss: Waltz *Roses from the South*

16 December 1956
Valencia, Spain
Orquesta Municipal de Valencia

Weber: Overture to *Der Freischütz*; Mario Zafred: *Sinfonietta* (Valencia premiere); Tchaikovsky: Symphony no. 6 (*Pathetique*)

20 December 1956
Valencia, Spain
Orquesta Municipal de Valencia
Wagner: Overture to *Die Meistersinger*, Prelude and Death from *Tristan und Isolde*; Dvořak: Symphony no. 9 (*From the New World*); J. Strauss: *The Blue Danube* Waltz, *Roses from the South* Waltz; Chapí: Prelude to *La Reveltosa*

21 December 1956
Valencia, Spain
Orquesta Municipal de Valencia
Weber: Overture to *Der Freischütz*; Tchaikovsky: Symphony no. 6 (*Pathetique*); Pino Donatti: *Tre Acquarelli Paesani*; Catalani-Zandonai: *In Sogno*; Rossini: *Sonata for Strings*; J. Strauss: Waltz *Roses from the South*

17 January 1957
Oslo, Norway
Filharmonisk Selskaps Orchester
Dittersdorf: Sinfonia no. 3 (*Actaeon*); Schubert: Symphony no. 5; Mahler: *Das Lied von der Erde*
Soloists: Kerstin Meyer (alto), Arne Hendriksen (tenor)

18 January 1957
Oslo, Norway
Filharmonisk Selskaps Orchester
Schubert: Symphony no. 5; Mahler: *Das Lied von der Erde*
Soloists: Kerstin Meyer (alto), Arne Hendriksen (tenor)

23 January 1957
Willowdale, Canada
Metro Orchestra
Cimarosa: Overture to *Il Matrimonio Segreto*; Beethoven: Piano Concerto no. 2; Schubert: Symphony no. 4 (*Tragic*)
Soloist: Dorene Uren (piano)

30 April 1957
Toronto, Canada
York Concert Society

Mozart: *Eine Kleine Nachtmusik*, Recitativo and Susanna's Aria ("Deh vieni, non tardar") from *The Marriage of Figaro*, Aria of Constanza ("Martern aller Arten") from *Il Seraglio*; Mahler: Symphony no. 4
Soloist: Lois Marshall (soprano)

7 May 1957
Toronto, Canada
York Concert Society
Reznicek: Overture to *Donna Diana*; F. Valen: *The Silent Island*; Prokofiev: Piano Concerto no. 3; Tchaikovsky: Symphony no. 4
Soloist: Moura Lympany (piano)

14 May 1957
Toronto, Canada
York Concert Society
Mendelssohn: Overture "Athalia," Violin Concerto in E minor; Pino Donatti: *Tre Acquarelli Paesani*; Brahms: Symphony no. 3; Weinberger: Polka and Fugue from *Schwanda the Bagpiper*
Soloist: Michael Rabin (violin)

21 May 1957
Toronto, Canada
York Concert Society
Beethoven: *Coriolan Overture*, Piano Concerto no. 5 (*Emperor*), Symphony no. 3
Soloist: Boris Roubakine (piano)

24 June 1957
Canada (city unknown)
CBC Strings
Handel: Concerto Grosso no. 5; J.S. Bach: *Brandenburg Concerto* no. 3; Bloch: Concerto Grosso no. 2; Rossini: *Sonata for Strings*

31 June 1957 (CBC broadcast)
Stratford, Canada
CBC Symphony Orchestra
Violet Archer: *Fanfare and Passacaglia*; R. Strauss: *Four Last Songs*, *Death and Transfiguration*; Nielsen: Symphony no. 4 (*The Inextinguishable*)
Soloist: Lois Marshall (soprano)

22 January 1958
Toronto, Canada

Toronto Symphony Orchestra
Beethoven: Overture to *The Creatures of Prometheus*; Mahler: three *Rückert* songs ("Ich atmet' eienen linden Duft," "Ich bin der Welt abhanden gekommen," "Um Mitternacht"), Symphony no. 2 (*Resurrection*) (Canada premiere)
Soloists: Elizabeth Benson-Guy (soprano), Mary Simmons (soprano)

9 February 1958
Toronto, Canada
Toronto Symphony Orchestra
Weber: Overture to *Der Freischütz*; songs with piano (Purcell: "I attempt from love's sickness"; P. Warlock: "Cradle Song"; R. Strauss: "Einerlei," "Schlechtes Wetter"); J.S. Bach: Air from Suite no. 3 in D; Mozart: Aria "Et incarnatus est" from *Great Mass in C minor* (K. 427); Mahler: Second Movement from Symphony no. 2 (*Resurrection*); Donizetti: Aria "O luce di quest' anima" from *Linda di Chamounix*; Liszt: *Les Préludes*; J. Strauss: *Roses from the South* Waltz
Soloist: Elizabeth Benson Guy (soprano)

12 February 1958
Toronto, Canada
Toronto Symphony Orchestra
Weber: Overture to *Der Freischütz*; W. Braunfels: *Phantastic Apparitions of a Theme by Hector Berlioz* (Canada premiere); Beethoven: Symphony no. 7

22 April 1958
Toronto, Canada
York Concert Society
Pfitzner: three preludes from *Palestrina*; Schumann: Piano Concerto; Berlioz: *Symphonie fantastique*
Soloist: Patricia Parr (piano)

29 April 1958
Toronto, Canada
York Concert Society
Handel: Concerto Grosso, Op. 6, no. 5; Vaughan Williams: Violin Concerto in D minor (*Concerto Academico*); Vivaldi: Violin Concerto in E major (*La Primavera*); Schoenberg: *Transfigured Night*
Soloist: Betty-Jean Hagen (violin)

6 May 1958
Toronto, Canada

York Concert Society
H. Somers: *Passacaglia and Fugue*; Tchaikovsky: Piano Concerto no. 1; Dvořak: Symphony no. 8
Soloist: Alexander Uninsky (piano)

13 May 1958
Toronto, Canada
York Concert Society
Beethoven: Overture to *Fidelio*, Symphony no. 1, Symphony no. 4, *Leonore No. 3* Overture

21 October 1958
Etobicoke, Canada
York Concert Society
Handel: Concerto Grosso Op. 6, no. 5; J.S. Bach: Suite in B minor; Corelli: Concerto Grosso Op. 6, no. 8; Harry Freedman: *Tableau*; Tchaikovsky: *Serenade for Strings*, Op. 48; Rossini: Sonata in C major

30 November 1958
Valencia, Spain
Orquesta Municipal de Valencia
Mozart: Symphony no. 33; R. Strauss: *Metamorphosen* (Valencia premiere); Beethoven: Symphony no. 7

7 December 1958
Valencia, Spain
Orquesta Municipal de Valencia
Weber: Overture to *Der Freischütz*; O. Morawetz: Divertimento (Spain premiere); Turina: *Fantastic Dances*; Tchaikovsky: Symphony no. 5

14 December 1958
Valencia, Spain
Orquesta Municipal de Valencia
R. Strauss: *Death and Transfiguration*; Berlioz: *Symphonie fantastique*

15 December 1958
Valencia, Spain
Orquesta Municipal de Valencia
Mozart: Symphony no. 33; R. Strauss: *Metamorphosen*; Tchaikovsky: Symphony no. 5

4 January 1959 (recording date)
London, England

London Symphony Orchestra
Mahler: *Das Lied von der Erde*
Soloists: unknown

25 February 1959
Toronto, Canada
Toronto Symphony Orchestra
Mozart: Overture to *The Marriage of Figaro*; Beethoven: Piano Concerto no. 4; Mahler: Symphony no. 5 (Canada premiere)
Soloist: Moura Lympany (piano)

15 March 1959
Toronto, Canada
CBC Symphony Orchestra
Handel: Cantata *Apollo e Dafne*; Brahms: *Variations on a Theme by Haydn*; R. Strauss: closing scene from *Capriccio*
Soloists: Elizabeth Benson-Guy (soprano), Norman Farrow (bass-baritone)

21 April 1959
Toronto, Canada
York Concert Society
Mendelssohn: *Calm Sea and Prosperous Voyage* Overture; Mahler: *Songs of a Wayfarer*; Bruckner: Symphony no. 4 (*Romantic*)
Soloist: Elena Nikolaidi (mezzo-soprano)

5 May 1959
Toronto, Canada
York Concert Society
J.S. Bach: Suite in G minor, Keyboard Concerto in F minor; R. Strauss: *Metamorphosen*; Haydn: Keyboard Concerto in D major; Mozart: Symphony no. 33
Soloist: Greta Kraus (harpsichord)

12 May 1959
Toronto, Canada
York Concert Society
Schubert: Overture to *Rosamunde*; Mozart: Adagio for Solo Violin (K. 261); Menotti: Violin Concerto (Canada premiere); Tchaikovsky: Symphony no. 6 (*Pathetique*)
Soloist: Tossy Spivakovsky (violin)

20 May 1959
Toronto, Canada

York Concert Society
Beethoven: Symphony no. 8, no. 9
Soloists: Elizabeth Benson-Guy (soprano), Irene Byatt (?), Alan Crofoot (tenor), Jan Simons (baritone)

29 May 1959
Lima, Peru
Orquesta Sinfónica Nacional
Handel: Concerto Grosso, Op. 6, no. 5 (Lima premiere); Mozart: Piano Concerto no. 24 (K. 491); Beethoven: Symphony no. 3 (*Eroica*)
Soloist: André Tschaikovsky (piano)

5 June 1959
Lima, Peru
Orquesta Sinfónica Nacional
Auber: Overture to *Fra Diavolo* (Lima premiere); Mozart: Symphony no. 33; R. Strauss: *Death and Transfiguration*; Schumann: Symphony no. 3 (*Rhenish*) (Lima premiere); Wagner: Overture to *Rienzi*

15 July 1959
Toronto, Canada
Toronto Summer Symphony Orchestra
Auber: Overture to *Fra Diavolo*; Mozart: Symphony no. 23; Dvořak: Symphony no. 9 (*From the New World*); J. Strauss: Waltz *Roses from the South*

October 1959 (precise date unknown)
Cologne, Germany
Westdeutschen Rundfunks
Repertoire unknown

25 November 1959
Stuttgart, Germany
Stuttgart Philharmonic
Mendelssohn: Overture to *A Midsummer Night's Dream*; Schumann: Piano Concerto; Brahms: Symphony no. 4
Soloist: Dorothea Braus (piano)

November/December 1959 (precise date unknown)
London, England
London Symphony Orchestra/BBC Choir
Mahler: Songs ("Ich atmet einen linden Duft," "Revelge," "Liebst du Schönheit," "Blicke mir nicht in die Lieder," "Ich bin der Welt

abhanden gekommen," "Der Tambourg'sell," "Um Mitternacht"), *Das Klagende Lied* (?)
Soloists: Richard Lewis (tenor), Kerstin Meyer (soprano)

13 January 1960
Geneva, Switzerland
L'Orchestre de la Suisse Romande
Beethoven: Overture to *Egmont*; Mozart: Violin Concerto no. 7 (apocryphal); Berlioz: *Symphonie fantastique*
Soloist: Charles Cyroulnik (violin)

12 February 1960 (CBC broadcast)
Toronto, Canada
CBC Symphony Orchestra
Busoni: Sarabande and Cortege from *Doktor Faust*; Mendelssohn: Symphony no. 3 (*Scottish*)

24 February 1960
Toronto, Canada
York Concert Society
Schubert: Symphony no. 8 (*Unfinished*); Mahler: *Das Lied von der Erde*
Soloists: Elena Nikolaidi (mezzo-soprano), David Lloyd (tenor)

15 April 1960 (CBC broadcast date)
Toronto, Canada
CBC Symphony Orchestra
Weber (arr. Mahler): excerpts from *The Three Pintos*; Mahler: Symphony no. 1

26 April 1960
Toronto, Canada
York Concert Society
Mozart: Serenade no. 7 (*Haffner Serenade*), Piano Concerto no. 26 ("Coronation"), Symphony no. 41 (*Jupiter*)
Soloist: Walter Susskind (piano)

3 May 1960
Toronto, Canada
York Concert Society
Vivaldi: Concerto no. 1 for Flute and Strings (*La Tempesta di Mare*); R. Strauss: Sextet for Strings (Introduction to *Capriccio*) (Canada premiere); J.S. Bach: *Brandenburg Concerto* no. 4; Healey Willan: *Poem*

*for Strings*; J.S. Bach: *Brandenburg Concerto* no. 5; Vivaldi: *Concerto alla Rustica*
Soloists: Gordon Day (flute), Nicholas Fiore (flute), Greta Kraus (harpsichord), Albert Pratz (violin)

10 May 1960
Toronto, Canada
York Concert Society
Pergolesi-Stravinsky: *Pulcinella* Suite; Chopin: Piano Concerto no. 1; Franck: Symphony in D minor
Soloist: Mieczyslaw Horszowski (piano)

17 May 1960
Toronto, Canada
York Concert Society
Beethoven: *Leonore No. 3* Overture, Violin Concerto, Symphony no. 5
Soloist: Betty-Jean Hagen (violin)

13 November 1960
Valencia, Spain
Orquesta Municipal de Valencia
Mozart: Symphony no. 39; Boris Blacher: *Concertante Music for Orchestra*, Op. 10 (Valencia premiere); Beethoven: Symphony no. 3 (*Eroica*)

20 November 1960
Valencia, Spain
Orquesta Municipal de Valencia
Schubert: Symphony no. 8 (*Unfinished*); Mahler: Symphony no. 1

21 November 1960
Valencia, Spain
Orquesta Municipal de Valencia
Boris Blacher: *Concertante Music for Orchestra*, Op. 10; Mozart: Symphony no. 39; Mahler: Symphony no. 1

1 March 1961 (CBC broadcast 8 March 1961)
Toronto, Canada
Toronto Symphony Orchestra
Brahms: *Variations on a Theme by Haydn*; Mahler: Symphony no. 1

10 May 1961 (CBC broadcast)
Toronto, Canada

CBC Symphony Strings
A. Hamerik: *Symphonie Spirituelle*

17 May 1961 (CBC broadcast)
Toronto, Canada
CBC Symphony Strings
R. Strauss: *Metamorphosen*; Handel: Minuet from Concerto Grosso, Op. 6, no. 5

5 November 1961
Valencia, Spain
Orquesta Municipal de Valencia
Weber: Overture to *Oberon*; Dvořak: Symphony no. 9 (*From the New World*); Wagner: Prelude to Act I from *Lohengrin*, Prelude and Death from *Tristan und Isolde*, Overture to *Die Meistersinger*

12 November 1961
Valencia, Spain
Orquesta Municipal de Valencia
Beethoven: Overture to *The Creatures of Prometheus*; Tchaikovsky: Symphony no. 6 (*Pathetique*); Turina: *Fantastic Dances*; R. Strauss: *Till Eulenspiegels lustige Streiches*

13 November 1961
Valencia, Spain
Orquesta Municipal de Valencia
Weber: Overture to *Oberon*; Tchaikovsky: Symphony no. 6 (*Pathetique*); Wagner: Prelude to Act I from *Lohengrin*, Prelude and Death from *Tristan und Isolde*, Overture to *Die Meistersinger*

8 April 1962 (CBC broadcast date)
Toronto, Canada
CBC Concert Orchestra
Auber: Overture to *Fra Diavolo*; Mozart: *Haffner* Serenade (excerpts); Bizet: Suite *L'Arlésienne No. 2*; J. Strauss: Waltz *Roses from the South*

12 April 1962
Toronto, Canada
York Concert Society
Mozart: Symphony no. 40, Ilia's Aria ("Zeffiretti lusinghieri") from *Idomeneo*, Aria of the Queen of the Night ("O zitt're nicht, mein lieber Sohn") from *The Magic Flute*; Mahler: Symphony no. 4
Soloist: Elizabeth Benson-Guy (soprano)

25 April 1962
Toronto, Canada
York Concert Society
A. Hamerik: *Symphonie Spirituelle*; J.S. Bach: Violin Concerto in E major (BWV 1042); Haydn: Violin Concerto no. 1 in C major; Schoenberg: *Transfigured Night*
Soloist: Oscar Shumsky (violin)

2 May 1962
Toronto, Canada
York Concert Society
Gluck: Chaconne from *Orpheus and Eurydice*; Danzi: Sinfonia Concertante for Clarinet and Bassoon (Canada premiere); Schumann: Introduction and Allegro for Piano and Orchestra, Op. 134 (Canada premiere); Mendelssohn: Serenade and Allegro Giocoso for Piano and Orchestra, Op. 43 (Canada premiere); Schubert: Symphony no. 6
Soloists: Abe Galper (clarinet), Nicholas Kilburn (bassoon), Anton Kuerti (piano)

16 May 1962
Toronto, Canada
York Concert Society
Beethoven: Music to *Egmont* (complete), *Leonore No. 2* Overture, Aria of Leonore ("Absceulicher, wo eilst du hin") from *Fidelio*, Symphony no. 7
Soloist: Mary Simmons (soprano)

15 July 1962
Toronto, Canada
Toronto Summer Symphony Orchestra
Berlioz: *Le Carnaval Romain* Overture; Tchaikovsky: Fantasy Overture *Romeo and Juliet*; Bizet: Suite from *Carmen*; Liszt: *Les Préludes*: Wagner: Overture to *Tannhäuser*

28 October 1962
Valencia, Spain
Orquesta Municipal de Valencia
Mozart: Symphony no. 40; Berlioz: *Symphonie fantastique*

4 November 1962
Valencia, Spain
Orquesta Municipal de Valencia

Mendelssohn: Overture and Scherzo to *A Midsummer Night's Dream*; Mahler: Adagietto from Symphony no. 5; Schubert: Symphony no. 6; J. Strauss: *The Blue Danube* Waltz

5 November 1962
Valencia, Spain
Orquesta Municipal de Valencia
Mozart: Symphony no. 40; Mahler: Adagietto from Symphony no. 5; Schubert: Symphony no. 6

11 November 1962
Valencia, Spain
Orquesta Municipal de Valencia
Wagner: Prelude to *Lohengrin*; R. Strauss: *Death and Transfiguration*; Beethoven: Symphony no. 5

22 January 1963
Toronto, Canada
Toronto Symphony Orchestra
Wagner: Prelude to *Lohengrin*, Aria of Elisabeth from *Tannhäuser*, Ballade of Senta from *The Flying Dutchman*; Mahler: Scherzo and Burlesque from Symphony no. 9
Soloist: Lois Marshall (soprano)

23 January 1963
Toronto, Canada
Toronto Symphony Orchestra
Wagner: Prelude and Elsa's Dream from *Lohengrin*, Elisabeth's Aria and Prayer from *Tannhäuser*, Santa's Ballade from *The Flying Dutchman*; Mahler: Symphony no. 9 (Canada premiere)
Soloist: Lois Marshall (soprano)

4 April 1963
Toronto, Canada
York Concert Society
Haydn: Symphony no. 100 (*Military*); Mozart: Piano Concerto no. 20 (K. 466); Stravinsky: *Eight Instrumental Miniatures*; Beethoven: Symphony no. 2
Soloist: Paul Helmer (piano)

18 April 1963
Toronto, Canada
York Concert Society

Bettinelli: *Sinfonia da Camera* (Canada premiere); Boccherini: Cello Concerto; Saint-Saens: Cello Concerto no. 1; Bizet: Symphony no. 1
Soloist: Leonard Rose (cello)

2 May 1963
Toronto, Canada
York Concert Society
Mendelssohn: Overture to *A Midsummer Night's Dream*; Harry Somers: *Fantasia for Orchestra* (Toronto premiere); Prokofiev: Violin Concerto no. 2; Brahms: Symphony no. 4
Soloist: Hyman Bress (violin)

18 October 1963
Stuttgart, Germany
Stuttgart Philharmonic
Mozart: Overture to *The Magic Flute*; Mendelssohn: Violin Concerto in E minor, Op. 64; Tchaikovsky: Symphony no. 5
Soloist: Shmuel Ashkenasi (violin)

3 November 1963
Valencia, Spain
Orquesta Municipal de Valencia
Beethoven: *Coriolan Overture*, Symphony no. 2, Symphony no. 7

11 November 1963
Valencia, Spain
Orquesta Municipal de Valencia
Bruckner: Symphony no. 4 (*Romantic*); Wagner: Overture to *Tannhäuser*, "Good Friday Spell" from *Parsifal*, Overture to *Rienzi*

17 November 1963
Valencia, Spain
Orquesta Municipal de Valencia
Weber: Overture to *Der Freischütz*; R. Strauss: *Don Juan*; Tchaikovsky: Symphony no. 5

5 January 1964 (CBC broadcast date)
Toronto, Canada
CBC Symphony Orchestra
Bruckner: Symphony no. 4 (*Romantic*)

4 February 1964
Toronto, Canada
Toronto Symphony Orchestra/Toronto Mendelssohn Choir
Schubert: Overture to *Rosamunde*; Mahler: Symphony no. 3 (Toronto premiere)
Soloists: Mary Simmons (soprano)

12 March 1964
Toronto, Canada
York Concert Society
Weber: Overture to *Der Freischütz*, Agatha's Aria from *Der Freischütz*; Mendelssohn: Symphony no. 4 (*Italian*); R. Strauss: *Four Last Songs*, *Death and Transfiguration*
Soloist: Lois Marshall (soprano)

2 April 1964
Toronto, Canada
York Concert Society
J.S. Bach: Suite in G minor; Stamitz: Symphony in F major; Mozart: Violin Concerto no. 4 (K. 218); Morawetz: Divertimento; Bloch: Concerto Grosso no. 2; Rossini: *Sonata for Strings*
Soloist: Betty-Jean Hagen (violin)

30 April 1964
Toronto, Canada
York Concert Society
Beethoven: Symphony no. 1, Piano Concerto no. 5 (*Emperor*), Symphony no. 8
Soloist: Anton Kuerti (piano)

10 May 1964
Toronto, Canada
York Concert Society
Beethoven: Overture to *The Creatures of Prometheus*, Symphony no. 1, Symphony no. 8

23 June 1964
Toronto, Canada
Members of the CBC and Toronto Symphony Orchestras
Villa Lobos: *Bachianas Brasileiras* no. 5 (Mary Morrison [soprano]); Schubert: Serenade (Maureen Forrester [contralto]); S. Barber:

*Reincarnations* (Festival Singers of Toronto, Elmer Iseler, cond.); R. Strauss: "Beim Schlafengehen im Abendrot" from *Four Last Songs* (Lois Marshall [soprano]); Beethoven: Symphony no. 9
Soloists: Lois Marshall (soprano), Maureen Forester (contralto), Garnet Brooks (tenor), Jan Simons (baritone)

24 June 1964 (CBC TV broadcast date)
Toronto, Canada
CBC Symphony Orchestra
R. Strauss: *Till Eulenspiegels lustige Streiche, Four Last Songs*
Soloists: Lois Marshall (soprano), Hermann Prey (baritone)

2 February 1965 (CBC broadcast 7 February 1965)
Toronto, Canada
Toronto Symphony Orchestra
Schubert: Symphony no. 8 (*Unfinished*); Mahler: *Das Lied von der Erde*
Soloists: Lili Chookasian (contralto), Garnet Brooks (tenor)

28 February 1965 (CBC broadcast)
Toronto, Canada
Toronto Symphony Orchestra
Mahler: Symphony no. 6 (*Tragic*) (first three movements) (Canada premiere)

**Other Significant Concerts (Unknown Dates)**

Circa 1920s
Vienna, Austria
Vienna Symphony Orchestra
Mahler: Symphony no. 1

**Known Concerts in the Soviet Union**

Winter 1924
Ukraine, Soviet Union
Seven concerts (2 in Kiev, 2 in Kharkov, 3 in Odessa)
Repertoire unknown

Spring 1926
Leningrad and Moscow, Soviet Union
Seven concerts (six in Leningrad – including a performance of Bruckner: Symphony no. 9 – one in Moscow); further repertoire unknown

Summer 1928
Ukraine, Soviet Union
Unknown number of concerts in Kharkov and Kiev
Tchaikovsky: Symphony no. 6 (*Pathetique*); further repertoire unknown

August 1929
Baku, Soviet Union
Unknown orchestra (possibly Leningrad Philharmonic Orchestra on tour)
Approx. twelve concerts
Repertoire Unknown

Summer 1930
Kislovodsk, Soviet Union
Leningrad Philharmonic Orchestra
Five concerts (of ten scheduled)
Repertoire unknown

Summer 1933
Moscow, Leningrad, Kiev, and Baku, Soviet Union
Unknown repertoire

30 January 1935
Leningrad, Soviet Union
Leningrad Symphony Orchestra
Mozart: Requiem

31 January 1935
Leningrad, Soviet Union
Leningrad Symphony Orchestra
Mozart: Requiem

27 February 1935
Leningrad, Soviet Union
Leningrad State Academic Philharmonic
J.S. Bach: *St. Matthew Passion*

1 March 1935
Leningrad, Soviet Union
Leningrad State Academic Philharmonic
J.S. Bach: *St. Matthew Passion*

22 November 1935
Leningrad, Soviet Union
State Philharmonic Academic Choir
Haydn: *The Seasons*

26 November 1935
Leningrad, Soviet Union
State Philharmonic Academic Choir
Haydn: *The Seasons*

1935 or 1936 (precise date unknown)
Tbilisi, Soviet Union
State Symphonic Orchestra
Berlioz: *Symphonie fantastique*; Chopin: Piano Concerto (No. 1 or 2); Tchaikovsky: Fantasy Overture *Romeo and Juliet*
Soloist: Bublikov (piano)

1935 or 1936 (precise date unknown)
Tbilisi, Soviet Union
State Symphonic Orchestra
Berlioz: *Symphonie fantastique*; Wagner: Isolde's Death from *Tristan und Isolde*; Liszt: *Les Préludes*
Soloist: Beatrice Valatstsi (?) (soprano)

5 March 1937
Leningrad, Soviet Union
Leningrad Philharmonic Orchestra (?)
Smetana: "Vltava"; Kabalevsky: Piano Concerto no. 2; Dvořak: Symphony no. 9 (*From the New World*)
Soloist: Kabalevsky (piano)

1–10 April 1937 (precise date unknown)
Leningrad, Soviet Union
Leningrad Radio Orchestra or Leningrad Symphony Orchestra
B. Savelyev: *Red Army Suite*; V. Sheherbachev: *The Storm*

Date unknown
Leningrad, Russia
Leningrad Conservatory and Opera Studio
Weber: *Der Freischütz*

# Notes

### Introduction

1 In her now classic article on the differences between biography and microhistory, Jill Lepore outlines the complexity of writing microhistory, ultimately concluding that she may be unable to ever write such a work due to her inability to treat her subjects as “only devices.” Jill Lepore, “Historians Who Love Too Much: Reflections on Microhistory and Biography,” *Journal of American History* 88, no. 1 (2001): 129–44.

2 Franz Rosenzweig and Gershom Scholem both came from German Jewish families that had effectively assimilated. As young men, both turned back to Judaism, Rosenzweig being instrumental in the creation of the Freie Jüdische Lehrhaus (The Free House of Jewish Learning), while Gershom Scholem remained a vital intellectual force among German Jewry for decades to come. For a closer examination of the Freie Jüdische Lehrhaus, see, for instance, Michael Brenner, *The Renaissance of Jewish Culture in Weimar Germany* (New Haven, CT: Yale University Press, 1996), wherein the author discusses the Lehrhaus as part of an ambitious and concerted project of Jewish cultural invention. Noah Isenberg explores a similar set of themes in his highly thoughtful *Between Redemption and Doom: The Strains of German-Jewish Modernism* (Lincoln: University of Nebraska Press, 1999).

A useful compendium of Gershom Scholem’s writing that ranges through the entirety of his long life and career as a Jewish philosopher and historian can be found in Gershom Scholem, *On Jews and Judaism in Crisis: Selected Essays*, ed. Werner J. Dannhauser (New York: Schocken Books, 1976).

3 For an example of a work that rejects the older construction of German-Jewish symbiosis, see Todd Samuel Presner, *Mobile Modernity: Germans, Jews, Trains* (New York: Columbia University Press, 2007).

4 Carlo Ginzburg, *The Cheese and the Worms: The Cosmos of a Sixteenth-Century Miller* (Baltimore, MD: John Hopkins University Press, 1980) (originally published as *Il formaggio e i vermi: Il cosmo di un mugnaio del'500* [Turino: Giulio Einaudi Editore, 1976]).

5 I engage with the subject in this manner cognizant of Jolanta T. Pekacz's understanding that "the cause-and-effect linearity implied by the chronological plot is considered a reliable way of ordering the subject's life, and the author a trustworthy narrator who understands the relationship between the private self and the public world." See Jolanta T. Pekacz, "Memory, History and Meaning: Musical Biography and its Discontents," *Journal of Musicological Research* 23 (2004): 39–80.

6 Hundert argues that "a combination of elements in the experience of eighteenth-century Eastern European Jews, including the concentration of large numbers, a continuing attitude of superiority to their neighbours, the secure place of and indispensable role played by Jews in the economy of the region, and the general absence of what I call the 'beckoning bourgeoisie,' strengthened and deepened a positive sense of Jewish identity. This became the central ingredient of the *mentalité* of East European Jews and constituted a kind of social-psychological translation of the concept of chosenness ... In subsequent centuries, despite ideological, geographical, economic, political, and even linguistic and cultural change, and for all the exceptions that might be cited, the vast majority of East European Jews and their descendants carried this core, even if transvalued, sense of chosenness within them." Gershon David Hundert, *Jews in Poland-Lithuania in the Eighteenth Century: A Genealogy of Modernity* (Berkeley: University of California Press, 2004), 4.

7 The Bund's importance as a nationalist movement is hotly contested. Jonathan Frankel insists that the Bund did not at first indicate the existence of a national consciousness. Jonathan Frankel, *Prophecy and Politics: Socialism, Nationalism, and the Russian Jews, 1862–1917* (Cambridge: Cambridge University Press, 1981). Henry J. Tobias, however, posits that the formation of the Bund marked and enabled the growth of a Jewish ethnic community that, for all intents and purposes, meant the creation of a nationalist ethos among Eastern European and Russian Jews. Henry J. Tobias, *The Jewish Bund in Russia from its Origins to 1905* (Stanford, CA: Stanford University Press, 1972), xv. Zvi Gitelman, meanwhile, endorses a moderate middle position between Frankel and Tobias, arguing that the Bund's growth was premised upon a pre-existing Jewish/Yiddish culture that continued to unfold due to the Bund's vibrancy in meeting explicit socio-economic and nationalist challenges to Jewish labourers. Zvi Gitelman, "A Century of Jewish Politics in Eastern Europe: The Legacy of the Bund and the Zionist Movement," and David Fishman, "The Bund and

Modern Yiddish Culture," both essays in Zvi Gitelman, ed., *The Emergence of Modern Jewish Politics: Bundism and Zionism in Eastern Europe* (Pittsburgh: University of Pittsburgh Press, 2003).

8 The waves of Eastern European Jews emigrating to Canada had, as Gerald Tulchinsky points out, actually begun in the 1880s following a series of pogroms stimulated by an antisemitism that had seen Jews blamed for the assassination of Tsar Alexander II. See Gerald Tulchinsky, *Taking Root: The Origins of the Canadian Jewish Community* (Hanover, NH: Brandeis University Press, 1993).

9 Ibid.

10 While seemingly lamenting that "Holocaust survivors who abandoned Judaism and Jewish organizational life do not occupy a central voice in the broader [Canadian Jewish] narrative," Goldberg seems compelled to lump what to my eyes are two very different groups – those who abandoned Judaism altogether and those who simply left Jewish organizational life – into one seemingly dismissive category. See Adara Goldberg, *Holocaust Survivors in Canada: Exclusion, Inclusion, Transformation, 1947–1955* (Winnipeg: University of Manitoba Press, 2015), 166–7.

11 Such an idea, while perhaps novel among historians, is not unknown in other fields. Philip Bohlman employs this methodological approach in his musicological study of German Jews in Israel; see Bohlman, *The Land Where Two Streams Flow: Music and the German-Jewish Community of Israel* (Chicago: University of Illinois Press, 1989).

12 In her work on German Jews who settled in New York between 1933 and 1945, Judith Gerson argues that their identity was constructed via what she calls "identity practices." As Gerson says, "I argue that we can best understand identities in their full complexity by carefully attending to how people routinely practice those identities." See Judith M. Gerson, "In Between States: National Identity Practices among German Jewish Immigrants," *Political Psychology* 22, no. 1 (2001): 179–98.

13 Israel Rabinovitch, *Of Jewish Music, Ancient and Modern*, trans. A.M. Klein (Montreal: Book Center, 1952), 143.

14 The title of the piece, "Das Judenthum in der Musik," is most accurately translated as "Jewishness in Music" but is more commonly translated as "Judaism in Music," an alteration that lessens the visceral nature of Wagner's antisemitism and paints the diatribe as less a blatantly antisemitic attack than a seeming critique of the formal aspects of Jewish religiosity in music.

15 For discussion of the rhetorical similarities shared by antisemites and early proponents of Jewish music, see Klara Moricz, *Jewish Identities: Nationalism, Racism, and Utopianism in Twentieth-Century Music* (Berkeley: University of California Press, 2008). James Loeffler also provides a fascinating discussion of the role that Wagner's thinking played in the development of the ideas

of Jewish musicological pioneers Abraham Idelsohn and Lazare Saminsky, arguing that "Wagner's iconic hate-text" lay "at the very center of the emerging Jewish musical imagination." See Loeffler, "Richard Wagner's 'Jewish Music': Antisemitism and Aesthetics in Modern Jewish Culture," *Jewish Social Studies* 15, no. 2 (2009): 2–36. Loeffler has also developed this idea in relation to the music (and musicology) of Israel; see Loeffler, "Do Zionists Read Music from Right to Left? Abraham Tsvi Idelsohn and the Invention of Israeli Music," *Jewish Quarterly Review* 100, no. 3 (2010): 385–416.

16 Abraham Idelsohn, *Jewish Music: Its Historical Development* (New York: Henry Holt and Co., 1929; New York: Dover Publications, 1992), xix. I'm citing here from the 1992 edition.

17 Ernest Bloch also wrote liturgical music, composing the *Avodath Ha-Kodesh: The Sacred Service* for San Francisco's Reform Congregation Temple Emanu-El between 1930 and 1933. See Seth Ward, "The Liturgy of Bloch's 'Avodath Ha-Kodesh,' " *Modern Judaism* 23, no. 3 (2003): 243–63.

18 Israel Rabinovitch, "Ernest Bloch," trans. A.M. Klein, in *Canadian Jewish Chronicle* (Montreal), 11 July 1947, 18 July 1947, 25 July 1947.

19 See Mathew Baigell and Milly Heyd, *Complex Identities: Jewish Consciousness and Modern Art* (New Brunswick, NJ: Rutgers University Press, 2001); David Biale, Michael Galchinsky, and Susan Henschel, *Insider/Outsider: American Jews and Multiculturalism* (Berkeley: University of California Press, 1998).

20 See Philip Bohlman, *Jewish Music and Modernity* (Oxford: Oxford University Press, 2008).

21 Eric Werner, "Felix Mendelssohn – Gustav Mahler: Two Borderline Cases of German-Jewish Assimilation." See also Henry A. Lea, *Gustav Mahler: Man on the Margin* (Bonn: Bouvier Verlag Herbert Grundmann, 1985); Kurt Blaukopf, *Gustav Mahler*, trans. Inge Goodwin (New York: Limelight Editions, 1985); Henry-Louis de la Grange, *Gustav Mahler, Vol. 2: Vienna: The Years of Challenge, 1897–1904* (Oxford: Oxford University Press, 1995); Michael Kennedy, *Mahler* (London: J.M. Dent, 1990); and Peter Heyworth, *Conversations with Klemperer* (New York: Faber and Faber, 1985). It should also be noted that certain scholars argue that Mahler's conversion was in fact not required. See, for example, Daniel Jütte, "His Majesty's Mahler: Jews, Courts, and Culture in the Nineteenth Century," *Simon Dubnow Institute Yearbook* 11 (2012): 149–62.

22 This quotation has become Mahler's most famous utterance, though the time and place of its genesis – or whether he even said it – is not entirely known. It may have in fact only been attributed to Mahler by his wife Alma. See Alma Mahler, *Gustav Mahler: Memories and Letters*, trans. Basil Creighton (New York: Viking Press, 1969), 109.

23 Theodor Adorno, *Mahler: A Musical Physiognomy*, trans. Edmund Jephcott (Chicago: University of Chicago Press, 1996), 149.

24 Arnold J. Band, "Kafka: The Margins of Assimilation," *Modern Judaism* 8, no. 2 (1988): 139–55; the quotation from Kafka appears on page 144. Numerous commentators have posited that the rapid shifts, or "lurchiness," of Mahler's music suggests a discomfort not only with the symphonic form but also a discomfort with society more broadly and a sense of being an outsider, an opinion presented as long ago as 1920, when the American music critic Paul Rosenfeld wrote that Mahler's music bore a certain sterility as a result of "the superficial assimilation of the traits of the people among who he is condemned to live." See Paul Rosenfeld, *Musical Portraits: Interpretations of Twenty Modern Composers* (New York: Harcourt, Brace and Howe, 1920), 221. Or, as his devoted admirer Max Brod would put it, "It may be that Mahler's music, though apparently German, is instinctively recognized as non-German – which is indeed the case." See Brod, *Israel's Music* (Tel Aviv: Sefer Press, 1951), 31.

25 In "Whose Gustav Mahler? Reception, Interpretation, and History," Leon Botstein argues that "For [Leonard] Bernstein, Mahler had pioneered a vision of a diaspora for Jews that, after defeat and tragedy, had ultimately found fulfillment in post-1960 America." See Botstein, "Whose Gustav Mahler? Reception, Interpretation, and History," in *Mahler and His World*, ed. Karen Painter, 1–54 (Princeton, NJ: Princeton University Press, 2002). In the same edited volume, Talia Pecker Berio also discusses the nexus between Bernstein and a post-war understanding of Jewish history; see: Talia Pecker Berio, "Mahler's Jewish Parable," in Painter, ed., *Mahler and his World*, 87–110. See also Adam J. Sacks, "Toward an Expansion of the Critique of the Mahler Revival," *New German Critique* 40, no. 2 (2013): 113–36.

26 Sacks, "Toward an Expansion of the Critique of the Mahler Revival."

27 Interestingly, Karen Painter suggests that the Jewish element in Mahler's life and work might not have been as central as others have made it out to be and that even the early spotlighting of the Jewish in relation to Mahler is at least in part a function of "the desire to find an interplay between religion, secularization and art [that] emerged perhaps from their effort to sacralize the memory of a composer who had become so important." See Painter, "From Biography to Myth: The Jewish Reception of Gustav Mahler," *Simon Dubnow Institute Yearbook* 11 (2012): 259–82. Whether Unger's veneration of Mahler suffered from a similar myopia is an interesting question to which the archives have not provided an answer, but my feeling is that Painter's fascinating argument misses one very key element: namely, the very fact that Mahler's defenders were often Jewish suggests some sort of common outlook, whether or not their explicit articulation or understanding of the composer's German Jewish meaning had to wait until later in the twentieth century.

## 1. A Thoroughly German Youth, Early Trips to the Soviet Union, and an Unfortunate Exile (1895–1933)

1 LAC. MUS 56, Box 4, File 69.
2 Sydney M. Bolkosky, *The Distorted Image: German Jewish Perceptions of Germans and Germany, 1918–1935* (New York: Elsevier Scientific, 1975), 68. Of course, many Jews had long before lost their explicitly religious affiliation with Judaism but had remained Jewish nevertheless, a reality underscored by the cultural values that they shared as well as the periodic discrimination that they experienced.
3 Unger never noted this. The only record of this having occurred comes from a letter written by his wife many years later. See LAC, MUS 56, Box 1, File 12.
4 LAC, MUS 56, Box 4, File 69.
5 Sylvia Cresti, "German and Austrian Jews' Concept of Nation, Culture and *Volk*," in *Towards Normality? Acculturation and Modern German Jewry*, ed. Rainer Liedtke and David Rechter (Tübingen, DE: Mohr Siebeck, 2003), 271–90.
6 James F. Brennan, *The Reflection of the Dreyfus Affair in the European Press, 1897–1899* (New York: P. Lang, 1998).
7 LAC, MUS 56, Box 1, File 23.
8 LAC, MUS 56, Box 1, File 12.
9 LAC, MUS 56, Box 1, File 12.
10 The details pertaining to the early years of the friendship between Bruno Walter and Heinz Unger are provided by Hella Unger in a speech she made circa 1959. The exact date and place of the speech is not known, though in the speech itself Hella notes it fell sometime after her husband's performance of Mahler's Fifth Symphony. Given the furore that surrounded Unger's Canadian premiere performance in February 1959, it seems highly likely that the speech falls just after this event. The full speech runs just under forty-two minutes and is a summation of Unger's achievements until that time. This speech is uncatalogued but is a part of the Heinz Unger Fonds (MUS 56) at LAC. The confirmation of their lifelong friendship resides in the extensive correspondence exchanged between the two men, which can also be found in the Heinz Unger Fonds.
11 Unger would count as one of the 100,000 out of a total population of 550,000 Jews in Germany that joined the army during the First World War. Thomas Levenson, *Einstein in Berlin* (New York: Bantam Dell, 2003), 167.
12 Ibid., 166. It should be noted that, while the myth of war enthusiasm has been brought into question by numerous scholars like Roger Chickering, the standard (albeit perhaps oversimplified) trope is that German Jews were excessively enthusiastic about the war as it provided them with an

opportunity to prove themselves as vital, heroic components of the German nation. See Chickering, " 'War Enthusiasm?' Public Opinion and the Outbreak of War in 1914," in *An Improbable War: The Outbreak of World War I and European Political Culture Before 1914*, ed. Holger Afflerbach and David Stevenson (New York: Berghahn Books, 2007), 200–12; Levenson, *Einstein in Berlin*, 170. See also Amos Elon, *The Pity of it All: A Portrait of the German-Jewish Epoch, 1743–1933* (New York: Picador, 2002), 338–9.

13 Helmut Kallmann, "Heinz Unger" in *The Encyclopedia of Music in Canada* (Toronto: University of Toronto Press, 1981), 943. Interestingly, his wife would recount that he had undertaken his studies privately although all the instructors were associated with the famous Stern Conservatory, founded in 1850 by Julius Stern, Theodor Kullak, and Adolf Marx. Given that Unger's mentor, Bruno Walter, had studied at the Stern Conservatory, it seems entirely reasonable to surmise that he encouraged Unger to undertake his studies with these professors.

14 See the Hella Unger speech in MUS 56.

15 The companion piece to the first concert was Wagner's *Faust Overture* while the second concert opened with Gluck's *Iphigenia in Aulis* Overture. Mention should also be made of the fact that the second concert coincided with what was dubbed a "Mahler woche" by the popular press, a week in which Unger's performance of *Das Lied* was accompanied by a performance of Mahler's Second Symphony led by Unger's close friend and mentor Bruno Walter. Indeed, Walter's support could not have but helped Unger secure his first performances with the Berlin Philharmonic. See LAC, MUS 56, Box 3, File 51.

16 LAC, MUS 56, Box 3, File 37.

17 "Ein junger Jurist unternahm es, den Befähigungnachweis als Orchesterdirigent zu erbringen und darzutun, dass die kunstlerische Begabung bei ihm eine urkraftig quellende, mit gebieterischer Kraft sich geltenmahhende sei ..." Max Chop, "Dr. Heinz Unger," *Signale für die musickalische Welt*, 17 September 1919, LAC, MUS 56, Box 3, File 51. My translation.

18 "Einen jungen Dirigenten, Dr. Heinz Unger, konnte man mit Interesse beobachten. Wie er Die Philharmoniker Wagners Faust Ouverture und Mahlers D-Dur-Sinfonie spielen ließ, zeugte von musikalischer Reife und Gestaltungsvermogen. Und das alles mit den Allüren eines Routiniers und einer selbstbewußten Sicherheit, die beinahe Besorgnis erweckt. Dr. Unger, von Hause aus ein Jurist, soll zum erstenmal ein Orchester leiten. Ist dem so, dann liegt allerdings ein starke Begabung vor." Leopold Schmidt, "Untitled," *Berliner Tageblatt* (No. 435), 16 September 1919, LAC, MUS 56, Box 3, File 51. My translation.

19 Kallmann, "Heinz Unger," in *The Encyclopedia of Music in Canada*.

20 Peter Muck, *Einhundert Jahre Berliner Philharmonisches Orchester: Darstellung in Dokumenten* (Tutzing, DE: Hans Schneider, 1982), 188.

21 Ibid., 194.
22 In a letter written 5 July 1958 to the vice-president of the Concertgebouw Orchestra, whose purpose it was to see if he might be granted the opportunity of conducting a Mahler work with the Concertgebouw in conjunction with the Mahler centenary of 1960, Unger writes: "As a very young man I belonged to the officially invited guests of your Mahler Festival of 1920. This honour was bestowed on me because in my very first season of subscription concerts with the Berlin Philharmonic Orchestra (1919/20) I had the courage to devote all my four programmes to different symphonies of the composer with whose works I am still to-day most closely associated: Gustav Mahler." LAC, MUS 56, Box 1, File 11.
23 Oskar Bie, "A Second Letter from Amsterdam," as quoted in Painter, ed., *Mahler and His World*, 367–8 (originally printed in the *Dresdner Neueste Nachrichten*, 25 May 1920). Oskar Bie (1864–1938) was a journalist and newspaper editor who devoted himself to the coverage of the arts, serving as chief editor of the literary magazine *Die neue Rundschau* between 1894 and 1922. Bie was progressive in his views, the journals that he ran reflecting this position. He was also Jewish and an early supporter of Gustav Mahler's music.
24 Despite the existence of earlier works, *Das klagende Lied* ("Song of Lamentation") was the first work that Mahler recognized, designating it as his Opus 1. The work was written between 1878 and 1880 and revised extensively in the subsequent decades, the composer excising the first of the work's three parts. Until recently, it was known in its revised bipartite form. In recent times, the first movement Mahler removed has been reintegrated into the work, resulting in a more balanced structure. Though no longer a rarity, it was rarely performed for a large part of the twentieth century.
25 The state certificate of marriage is signed 13 October 1923; see MUS 56, Box 4, File 69. Their marriage would produce one child, a daughter by the name of Ines, born 28 April 1928.
26 For Hella Unger's account of their meeting, see MUS 56, Box 1, File 12.
27 Hella Unger had taken advantage of the new freedoms that the Weimar Constitution afforded to women, and had finished her studies around the time of their marriage. According to Hans Joachim Hahn, "by 1925, women accounted for 100,000 teachers, 2,572 medical doctors, 4,000 dentists, 2,720 pharmacists and 1,000 chemists." See B. Beuys, *Familienleben in Deutschland* (Hamburg: Reinbeck, 1980), as cited in Hans Joachim Hahn, *Education and Society in Germany* (Oxford: Berg Publishers, 1998).
28 Unfortunately, all records of these travels have been lost and we must be content knowing that Unger appeared in Vienna during the 1920s, leading the Vienna Symphony Orchestra in Mahler's Symphony no. 1.
29 No entity with the title "the cultural State Institute of the Ukraine" is known to have existed. It is more than likely that Unger was referring to the

Leontovych Music Society (Muzychne Tovarystvo im. Leontovycha), which Dagmara Turchyn-Duvirak calls "the main creative musical association of those years." See Turchyn-Duvirak, "Kyiv, the 1920s, and Modernism in Music," in *Modernism in Kiev: Kyiv/Kyïv/Kiev/Kijów/Ķiev: Jubilant Experimentation,* ed. Irena R. Makaryk and Virlana Tkacz (Toronto: University of Toronto Press, 2010), 322–41.

30 Heinz Unger, *Hammer, Sickle and Baton* (London: The Cresset Press, 1939), 3–4. Unger's memoir of his experiences in the Soviet Union forms the heart of what we know of his time there from 1924 until the end of his regular visits to the USSR in 1937. Written as a travelogue and an evolving critical reflection of his many years working in Stalin's Russia, *Hammer, Sickle and Baton* illustrates the rising frustrations of a musician who had travelled "into the unknown" and become increasingly distraught by what he experienced during his many regular visits. Being a memoir, however, *Hammer, Sickle and Baton* presents a subjective and incomplete picture of the period and Unger's place within it. As a consequence, while the work serves as a guide, it fails to answer critical questions such as the original reasons for Unger's travels to the Soviet Union or why he would continue to return to a place that caused him so much frustration over such an extended period of time.

31 Sheila Fitzpatrick in fact contests the end date of the Russian Revolution, arguing that it did not truly end until Stalin's purges in the mid- to late 1930s; see Fitzpatrick, *The Russian Revolution* (Oxford: Oxford University Press, 1994).

32 Unger, *Hammer, Sickle and Baton,* 11.

33 Ibid.

34 Boris Schwarz notes that guest artists had begun to appear in the Soviet Union in 1921. By the mid-1920s, this trickle of foreign experts – musical or otherwise – had become a flood. "Foreign artists were invited to perform in Russia; often they brought a new repertoire and so provided a new stimulus ... Among guest artists who visited the Soviet capitals, orchestral conductors predominated. Most of them belonged to the Austro-German school. Even in Tsarist days, Russia had imported many foreign conductors. Now, after years of isolation and weakened orchestral discipline, the foreign visitors revived vanishing traditions, renewed the repertoire, and brought new excitement to the Russian musical scene. Among the guests were Bruno Walter, Otto Klemperer, Pierre Monteux, Hermann Scherchen, and William Steinberg." Unger is not mentioned in this context but was among this wave of Austro-German guests. Boris Schwarz, *Music and Musical Life in Soviet Russia, 1917–1970* (London: Barrie and Jenkins, 1972), 43–4.

35 Unger, *Hammer, Sickle and Baton,* 55–7.

36 Ibid., 59–60.

37 Ibid., 60.

38 Ibid.
39 Unger mentions these two works as examples of "modern" music; see Ibid., 64.
40 Ibid., 66–7.
41 Ibid., 69.
42 Ibid., 81. Unger notes that he was asked to repeat Anton Bruckner's Ninth Symphony in Moscow but declined on account of limited rehearsal time, opting instead to conduct Beethoven's Fifth Symphony, a work with which the musicians in Moscow would have been far more familiar.
43 Ibid., 85. Of course, we now know that the Soviet Union of the late 1920s and early 1930s was far from a place where great freedoms were allowed. Compared to the repression and culture of fear that was to come in the mid- to late 1930s, however, Unger's comments are most certainly close to the mark. For a fuller discussion of the period, see Amy Nelson, *Music for the Revolution: Musicians and Power in Early Soviet Russia* (University Park: Pennsylvania State University Press, 2004).
44 "Stimulated by the influx of musical ideas, encouraged by the tolerant view of the Soviet government, Russian musicians – composers, conductors, musicologists, and performers – joined forces to explore modern music, both foreign and Russian." Schwarz, *Music and Musical Life in Soviet Russia,* 45
45 Unger, *Hammer, Sickle and Baton,* 92.
46 Ibid.
47 Ibid., 93.
48 Ibid., 88. In her article on the period, Amy Nelson advances a similar view but cites 1931 as the year in which Stalin made a speech that liberated the arts. See Nelson, "The Struggle for Proletarian Music: RAPM and the Cultural Revolution," *Slavic Review* 59, no. 1 (2000): 101–32. A further discussion of the Soviet musical culture of the early to mid-1930s is found in chapter 2 of the present volume.
49 Unger, *Hammer, Sickle and Baton,* 98.
50 Ibid., 99.
51 Ibid., 125.
52 Ibid., 143.
53 Ibid., 185.
54 Ibid., 186. While Unger does not make clear the exact time of which he is speaking, we know that he is referring to the Reichstag elections of 14 September 1930, in which the number of seats won by the Nazi Party rose sharply, from 12 to 107.
55 Ibid.
56 Unger was set to open the 1930–1 Gesellschaft der Musikfreunde season on 16 October 1930 with a concert that consisted of Mozart's Symphony no. 38 (*Prague*) and Gustav Mahler's *Das Lied von der Erde.* The vocal soloists in the

Mahler were to have been Sarah Charles-Cahier (alto) and, in one of his final appearances, Jacques Urlus (tenor) (1867–1935). The second concert of the season, meanwhile, should have included the Berlin premiere of Ernest Bloch's *America, an Epic Rhapsody*. See Muck, *Einhundert Jahre Berliner Philharmonisches Orchester*, 245. Due possibly to ill health, Unger's 1930–1 season with the Berlin Philharmonic was limited to two engagements, the other two concerts of this season being led by guest conductors: on 15 January 1931, Igor Stravinsky appeared in a concert that included his suites from *Pulcinella* and the *Firebird* as well as the "eight pieces for small orchestra," while on 19 March 1931 the music director of the Bremen Philharmonic Orchestra, Ernst Wendel (1876–1938), led a program that included Richard Strauss's *Don Juan*, Beethoven's Fifth Piano Concerto (*Emperor*), and Brahms's Fourth Symphony. In the following season, Unger continued his pattern of sprinkling novelties in among the more familiar fare on his programs. On 15 October 1931, he led the first concert of the Gesellschaft der Musikfreunde series, a concert that consisted of J.C. Bach's Sinfonia in B-flat major, Beethoven's Piano Concerto no.1 (Georg Bertram, piano), and Bruckner's Eighth Symphony. The second concert of the season, held on 10 December, was a potpourri of sorts, including a series of arias by Bruch (from *Achilleus*) and Verdi (from *Don Carlos*) sung by Sigrid Onegin, orchestral music from Prokofiev's opera *The Love of Three Oranges*, Saint-Saens's Piano Concerto no. 2, and Tchaikovsky's Sixth Symphony. The novelty on the program was the Berlin premiere of Cesar Franck's Symphonic Poem for Piano and Orchestra *Les Djinns*. The fourth concert of the season was even more interesting, including Ernst Toch's *Bunte Suite für Orchester* placed between two war horses: Brahms's Violin Concerto (played by Carl Flesch) and Beethoven's Fifth Symphony. This concert was held on 3 March 1932 and opened with Mozart's *Maurerische Trauermusik* in honour of the passing of the influential musicologist Walther Schrenk. All information pertaining to the 1931 concerts is to be found in LAC, MUS 56, Box 3, File 47.

57 According to a German Bundestag study conducted in March 2006, "the NSDAP emerged as the strongest party [in the elections of 31 July and 6 November] with 37.4% (230 seats) and 33.1% (196 seats) respectively. In the July election it [the NSDAP] sent shock waves reverberating through the political landscape by more than doubling its number of votes; its relatively small loss of 4.3 percentage points in the November election did little to blunt the impact of the July vote." Administration of the German Bundestag, Research Section WD1, "Elections in the Weimar Republic," (March 2006), 2, available at https://www.bundestag.de/resource/blob/189774/7c6dd629f4afff7bf4f962a45c110b5f/elections_weimar_republic-data.pdf. The discrepancies between the dates and numbers is accounted for by the "much-debated dual system whereby both the Reichstag

and the Reich President were elected by direct popular vote." Detlev J.K. Peukert, *The Weimar Republic: The Crisis of Classical Modernity*, trans. Richard Deveson (New York: Hill and Wang, 1987), 38. Nevertheless, the numbers are all presented in Peukert's magisterial account of the Weimar Republic, 262–68.

58 Wilhelm Guttmann was one of the last German Jewish musicians working in the Third Reich, dying during a concert in Berlin in 1941. Michael Kater, *The Twisted Muse: Musicians and their Music in the Third Reich* (Oxford: Oxford University Press, 1997), 100.

59 The three orchestral songs were "Revelge," "Ich bin der Welt abhanden gekommen," and "Um Mitternacht." The soloist was baritone Alexander Kipnis. The concert was held on 13 October 1932. This concert also represents the last time that Unger would conduct Mahler on German soil for over two decades and one of the last examples of a German performance of Mahler's music before Nazi prohibitions against this "non-Aryan" composer went into force.

**2. European Exodus: USSR, England, Spain, and the World (1933–1954)**

1 Unger, *Hammer, Sickle and Baton*, 187.

2 Ibid.

3 Nelson, "The Struggle for Proletarian Music." Nelson also rightly notes that the RAPM failed to establish its desired "monopoly in musical affairs" and that its role in shaping musical culture in the period was rivalled by other agencies such as the Association for Contemporary Music (which reorganized as the All-Russian Society of Contemporary Music in July 1928) and the Organization of Revolutionary Composers and Musical Activists.

4 Nelson points to Stalin's 23 June 1931 speech to industrial managers as critical to the beginning of a greater period of freedom and the end of the cultural revolution by way of his direct call for "better relations with the intelligentsia" and a "denouncing [of] the radical theorizing of communist intellectuals." See Nelson, "The Struggle for Proletarian Music," 128. In a detailed discussion of the period, Boris Schwarz describes the climate and debates of the time, noting the pleasure with which these developments were greeted by those working in the field of music. Nevertheless, Schwarz points out that the abandonment of musical modernism led to "a general retreat into rose-coloured 'realism'" that in turn resulted in a "plateau of safe conservatism" that reflected the "new respectability" of Soviet life in the first half of the 1930s. See Schwarz, *Music and Musical Life in Soviet Russia*, 109–16. Unger's quote appears in *Hammer, Sickle and Baton*, 186.

5 Unger, *Hammer, Sickle and Baton*, 188.

6 The Leningrad Radio Orchestra had been founded as recently as 1931 and was a vital organ of musical culture for the remainder of the century until the present day. Its highlight was the premiere of Dmitri Shostakovich's Seventh Symphony ("Leningrad") on 9 August 1942 while the city was under German siege. After the Second World War, the orchestra's activities were merged with those of the Leningrad Philharmonic. In the post-Communist period, the Symphony Society of Leningrad was renamed the St. Petersburg Symphony Orchestra, which remains to this day one of the most important and well-respected ensembles in the world of music.

7 Unger, *Hammer, Sickle and Baton,* 189–90.

8 Ibid., 191. Unger mentions that there was more than enough work to go around for the many conductors working in the city, including Austrian Fritz Stiedry (1883–1968), German Oskar Fried (1871–1941), and a great many Russian conductors. Boris Schwarz confirms Unger's verdict, also noting his directorship of the Leningrad Radio Orchestra. See Schwarz, *Music and Musical Life in Soviet Russia,* 138.

9 Unger, *Hammer, Sickle and Baton,* 195. Unger fails to provide any evidence of this. We may therefore question whether such an accusation had less to do with reality and more to do with Unger's characteristic paranoia.

10 Ibid., 215. A part of Unger's contentment during this period must have come from playing a part in the Russian discovery of Mahler's music. As Inna Barsova notes, "throughout the ... [1920s] and the 1930s, Mahler's symphonies and songs were performed in Leningrad and (less frequently) Moscow by Heinz Unger, Fritz Stiedry, Hans Steinberg, Albert Coates, Bruno Walter, Otto Klemperer, Alexander Zemlinsky, Joseph Rosenstock, Václav Talich, Eugen Szenkar and Jascha Horenstein, and by such Soviet conductors as Aleksander Gauk, Karl Eliasberg, Natan Rakhlin, Nikolay Rabinovich, and Evgeny Mravinsky. See Barsova, "Mahler and Russia," in *The Mahler Companion,* ed. Donald Mitchell and Andrew Nicholson (Oxford: Oxford University Press, 1999), 517–30; the quote is from p. 526, with Barsova citing the original source of the information as Sollertinsky's "Khronograf ispol'neniya proizvedeniy Malera I Bruknera v SSSR," in *Pamyati I.I. Sollertinskogo, vospominaniya, materialy, issledovaniya,* ed. Ludmila Mikheyeva (Leningrad and Moscow: Sovetskiy kompozitor, 1974), 232–4. In light of the dearth of information pertaining to Unger's years in the Soviet Union, this passage accounts for the only list – albeit an undetailed one – of Unger's repertoire during this period.

11 *Lady Mcbeth of Mtsensk* was triumphantly premiered in Leningrad on 22 January 1934 and, according to Schwarz, "was hailed as a great achievement of Soviet culture." See Schwarz, *Music and Musical Life in Soviet Russia,* 119; for a fuller discussion of the opera, see pp. 119–32.

12 While there is no evidence by which to ascertain the identity of the author, it is often claimed that Stalin had a large part in the composition of the article, titled "Chaos instead of Music." Boris Schwarz notes the "article [was] unsigned which gave [it] the standing of official policy pronouncements, and it was revealed in 1948 that [it] was written on instructions from the Party's Central Committee. Whether Stalin personally was involved in giving these instructions, whether Zhdanov was the actual author of the articles, cannot be ascertained though these facts were widely rumoured." Schwarz, *Music and Musical Life in Soviet Russia,* 122.

13 Unger, *Hammer, Sickle and Baton,* 225. Echoing Unger's position, Schwarz provides us with information on Stalin's preferences in the realm of opera, noting that Stalin's requisites for a "good" Soviet opera were "a libretto with a Socialist topic, a realistic musical language with stress on a national idiom, and a positive hero typifying the new Socialist era." Schwarz, *Music and Musical Life in Soviet Russia,* 123. Needless to say, Shostakovich's *Lady Macbeth of Mtsensk* met none of those requirements.

14 Boris Schwarz links the above-mentioned attack on Shostakovich's opera *Lady Macbeth of Mtsensk* to the assassination of Kirov, noting that 1936 "brought an intensification of political terror, culminating in the great purge that cut deeply into every stratum of Soviet life." Schwarz, *Music and Musical Life in Soviet Russia,* 119. In her far more wide-ranging discussion, Sheila Fitzpatrick describes the political machinations and terror that followed Kirov's assassination and the exploitation of the event as an example of the alleged "terrorist activity of the Troskyite-Zinovievite counter-revolutionary bloc." See Fitzpatrick, *The Russian Revolution,* 163–70.

15 Unger, *Hammer, Sickle and Baton,* 243.

16 Ibid., 267.

17 Ibid., 268.

18 Ibid., 271.

19 Ibid., 273.

20 LAC, MUS 56, Box 3, File 48. The Northern Philharmonic Orchestra had been formally constituted in 1935, having changed its name that year from the Leeds Symphony Orchestra (est. 1908). Due to artistic discontinuities, the Northern Philharmonic was disbanded after the Second World War and re-formed in 1978 as the English Northern Philharmonia. It continues to function today as the Orchestra of Opera North.

21 John Barbirolli (1899–1970) was one of the eminent British conductors of the twentieth century. He was conductor of the New York Philharmonic between 1937 and 1942 and then assumed command of the Hallé Orchestra (Manchester), which he led between 1942 and 1970. Sir Hamilton Harty (1879–1941) was a British conductor and composer who held the post of conductor of the Hallé Orchestra from 1920 to 1933. He was knighted in

1925 and had long career conducting in England and abroad. Malcolm Sargent (1895–1967) is also one of the most renowned British conductors of the twentieth century, having worked with all of England's major orchestras during his career. He became conductor of the famous Proms concerts, serving in that capacity between 1948 and 1967.

22 LAC, MUS 56, Box 5, File 74. The praise for Unger's conducting comes from the uncredited article entitled "The Northern Orchestra," *Yorkshire Post,* 24 January 1938, LAC, MUS 56, Box 5, File 74. For details pertaining to the TSO concert, see chapter 3 of this volume.

23 "Musician in Russia," *Daily Telegraph* (London), 16 May 1939, LAC, MUS 56, Box 5, File 74. The book was reviewed by nearly every major and minor newspaper across England.

24 The *Jüdische Welt-Rundschau* was the successor to the *Jüdische Rundschau,* the official weekly of the *Zionistische Verein für Deutschland* that had been published between 1897 and 1938. Suspended by official order of the Gestapo after Kristallnacht, the newspaper was reorganized as the *Jüdische Welt-Rundschau* and published in Paris and printed in Tel Aviv for a short time before suspending operations. See Abraham J. Edelheit and Hershel Edelheit, *A History of the Holocaust: A Handbook and Dictionary* (Boulder, CO: Westview Press, 1994), 378.

25 "Ein Dirigent in Russland," *Jüdische Welt-Rundschau* (Jerusalem), 23 June 1939, LAC, MUS 56, Box 5, File 74.

26 Heinz Unger's acceptance speech upon being awarded the West German Commander's Cross, January 1965, LAC, MUS 56, Box 1, File 16. For a fuller discussion of the event itself, see chapter 5 in this volume.

27 S.F.C.H. (contributor's true identity unknown), "The West London Amateur Orchestra," *Synagogue Review,* August 1940. According to the *Edinburgh Evening News,* the West London Amateur Orchestra was "an amateur orchestra, formed from among the most famous musicians of Germany, Austria, and Czechoslovakia, who are now refugees in Great Britain." This may have been a case of hyperbole, perhaps on the part of Unger himself. See "Exiled Musicians," *Edinburgh Evening News,* Winter 1940 (exact date unknown).

28 "A First-Class Conductor," *Jewish Chronicle* (London), 2 February 1940, LAC, MUS 56, Box 5, File 74.

29 Jutta Raab Hansen, *NS-verfolgte Musiker in England: Spuren deutscher und österreichischer Flüchtlinge in der britischen Musikkultur* (Hamburg: von Bockel, 1996). The review of the concert appears in "The West London Amateur Orchestra," *Synagogue Review,* March 1940, LAC, MUS 56, Box 5, File 74.

30 S.F.C.H., "The West London Amateur Orchestra."

31 In the words of the association's chairman, Lord Phillimore, "The Finland Fund was formed on a strictly non-party basis with the specific objects of

succouring the sick and wounded and affording relief to civilians who suffered owing to the invasion of their country." The president of the fund was Lord Plymouth. See Session of Parliament: Relations with Finland, 22 July 1941, available at http://hansard.millbanksystems.com/lords/1941/jul/22/relations-with-finland.

32 The music for this concert is not known beyond the fact that Mozart's *Eine Kleine Nachtsmusik* was included on the program. S.F.C.H., "The West London Amateur Orchestra." According to the *Edinburgh Evening News,* two further concerts in aid of the British Sailors' Society and the University College Hospital were arranged. A lack of material prevents us from knowing whether these concerts were ever actually held.

33 "The Northern Philharmonic is one of the seven National Orchestras to receive the grant from the Government, administered through the Council for the Encouragement of Music and the Arts (C.E.M.A.) to give performances of orchestral music in [communities] where such is not frequently provided." B.L. "Orchestral Concert at the Ritz," *Barnsley Chronicle,* 2 October 1943, LAC, MUS 56, Box 5, File 74.

34 H.H.W., "Leeds Sunday Concert: Mr. Heinz Unger's Conducting," *Yorkshire Post,* 28 December 1942.

35 Unger's upturn in fortunes with the London Philharmonic began in 1943 and extended through the remainder of the war years. The London Philharmonic Orchestra was founded in 1932 by the conductor Sir Thomas Beecham (1879–1961) and is considered even today one of Britain's, if not the world's, greatest orchestras.

36 In each of these concerts, a similar program was repeated with minimal changes, the touring program almost always including Brahms's Fourth Symphony. Works with a guest soloist and/or another shorter overture or symphony usually took up the bulk of the first half of the concerts. That said, it should also be noted that on some occasions Unger made a point of programming less popular material, as was the case on 16 January 1944, when the concert included Anton Bruckner's Fourth Symphony (*Romantic*), the work of a composer that, judging from reviews, had yet to be accepted in England. On more than one occasion, Unger also programmed Elgar's Violin Concerto, a work still deemed "modern" decades after its composition and premiered by the remarkable young violinist Yehudi Menuhin, LAC, MUS 56, Box 5, File 74.

37 In Nottingham, Unger was praised for his "assurance and attention to detail," while in Bristol the admiration for the conductor was even more effusive: "This gift is Dr. Heinz Unger, a real performer and conductor on [*sic*] the orchestra. Musical understanding, depth of feeling, sensitiveness, rightness of tempi, beauty of phrasing and control of his instrument are all displayed by this Master of Music." See M.E., "Brahms Artistry," *Nottingham*

*Journal*, 13 January 1944, LAC, MUS 56, Box 5, File 74; M.A., "A Master of Music: Heinz Unger and the L.P.O.," *Western Press* (Bristol), 27 January 1944, LAC, MUS 56, Box 5, File 74. The Nottingham concert was held in Nottingham's Albert Hall on 12 January 1944 and included Mendelssohn's *Calm Sea and Prosperous Voyage* Overture, Schumann's Piano Concerto (with Eileen Joyce as soloist), and Brahms's Fourth Symphony. The Bristol concert was held at Colston Hall, on 26 January 1944, the second of two concerts held by Unger and the LPO on the same day (the first being a lunchtime affair). The evening concert consisted of Mendelssohn's *Calm Sea and Prosperous Voyage* Overture, Grieg's Piano Concerto (with Eileen Joyce as soloist), and Brahms's Fourth Symphony.

38 Hugh Liversidge, "London," *Musical Courier*, February 1944, LAC, MUS 56, Box 5, File 74.

39 The works performed at the 21 February 1942 matinee concert were: Weber's *Oberon* Overture, Schumann's Piano Concerto (performed by Dame Myra Hess), Dvořak's Eighth Symphony, and the aforementioned Mahler excerpt. See "Dame Myra Hess in Leeds," *Yorkshire Post*, 23 February 1942, LAC, MUS 56, Box 5, File 74.

40 The full concert consisted of Mendelssohn's *Athalie* Overture, Mahler's *Songs of a Wayfarer*, Tchaikovsky's *Romeo and Juliet*, Brahms's Third Symphony, and Glinka's *Russlan and Ludmilla* Overture. The program was performed on 6 September at the Orpheum in the London borough of Barnet, LAC, MUS 56, Box 5, File 74. The London Symphony Orchestra was founded in 1904 and its conductors have included leading luminaries of twentieth-century music, including Hans Richter (1904–1911), Arthur Nikisch (1912–1914), Thomas Beecham (1915–1916), Albert Coates (1919–1922), Willem Mengelberg (1930–1931), and Hamilton Harty (1932–1935). In the post-war period, its conductors have included Pierre Monteux, André Previn, Claudio Abbado, Michael Tilson Thomas, and Colin Davis.

41 The uncredited reviewer was referring also to Adrian Boult's presentation of Mahler at an LPO concert earlier that summer. "More Mahler, Please," *Cavalcade*, 21 November 1942, LAC, MUS 56, Box 5, File 74.

42 E.H.W., "Dr. Unger Conducts Mahler Work at Liverpool," *Yorkshire Post*, 5 March 1945, LAC, MUS 56, Box 3, File 52.

43 "Philharmonic Concerts: 'The Song of the Earth,' " *Liverpool Post*, 5 March 1945; B.A., "The Song of the Earth," *Liverpool Echo*, 5 March 1945. Both LAC, MUS 56, Box 3, File 52.

44 The first such instance of this seems to have come at an LPO concert held on 28 December 1944 at Colston Hall Bristol, the local press greeting the performance as one in which "the grace and beauty of this movement was fully expressed." M.A., "L.P.O. Festival Week: Programme of Serious Music," *Western Daily Press* (Bristol), 29 December 1944, LAC, MUS 56, Box 3, File 52.

45 In a review of the performance, the unnamed critic mentions that Unger made "a number of cuts in the Scherzo and Finale of the Fifth." One wonders whether this was Unger's decision or the consequence of a "corrupted" score that he was using. In light of his familiarity with Mahler's music, one gets the impression that these cuts were made by Unger himself, perhaps in hopes of making a more favourable impression with British concertgoers. "Mahler and the Concert Season," *New Statesman*, 27 October 1945. Mahlerites might also be interested in the eminent Mahler musicologist Donald Mitchell's observation that "the orchestra's first horn, at the end of the second movement, took up his place (his seat) at the front of the platform, alongside – or close to – the leader of the orchestra" in the manner written into Mahler pioneer Willem Mengelberg's conducting score. Mitchell thus raises the interesting possibility that "this was a 'tradition' Mengelberg inherited from Mahler himself." Adding weight to the theory that this was an instruction inherited from Mahler himself is the fact that Unger was not a protégé of Mengelberg but of another of Mahler's own protégés, Bruno Walter. Donald Mitchell, "Mahler's Fifth Symphony," in *The Mahler Companion*, ed. Donald Mitchell and Andrew Nicholson (Oxford: Oxford University Press, 1999), 236–325. The aforementioned discussion appears on page 275.

46 The most critical review of the work appeared in the *Musical Times*: "In listening to a great symphony one has the impression that when the composer set about writing the first notes his mind had already a complete picture of the whole. That is an impression that Mahler's symphonies do not convey ... there were times during the performance when one felt that the composer, enamoured of his own emotion, lost touch with realities and was no longer thinking in terms of practical notes." See "Mahler's Fifth Symphony," *Musical Times*, date unknown. Other reviewers were far more receptive, recounting both the enthusiasm of the audience ("one has seldom witnessed such whole-hearted enthusiasm as that to which the audience gave vent at the conclusion") as well as the strength of the work itself ("Mahler's Fifth Symphony is a magnificent work"). That same reviewer then went on to praise the conductor's performance of this unfamiliar work – "it calls for playing of the utmost virtuosity and sensitivity, and this Dr. Unger secured." H.S.R., "London Philharmonic Orchestra," *Musical Opinion*, date unknown. One of Britain's most important music critics, Hugh Liversidge, appropriately characterized the conductor's work as being "in the true Mahler tradition" while also lamenting that "a rather more sensuous, and at other times, more biting and resonant tone from the strings would have made for even greater enjoyment." See Liversidge, "London: Lends Ear to Mahler Fifth," *Musical Courier*, n.d., ca. October/November 1945.

47 Donald Mitchell notes that performances such as Unger's British premiere of Mahler's Fifth Symphony "bring fascinating evidence that the English

Mahler 'boom' was struggling to get under way even during the inauspicious wartime years." Mitchell, "The Mahler Renaissance in England," in *The Mahler Companion,* ed. Donald Mitchell and Andrew Nicholson (Oxford: Oxford University Press, 1999), 550.

48 The reviews for the recording confirmed the musician's growing reputation in Britain, not only because of the confidence laid in him in granting him the opportunity but also by the reviews that demonstrated the high esteem in which he was held. "Ruy Blas," *Symphony,* July 1947, LAC, MUS 56, Box 5, File 75. The Mendelssohn was recorded with the National Orchestra and the Beethoven with the London Philharmonic.

49 LAC, MUS 56, Box 5, File 74, and "Art, Politics and a Conductor," *New York Times,* 31 October 1937, LAC, MUS 56, Box 5, File 74.

50 Historians of modern Spain have in recent years helped us better understand the nature of the relationship between Franco's "quasi-Fascist" Spain and Hitler's Nazi Germany, demonstrating that while Franco flirted with the idea of more closely aligning Spain with Nazi Germany early in the war, such a course was dashed by Hitler's assessment that Spain had little to offer the Axis as a fighting force and his desire to not alienate his precarious relationship with Vichy France by conceding the French territories in North Africa that Franco sought as compensation for entering the war. Perhaps as early as late 1943, and certainly by the spring and summer of 1944, Franco had begun a "tilt to the allies" as it became clear that Germany would lose the war. See Stanley Payne, *Franco and Hitler: Spain, Germany and World War II* (New Haven, CT: Yale University Press, 2008).

51 "The Department of Cultural Relations of the British Ministry of Foreign Affairs has had the courtesy of facilitating the travel of Unger to come to Spain, cordially attending as such to the petition made by our local government and other Spanish entities.

Maestro Unger has come to Spain on a cultural mission and one of the goals of this journey is to introduce in our country – by way of the artistic temperament of this illustrious director – works by English composers, some of which figure in the programs of our concerts."

This note is taken from an insert included in an appearance by Unger with the Valencia Orchestra in late fall 1945. "El Maestro Unger," LAC, MUS 56, Box 3, File 52. My translation.

52 In the immediate post-war period, Franco was already beginning to be seen as an ally in the common front against Soviet expansionism. Then, "the commencement of the Cold War in the final years of the 1940s dismantled whatever enthusiasm existed for forcing out a violently anti-Communist Franco who, whatever his evils, at least ensured that Spain would not fall into the Soviet sphere of influence." Florentino Portero, "Spain, Britain and

the Cold War," in *Spain and the Great Powers in the Twentieth Century*, ed. Sebastian Balfour and Paul Preston (London: Routledge, 1999), 210–28.

53 Bernd Rother notes: "No se le puede atribuir a la dictadura de Franco que haya apoyado la persecución judía llevada a cabo por el nacionalsocialismo. Este gobierno estaba tan lijado a los valores católicos tradicionales que no pudo compartir las terribles consequencias que los nacionalsocialistas extrajeron de su ideología racista desde el principio de la segunda guerra mundial." (One cannot attribute to Franco's dictatorship a support for the Jewish persecution carried out by National Socialism. This government was so tied to traditional Catholic values that it could not share in the terrible consequences that the National Socialists extracted from their racist ideology from the beginning of the Second World War). See Rother, *Franco y el Holocausto* (Tübingen, DE: Max Niemeyer Verlag, 2001), 405. My translation.

54 Raanan Rein, *In the Shadow of the Holocaust and the Inquisition: Israel's Relations with Francoist Spain* (London: Frank Cass and Co., 1997).

55 The Orquesta de Valencia had been founded as recently as 1943. At its inception it was known as the Orquesta Municipal de Valencia and only changed its name years later.

56 Federico, "Musica en la Sociedad Filarmónica: Unger es recibido de nuevo Clamorosamente," *Jornada* (Valencia) 11 December 1945. LAC, MUS 56, Box 3, File 52. My translation.

57 Benjamin's work appeared on 10 December 1945 alongside works by Dvořak, Smetana, Beethoven, and Liszt, while Unger performed Jacob's work with the Valencia Orchestra on 17 December 1945 and then again with the Symphonic Orchestra of Madrid on 30 December 1945.

58 "una encendida, cariñosisima y prolongada ovacion de despedida," *Jornada* (Valencia), 24 December 1945. LAC, MUS 56, Box 3, File 52.

59 The concert with the Orquesta Sinfónica de Madrid featured Brahms's First Symphony, Gordon Jacob's Passacaglia, Wagner's *Siegfried Idyll*, and Dvořak's *Carnival* Overture. The first of the two January 1946 concerts with the National Orchestra consisted of Weber's *Oberon* Overture, Smetana's "Vltava," Milane's *Suite Española*, and Tchaikovsky's Fifth Symphony, while the second was composed of Gluck's *Iphigenie in Aulis* Overture, Brahms's Fourth Symphony, Richard Strauss's *Don Juan*, and orchestral pieces from Berlioz's *The Damnation of Faust*. LAC, MUS 56, Box 3 File 52.

60 "El publico madrilèno ha sabido prestar la acogida mas entusiasta e incondicional a Heinz Unger, el maestro admirable, cuyos conciertos quedarán durante mucho tiempo como modelo de dificil copia." A. Fernadez-Cid, "Triunfal concierto de despedida de Heinz Unger," *Arriba* (Madrid), 26 January 1946. LAC, MUS 56, Box 3, File 52. My translation.

61 Hugh Liversidge, "Music in Spain," *Gramophone Record and Home Musician*, March 1946. LAC, MS 56, Box 3, File 52.

62 Ibid.

63 Antonio Cazorla-Sanchez, "Beyond They Shall not Pass: How the Experience of Violence Reshaped Political Values in Franco's Spain," *Journal of Contemporary History* 40, no. 3 (2005): 503–20. Cazorla-Sanchez's appraisal of Franco's Spain as not a truly fascist state is reflected by Stanley Payne, who notes that even the most fascist-leaning government formed by Franco in 1939 was not Falangist but, rather, a government that balanced the "various ideological 'families' of the regime." Payne, *Franco and Hitler*, 414. Writing at the time, Samuel Grover Rich, Jr., would note much the same thing:

> The present Spanish regime differs in several important characteristics from the fascism of other countries. First, its leader is no Hitler. He is a *Catholic militarist*, a man who belatedly allied himself with Spain's fascist party ... [Second] Franco's ascendancy to power has not changed the fundamental character of Spanish society. There has been no "fascist revolution" if one means by that a disturbance of the economic and social structure. On the contrary, Spain's traditional class system has been frozen. Franco served to solidify the *status quo* ... Indeed, the societal elements supporting the Franco dictatorship have been the bulwark of every Spanish government in modern times.

Grover Rich, Jr., "Franco Spain: a Reappraisal," *Political Science Quarterly* 67, no. 3 (1952): 397.

64 The Mahler concert with the Orquesta Nacional was held on 29 March 1946 and also included Schubert's *Rosamunde* Overture and Schumann's Piano Concerto (with José Cubiles as soloist). The performance of Mahler's First Symphony with the Orquesta Municipal de Valencia was held on 1 May 1946 and included Gluck's *Iphigenie in Aulis* Overture and Mozart's Serenade No.7. On the occasion of Mahler's performance in Madrid, the press noted: "Si esta sinfonía de Mahler no hubiera sido servida por un director como Unger, el resultado, aun favourable a la obra, hubiero sido muy otro. Con el, el interes fue creciendo desde el primer compas hasta terminar, en el ultimo tiempo, en las ovaciones mas delirantes." (If this symphony of Mahler's had not been presented by a conductor like Unger, the result, despite favourable to the work, would have been very different. With him, interest grew from the first bar until the end, the conclusion being greeted with the most delirious ovations.) A. de la H., "Clamoroso triunfo de Unger y Cubiles con la Orquesta Nacional," *Informaciones* (Madrid), 30 March 1946. My translation.

65 The first concert was with the Orquesta Nacional on 4 October 1946. The last concert was with the Orquesta Municipal de Valencia on 2 December 1946. LAC, MUS 56, Box 5, File 75.

66 On 18 and 19 October, Unger conducted the Orquesta Nacional (Madrid) and included Moeran's *Overture for a Masque* in a program of otherwise standard symphonic fare by Weber, Schumann, and Mendelssohn. LAC, MUS 56, Box 5, File 75.

67 A list would be superfluous here. Suffice it to say that Unger's concerts regularly included the standard symphonic works of the eighteenth, nineteenth, and early twentieth centuries. For the "Jewish" significance of this repertoire, see Bohlman's *The Land Where Two Streams Flow.*

68 LAC, MUS 56, Box 5, File 75.

69 The concert, which included Charles Stanford's *Irish Rhapsody*, Borodin's *In the steppes of Central Asia*, Chopin's Piano Concerto No.1 (Weingarten as piano soloist), and Beethoven's Sixth Symphony (*Pastorale*), was held on the afternoon of 8 December 1946. A.F., "Heinz Unger as Guest Conductor," *Birmingham Mail*, 9 December 1946, LAC, MUS 56, Box 5, File 75.

70 The first concert of this trip was on 14 March 1947 with the *Orquesta Nacional*, the last with the *Orquesta Municipal de Valencia* on 4 May 1947. LAC, MUS 56, Box 5, File 75.

71 The Philharmonia (founded in 1945 by the famous EMI producer Walter Legge) concert, held at Central Hall, Westminster, consisted of Gluck's *Iphigenia in Aulis* Overture, Mozart's Piano Concerto in A major (K. 488), and Tchaikovsky's Fifth Symphony. The piano soloist in the Mozart concerto was the Romanian (and Jewish) Mozart specialist Clara Haskil (1895–1960). LAC, MUS 56, Box 5, File 75.

72 The concerts were held on 14, 27, and 28 June, and 11 July 1948. The Cuban press commented on these concerts very favourably, noting in particular how Unger's style and force of personality made a quick impression on both musicians and non-musicians alike: "el estilo del maestro Unger acuso, enseguida, una recia personalidad para conducir immejorablemente el conjunto orquestal." (Maestro Unger's style at once showed a strong personality to conduct the orchestral group in an insuperable manner.) Vicente Bernardes, "Heinz Unger y la Filarmonica," *Pueblo* (Havana), 22 June 1948, LAC, MUS 56, Box 5, File 75 (picture 70). My translation.

73 Unger would return to Mexico in 1950 and lead the Orquesta Sinfónica de la Universidad on at least two more occasions in the fall of 1950.

74 E.L. Chavarri, "Estreno en Espana de la Segunda Sinfonía de Mahler," *Las Provincias* (Valencia), 22 February 1951. The critic, after a lengthy explanation of the work and performance, completes his review with the short phrase "Fue un exito completo." My translation. LAC, MUS 56, Box 5, File 75.

75 "Anoche, la Valencia ..., sensible al tremendo esfuerzo del insigne maestro Unger, la Orquesta Municipal, Coral Polifónica y Orfeón de Godella, contralto y soprano solistas ... es decir, correspondiendo a la tarea admirable de un conjunto de doscientos cincuenta ejecutantes ... saludó con unanime aplauso, clara expresión de afecto y admiración sin reserves, al eminente director." Federico, "Estreno en Espana de la sinfonia 'Resurrección,' de Mahler: Una Audicion Memorable Y un Exito Clamoroso," *Jornada* (Valencia), 22 February 1951. My translation.

76 LAC, MUS 56, Box 6, File 76.

77 "El maestro Unger ofreció su ultima audición," *La Nación* (Buenos Aires), 8 September 1951, LAC, MUS 56, Box 6, File 76.

78 LAC, MUS 56, Box 6, File 76.

79 Pearl McCarthy, "Argentinians in 5-Block Queue for Beethoven," *Globe and Mail* (Toronto), 1 October 1951, LAC, MUS 56, Box 6, File 76. The *Musical Courier* reported on these selfsame queues; see "Dr. Unger's Series in Buenos Aires Extended," *Musical Courier*, November 1951, LAC, MUS 56, Box 6, File 76.

80 Not all reviewers were completely won over – while the critic for *La Prensa* praised Unger for his "balanced rendition ... that adequately marked the contrast between the timbres and the choral mass," he also noted that the performance of Beethoven's Ninth Symphony lacked "profundity." See "Finalizó el Ciclo de Sinfonías de Beethoven," *La Prensa* (Buenos Aires), 8 October 1954, LAC, MUS 56, Box 6, File 76.

81 See "Dr. Unger Repeats," *Globe and Mail* (Toronto), 2 October 1954; "Un Hecho Cultural Altamente Signicativo," *Musica* (date unknown), LAC, MUS 56, Box 6, File 76.

### 3. Early Life in Canada and a Return to Germany (1937–1956)

1 "Conductor Balks at Swinging Bach: Soviet Ousts Him," *New York Post*, 26 October 1937, LAC, MUS 56, Box 5, File 74.

2 Ibid.

3 Ibid.

4 Ibid.

5 "Art, Politics and a Conductor," *New York Times*, 31 October 1937, LAC, MUS 56, Box 5, File 74.

6 This information comes only from Hella Unger's uncatalogued speech, circa 1959, to be found in the Heinz Unger Fonds (MUS 56) at LAC.

7 "Maestro Enjoys Jazz Provided It Is Good," *Globe and Mail* (Toronto), 3 November 1937. LAC, MUS 56, Box 5, File 74.

8 Ibid.

9 "Toronto's Musical Interest Delights Guest Conductor," *Evening Telegram* (Toronto), 5 November 1937, LAC, MUS 56, Box 5, File 74.

10 Ezra Schabas, *Sir Ernest MacMillan: The Importance of Being Canadian* (Toronto: University of Toronto Press, 1994), 122.

11 Ibid. Unger had in fact wanted more than the three rehearsals that he was granted but ultimately had to make do. Throughout his career, Unger would wage similar battles in what was often a futile attempt to secure what he considered to be the required time to adequately rehearse and prepare for a performance.

12 The evening was supposed to begin with Mozart's Overture to *The Marriage of Figaro* (K. 492) but this was omitted (despite being on the concert program) due to the length of the program.

13 Edward Wodson, "Visiting Artists Work Miracles with Orchestra" *Evening Telegram* (Toronto), 10 November 1937. The uncredited music reviewer for the *Globe and Mail* commended Unger in a similar manner:

> The hero of the evening was undoubtedly Heinz Unger, famous European conductor, who led our players superbly in two of the three major works that made up the fine program presented. He was recalled countless times, applauded and cheered to the echo, but steadily refused to accept for himself the extraordinary ovation tendered, always insisting upon making our players rise to share in acknowledgement of the ardent tribute. Our players did, indeed, distinguish themselves in their sensitive and vital response to his leadership, so that many passages throughout the evening could hardly have been bettered anywhere; but the chief honours, nevertheless, were Dr. Unger's.
> "A Splendid Concert," *Globe and Mail* (Toronto), 10 November 1937.

14 "Ocean Travellers," *New York Times*, 15 December 1937, LAC, MUS 56, Box 5, File 74.

15 Unger arrived in Montreal aboard the RMS *Ausonia* on 20 November 1938. LAC, MUS 56, Box 5, File 74.

16 Hector Charlesworth, "Visit of a Great Master," *Saturday Night*, 10 December 1938, LAC, MUS 56, Box 5, File 74.

17 Augustus Bridle, "Unger Makes Magic Aided by Symphony," *Toronto Daily Star*, 30 November 1938, LAC, MUS 56, Box 5, File 74.

18 Schabas states that the low point of MacMillan's relationship with the TSO fell in the latter parts of the 1930s and lasted into the early 1940s. See Schabas, *Sir Ernest MacMillan*, 146–54.

19 In trying to deny that Macmillan had grown uncomfortable with Unger's success, Schabas rather oddly and obliquely – and with no firm cited support – refers to the fact that even before Unger's second appearance in 1938 some suspected that MacMillan had grown jealous of Unger; ibid., 123.

20 For a fuller discussion of this émigré community, see Dorothy Lamb Crawford, *A Windfall of Musicians: Hitler's Émigrés and Exiles in Southern California* (New Haven, CT: Yale University Press, 2009). See also Ehrhard Bahr, *Weimar on the Pacific: German Exile Culture in Los Angeles and the Crisis of Modernism* (Berkeley: University of California Press, 2007), and Anthony Heilbut, *Exiled in Paradise: German Refugee Artists and Intellectuals in America, 1930s to the Present* (Boston: Beacon Press, 1983).

21 Lamentably little information is to be found on Unger's activities or even where he stayed in his year-long sojourn in New York. The single document in his Fonds relating to this period is the letter from Leopold Stokowski, dated 20 December 1947, LAC, MUS 56, Box 1, File 10.

22 See Hella Unger's uncatalogued speech, circa 1959, LAC, MUS 56.

23 Despite the fact that many of the players were culled from the TSO's ranks, the Toronto Philharmonic Orchestra was actually a separate entity, "established with the assistance of the Toronto Musical Protective Association to provide summer employment for musicians." See Robert W. Judge, "Promenade Symphony Concerts," in *The Encyclopedia of Music in Canada*. The 15 July concert was divided into two parts, the first half consisting of Beethoven's *Coriolan Overture* followed by three piano-accompanied songs performed by Ms. Carol Brice and then by Borodin's "Polovtsian Dances." The second half of the concert was broadcast on the CBC Dominion Network and consisted of Rossini's "Thieving Magpie" Overture, two Arias performed by Ms. Brice, Schubert's Symphony no. 5, and the Johann Strauss II waltz, *Roses from the South*. LAC, MUS 56, Box 5, File 75.

24 The *Evening Telegram*'s music critic called the performance of the Beethoven overture an interesting reading, the Borodin dances "quite fascinating," the Schubert "delightful," and the "almost banal" Strauss waltz "the reincarnation of the spirit of that musical city [Vienna] that has become almost a legend." See *Evening Telegram* (Toronto), 16 July 1948, LAC, MUS 56, Box 5, File 75. The unsigned reviews of the concert in both the *Globe and Mail* and the *Evening Telegram* (both 16 July 1948) each made a point of noting that Unger was handicapped by a lack of rehearsal time; LAC, MUS 56, Box 5, File 75.

25 Schabas, *Sir Ernest MacMillan*, 196.

26 For an account of the entire saga surrounding MacMillan's increasing frustration with the TSO and his desire to obtain a new position – including mention of the 6 September 1938 letter from MacMillan to Judson in which he told his agent that 1938 "would be his last TSO season" – see ibid., 149–56

27 Letter from Heinz Unger to Harry Newstone, 12 February 1962, LAC, MUS 56, Box 1, File 15. In this letter, Unger was trying to advise his friend

Newstone, who was seeking opportunities in Canada and trying to deduce whether Walter Susskind might be leaving the post of the director of the TSO.

28 In speaking of German Jews arriving in Canada during the Second World War and in the immediate post-war period, Adara Goldberg notes that some "felt that they faced discrimination as German and Austrian Jews and 'greenies,' ignorant newcomers in an unfamiliar foreign environment." See Adara Goldberg, *Holocaust Survivors in Canada: Exclusion, Inclusion, Transformation, 1947–1955* (Winnipeg: University of Manitoba Press, 2015), 31. Goldberg develops this same theme later in her text, pointing to how "unfamiliar liturgies and melodies, and the sense that their foreign languages, cultures, and religious traditions alienated them from local congregations, prompted the survivors to unite and form their own prayer centres and, subsequently, spiritual, social, and economic communities." This statement is part of a longer discussion of the establishment of Toronto's liberal Congregation Habonim in the early to mid-1950s. See: Goldberg, *Holocaust Survivors in Canada,* 139–43.

29 Franklin Bialystock, *Delayed Impact: The Holocaust and the Canadian Jewish Community* (Montreal: McGill-Queen's University Press, 2000), 69. It should be noted that Goldberg's more recent work points – albeit in passing – to how wartime German-speaking Jewish refugees "enriched Canadian-Jewish life and contributed greatly to secular society at large." Goldberg, *Holocaust Survivors in Canada,* 32. That said, the general sweep of her volume focuses principally on post-war European Jewish arrivals more in need of assistance.

30 In his magisterial account of Jewish life in the Americas, *World of our Fathers* (New York: Simon and Schuster, 1976), Irving Howe makes this precise point with a beautiful nuance that bears repeating:

> Cultures are slow to die; when they do, they bequeath large deposits of custom and value to their successors; and sometimes they survive long after their more self-conscious members suppose them to have vanished. A great many suburban Jews no longer spoke Yiddish, a growing number did not understand it, some failed to appreciate the magnitude of their loss; but their deepest inclinations of conduct, bias, manner, style, intonation, all bore heavy signs of immigrant shaping. What Jewish suburbanites took to be "a good life," the kinds of vocations to which they hoped to lead their children, their sense of appropriate conduct within a family, the ideas capable of winning their respect, the moral appeals to which they remained open, their modes of argument, their fondness for pacific conduct, their views of respectability and delinquency – all showed the strains of immigrant Yiddish culture, usually blurred, sometimes buried, but still at work. (618)

31 Bialystock, *Delayed Impact*, 69.

32 For a fuller discussion of the cultural difference between German and Eastern European Jews, see Bohlman's *The Land Where Two Streams Flow.*

33 "Heinz Unger Leads Village Symphony after All-Star Career," *Forest Hill Journal*, 1 July 1950, LAC, MUS 56, Box 5, File 75.

34 "Some more affluent Toronto Jews moved away from the areas of first and second settlement up to swanky Forest Hill ... Many of the new arrivals shed their 'old-fashioned' ways – abandoning Orthodox religious observances, for example – and adopted upper-class norms." Gerald Tulchinsky, *Canada's Jews: A People's Journey* (Toronto: University of Toronto Press, 2008), 417.

35 The German word *Bildung* is difficult to translate but is often understood as a concept that goes beyond merely "learning" and links to general moral improvement of the individual. According to George Mosse, *Bildung's* success in helping German Jews integrate into general society beginning in the late-Enlightenment period transformed it into a code of conduct that was retained by German Jews well into twentieth century and explains their posture during the Weimar era and – in Unger's case – beyond. See George L. Mosse, *German Jews beyond Judaism* (Bloomington: Indiana University Press, 1985). While scholars of German Jewry have begun to question certain facets of this thesis, it has – in the words of Shulamit Volkov – "with time almost turned self-evident, a commonplace among historians of German Jewry." See Volkov. "The Ambivalence of Bildung: Jews and Other Germans," in *The German-Jewish Dialogue Reconsidered: A Symposium in Honor of George L. Mosse*, ed. Klaus L. Berghahn (New York: Peter Lang, 1996), 81.

36 The goals were a) "To give to [the music lovers and amateur musicians] the deep enjoyment, that real understanding and appreciation of music and music performances in general, which can only be derived from meticulous studies of the works at hand and from the observance of the essential rules of true ensemble playing"; b) "To the student and the professional members of the orchestra we wish to give a valuable training ground for orchestral practice in general"; and c) "To our listeners we wish to bring performances of the masterworks of the musical literature." Gladys Allison, "Dr. Heinz Unger Directs Forest Hill Orchestra," *The Enterprise* (Lansing, ON), 6 July 1950.

37 Hugh Thomson, "Forest Hill Hails New Orchestra," *Toronto Star*, 18 November 1950.

38 Quote from Gladys Allison, "Dr. Heinz Unger Receives Ovation at Forest Hill," *The Enterprise* (Lansing, ON), 23 November 1950.

39 Paul Helmer, *Growing with Canada: The Émigré Tradition in Canadian Music* (Montreal: McGill University Press, 2009), 18. Gustav Mahler's nephew Alfred Rosé (b. Vienna 1902, d. London, ON 1975) is cited as another

example of a musician who failed to achieve the same heights they had attained in Europe before their emigration to Canada.

40 The program for the 31 May concert opened with Tchaikovsky's *Romeo and Juliet* Overture, a selection of songs and arias, and ended with Dvořak's Symphony no. 9 (*From the New World*). The guest soloist for the vocal selections was baritone Igor Gorin. Unger also led a second Proms concert the following week, the program being Mendelssohn's *Calm Sea and Prosperous Voyage*, a selection of lighter violin "encores" by Foster-Heifetz, Kreisler, and Sarasate (all performed with Simeon Joyce accompanying at the piano), Mozart's Violin Concerto no. 4 in D major, and Beethoven's Symphony no. 5. The soloist for the violin pieces on that occasion was Donna Grescoe. On 11 June 1951, Unger also led the Beaches Symphony in a public rehearsal at the Riverdale Collegiate Auditorium that consisted of Rossini's *Barber of Seville* Overture, Haydn's Symphony no. 100 (*Military*), and Mozart's Symphony no. 35 (*Haffner*). LAC, MUS 56, Box 6, File 76.

41 The reviewer in attendance paid particular attention to the fact that the orchestra's work blurred the lines between professional and amateur ensemble playing, concluding that "no such matter needed to be taken into consideration." Pearl McCarthy, "Community Orchestra Plays Mozart Concert," *Globe and Mail* (Toronto), 30 January 1952, LAC, MUS 56, Box 6, File 76.

42 *CBC Times*, 23 January 1952, LAC, MUS 56, Box 6, File 76. Unfortunately, the tapes for this performance seem not to have been preserved by the CBC.

43 The orchestral part of the 26 February program consisted of the following: Berlioz's *Le Carnaval Romain* Overture, Tchaikovsky's *Romeo and Juliet*, Wagner's *Rienzi* Overture, and Liszt's *Les Préludes*. Edward Wodson, "Police Concert Stars Baritone, TSO and Ballet," *Telegram* (Toronto), 27 February 1952, LAC, MUS 56, Box 6, File 76.

44 The 20 March program at Aeolian Hall consisted of Handel's Concerto Grosso in G major, Op. 6, no. 1, Franck's *Symphonic Variations*, Mozart's Piano Concerto in A major (K. 488), and Mozart's *Marriage of Figaro* Overture. The soloist was Helen Ingram. LAC, MUS 56, Box 6, File 76.

45 The two concerts took place on the Friday and Saturday evenings, 18 and 19 April 18. The Friday night concert consisted of Cantata no. 51 ("Jauchzet Gott in allen Landen") (soprano: Eunice MacDonald), Air in D from Suite no. 3, *Brandenburg Concerto* no. 3, and the Overture in G minor. Saturday's concert consisted of *Brandenburg Concerto* no. 4, the Trio in C major, the Harpsichord Concerto in F minor (soloist: Ray McIntyre), and Suite no. 2 for Orchestra. LAC, MUS 56, Box 6, File 76.

46 LAC, MUS 56, Box 6, File 76.

47 The London Chamber Orchestra works were Bach's Overture in G minor (BWV 1070), Schubert's Symphony no. 5 (D. 485), and Beethoven's Second

Piano Concerto (Op. 19) (soloist: Helen Ingram). At the concert with the Community Centre Orchestra, the Schubert works were the Overture In the Italian Style in C major (D. 590) and his *Unfinished* Eighth Symphony (D. 759). The Beethoven works performed were the *Egmont* Overture, Op. 84, and Symphony no. 2, Op. 36. LAC, MUS 56, Box 6, File 76.

48 "Society Concerts Fill Spring Gap" *Globe and Mail* (Toronto), 17 February 1953, LAC, MUS 56, Box 6, File 76.

49 LAC, MUS 56, Box 5, File 76. Lubka Kolessa (1902–1997) was a pianist born in the Ukraine who emigrated to Canada in 1940 and continued to concertize until 1954, after which she devoted herself entirely to teaching.

50 Ibid.

51 Ibid.

52 Ibid. The final program (held on 26 May) was to open with Mozart's Symphony no. 41 (*Jupiter*), continue with an Aria from Mozart's opera *Il Re Pastore*, and end with a performance of Mahler's Symphony no. 4. For unknown reasons, this program was changed prior to the concert date.

53 John Kraglund, "Small Orchestra, Conductor Score in First of Series," *Globe and Mail* (Toronto), 24 April 1953, LAC, MUS 56, Box 6, File 76. Kraglund was born in Denmark and, despite his family moving to Canada in 1929, had become a naturalized Canadian citizen as recently as 1949. After studying music theory and criticism with Leo Smith, he would embark on a decades-long career as a music critic, retiring from the *Globe and Mail* only in 1987. In his time as a critic, Kraglund contributed a great deal to the development of Canadian musical culture, expecting much from the concerts and events he attended. Indeed, his high expectations were rarely met and he was often guarded in his praise. In light of this, Kraglund's consistently positive views of the many Unger-led concerts he attended carry extra weight. See Alan H. Cowle and Kenneth Winters, "John Kraglund," in *The Encyclopedia of Music in Canada*. A further assessment of Kraglund's music criticism (along with those of his many colleagues at the *Globe and Mail*) can be found in Colin Eatock, "Classical Music Criticism at the *Globe and Mail*: 1936–2000," *Canadian University Music Review* 24, no. 2 (2004).

54 Edward Wodson, "Beethoven Music Delights Concert Audience," *Telegram* (Toronto), 24 April 1953, LAC, MUS 56, Box 6, File 76.

55 John Kraglund, "Harpsichordist, Small Orchestra Near Perfection," *Globe and Mail* (Toronto), 7 May 1953.

56 *CBC Times*, 5–11 December 1954, LAC, MUS 56, Box 7, File 77; "Mahler's Fourth," *Globe and Mail* (Toronto), 27 November 1954, MUS 56, Box 7, File 77. A longer discussion of Unger and his affiliation with Mahler can be found in "Gustav Mahler," *CBC Times*, 12–18 December 1954, LAC, MUS 56, Box 7, File 77. The soprano soloist in the final movement was Elizabeth Benson-Guy.

57 Ezra Schabas and Stuart Nall, *Musical Courier*, January 1955, LAC, MUS 56, Box 7, File 77.

58 "A CBC Wednesday Night Devoted to Mahler," *CBC Times*, 27 March–2 April 1955, LAC, MUS 56, Box 7, File 77. Unfortunately, the tapes of this program have either been lost, destroyed, or languish in some unknown corner of the CBC. Ezra Schabas, *Musical Courier*, May 1955, LAC, MUS 56, Box 7, File 77.

59 Unger's work with the YCS had resulted in Governor General Vincent Massey and the Lieutenant Governor Louis O. Breithaupt and his wife accepting honorary patronship of the society "in recognition of the achievements of the York Concert Society in the past three years and of its support for Canadian art and artists." See "Honorary Patrons of York Society," *Globe and Mail* (Toronto), 8 October 1955.

60 The full orchestral program, broadcast coast to coast, consisted of Auber's *Fra Diavolo* Overture, the Nocturne and Scherzo from Mendelssohn's "Midsummer Night's Dream," the Arias "Parto, parto, Ma tu ben mio" from Mozart's opera *La Clemenza di Tito* and "In Questa Reggia" from Puccini's *Turandot*, the aforementioned Adagietto from Mahler's Symphony no. 5, and Strauss II's *Roses from the South* Waltz. The guest vocal soloist was Lois Marshall. After an intermission, Marshall returned to the stage to sing a selection of songs with piano accompaniment. The evening then concluded with Tchaikovsky's *Romeo and Juliet* Overture. (The works performed after the intermission were not broadcast). LAC, MUS 56, Box 7, File 77.

61 Ibid.

62 John Kraglund, "Toronto," *Musical Courier*, December 1955.

63 Hugh Thompson noted how the performance pleased the crowd, as "three thousand concert-goers in Massey Hall last night took to clapping, cheering and stamping at the close of the Toronto Symphony subscription concert conducted by Dr. Heinz Unger." See Thomson, "Unger-led Tchaikovsky Wins Boisterous Ovation," *Toronto Daily Star*, 9 November 1955. George Kidd, meanwhile, noted how Unger "thrilled a near-capacity audience" and how his "approach was one of sincerity and deep feeling, and the orchestra's response was a labour of love for both composer and conductor." Kidd, "TSO Brass Section Correct, Precise under Dr. Unger," *Telegram* (Toronto), 9 November 1955.

64 The Ginastera work, commissioned by the Buenos Aires Society of Friends of Music, was receiving under Unger its Toronto (and presumably also Canadian) premiere. *CBC Times*, 18–23 December, LAC, MUS 56, Box 7, File 77.

65 The other works performed on that occasion were Carl Ditters von Dittersdorf's (1739–1799) *Actaeon* Symphony, and the obscure and now forgotten Norwegian composer Regnald Skrede's *Den Kvite Fuglen*. See "Riksprogrammet, Onsdag 8. Februar," *Program Bladet*, 8 February 1956. The Soloist in the

Mahler symphony was the Norwegian soprano Randi Helseth (1905–1991). LAC, MUS 56, Box 7, File 77.

66 "Here and There," *Musical Courier*, March 1956, LAC, MUS 56, Box 7, File 77. On the back of these successful performances, Unger is noted as having obtained engagements in Copenhagen, Göteborg, and Bergen for the subsequent season. Unfortunately, there are no confirmed details of these concerts.

67 Klaus Pringsheim led a performance on Mahler's *Lieder eines fahrenden Gesellen* and Symphony no. 5 on 30 May 1956. The singer in the Lieder was Hermann Prey. See Muck, *Einhundert Jahre Berliner Philharmonisches Orchester*, 352.

68 The 22 and 23 February 1956 concerts were held in the Konzertsaal der Hochschule für Musik and featured Anny Schlemm as the vocal soloist in the arias. LAC, MUS 56, Box 7, File 77.

69 Hugh Thomson, "Spain Bids Heinz Unger For Valencia Orchestra," *Toronto Daily Star*, 3 April 1956.

70 Ibid.

71 Ibid.

**4. A Jewish Renaissance: Life in Canada, the Israel Philharmonic, and the Mahler Centenary (1956–1960)**

1 For a fuller discussion of the role of nature in Mahler's music, see Julian Johnson, "Mahler and the Idea of Nature," in *Perspectives on Gustav Mahler*, ed. Jeremy Barham (Aldershot, UK: Ashgate, 2005), 23–36.

2 Alfredo Catalani and Riccardo Zandonai were both Italian opera composers who have failed to establish themselves in the mainstream repertoire except for the odd aria. Catalani is best known for his opera *La Wally* while Zandonai is more obscure. The particular work was a Zandonai arrangement of a Catalani aria.

3 Carl Maria von Weber (1786–1826) had begun the composition of his comic opera *Die Drei Pintos* in the summer and fall of 1821, after completing the Romantic opera *Der Freischütz*. After being refused permission to stage the work, Weber abandoned it. When Giacomo Meyerbeeer proved unable to complete the opera, it returned to the Weber family, who in turn passed it on to a young Gustav Mahler, who conducted his completion of the opera at Leipzig on 20 January 1888. Michael Kennedy, "Mahler's Only Opera?," Liner notes to Carl Maria von Weber (compl. Mahler) *Die Drei Pintos* (Naxos: 8.660142–43, 2004).

4 John Kraglund, "Music in Toronto," *Globe and Mail* (Toronto), 16 May 1956.

5 George Kidd's review of the concert also highlighted the beauty in the performance of the *Wayfarer* songs, not exactly stressing Unger's contribution

but noting with emphasis the excellent contribution made by Forrester: "Miss Forrester was heard in Mahler's Songs of a Wayfarer, and once again the beauty of this remarkable voice shone brilliantly throughout the four parts. She has apparently made a complete study of the work and it emerged with sincerity, beautiful control and an exciting imagination." See Kidd, "Final Concert in Series Proves Musical Treat," *Telegram* (Toronto), 16 May 1956, LAC, MUS 56, Box 7, File 77.

6 For further discussion of Strauss's activity during the Nazi period, see Michael Kater, *The Twisted Muse: Musicians and their Music in the Third Reich* (New York: Oxford University Press, 1997).

7 Violet Archer (b. Montreal 1913, d. Ottawa 2000) was an important Canadian composer and teacher of the last century. She studied with a number of composers of the first rank (including Béla Bartók and Paul Hindemith) and later served as chair of the theory and composition department at the University of Alberta between 1962 and 1978. See Barclay McMillan (revised Elaine Keillor), "Violet Archer," in *The Encyclopedia of Music in Canada.* Carl Nielsen (b. 1865, d. 1931) was a major Danish composer who, until the last few decades, was not well known in Canada despite being a part of the canon in Scandinavia and in other parts of Europe.

8 Unfortunately, Kraglund fails to give the occasion of this broadcast and no information is to be found in the remainder of the Unger Fonds. John Kraglund, "Nielsen Symphony at Festival Interprets a Composer's Credo," *Globe and Mail* (Toronto), 20 July 1957, LAC, MUS 56, Box 8, File 78.

9 Ibid.

10 A.J.L., "Mahler Award," *Jerusalem Post,* 8 July 1959, LAC, MUS 56, Box 8, File 78.

11 Ibid.

12 Letter from Arthur Lourie to Heinz Unger, 10 February 1958, LAC, MUS 56, Box 1, File 11. The performance was to be held 3 March 1958.

13 Letter from Heinz Unger to the Executive Council of the Israel Philharmonic Orchestra, 29 September 1960, LAC, MUS 56, Box 1, File 13.

14 Letter to Mrs. Mark Levy, 5 June 1958, LAC, MUS 56, Box 1, File 11. Uncatalogued documents in the archives of the Israel Philharmonic confirm that Unger had in fact been in contact with the IPO on a number of occasions since at least 1947 and that "excuses, pretexts, indefinite postponement" had indeed been the order of the day for at least a decade. In light of the fact that he was ultimately never invited to conduct an IPO concert despite the many promises made, his frustration by the end of the 1950s is certainly understandable. It is also interesting to note that Unger's first documented approaches to the IPO closely coincide with the State of Israel's birth, thereby granting a better understanding of his close attention to, if not intimate involvement with, the Jewish state. (Documents courtesy of the Israel Philharmonic Archive.)

15 The Israel Philharmonic Orchestra would appoint Zubin Mehta as its first music director in 1977 after decades of relying on "music advisors" and guest conductors to lead the orchestra.

16 It should be noted that this is but a partial list of conductors who worked with the IPO during the period, suggested to the author by Avivit Hochstadter at the IPO archives. And while I do not mean to denigrate in any way the achievement of the conductors who were granted opportunities with the IPO, it must be noted that our understanding of these musicians' achievements is often informed by their posthumous import built largely upon their recorded legacy. It is also important to recognize that some of these musicians worked under fascist dictatorships, a fact that did not seemingly trouble the directors of the IPO in appointing them; Maestro Molinari, for instance, retained his position with the Orchestra dell'Accademia Nazionale di Santa Cecilia (Rome) for the entirety of the Second World War, surely a greater "sin" than Unger choosing to conduct in Spain during the post-war years.

17 Letter to Mrs. Mark Levy, 5 June 1958, LAC, MUS 56, Box 1, File 11.

18 Ibid.

19 Ibid.

20 Ibid.

21 "Israel Bonds," *Canadian Jewish Review,* 8 February 1963, 9.

22 Letter from Arthur Lelyveld to Mark Levy, 10 December 1957, LAC, MUS 56, Box 1, File 10.

23 Ibid.

24 Ibid.

25 Letter from Mark Levy to Joseph Jacobson, 2 June 1958, LAC, MUS 56, Box 1, File 11.

26 Letter to Mrs. Mark Levy, 5 June 1958, LAC, MUS 56, Box 1, File 11.

27 Letter from Mark Levy to Joseph Jacobson, 9 June 1958, LAC, MUS 56, Box 1, File 11.

28 Letter from Mark Levy to Heinz Unger, 5 August 1958, LAC, MUS 56, Box 1, File 11.

29 Letter from Heinz Unger to Joseph Jacobson, 1 September 1958, LAC, MUS 56, Box 1, File 11.

30 Letter from Heinz Unger to Abe Cohen, 17 March 1959, LAC, MUS 56, Box 1, File 12.

31 Letter from Heinz Unger to the Executive Council of the Israel Philharmonic Orchestra, 29 September 1960, LAC, MUS 56, Box 1, File 13. It should be noted that Unger and his wife appear on the lengthy list of honorary patrons for the 7 November 1960 IPO concert at Massey Hall, despite their absence from the event. See *Canadian Jewish Review,* 21 October 1960, 15; *Canadian Jewish Review,* 18 November 1960, 13.

32 John Kraglund, "Concerts Renew Interests," *Globe and Mail* (Toronto), 18 January 1958, LAC, MUS 56, Box 8, File 78.
33 Leslie Bell, "Leslie Bell's Music: Unger and Mahler," *Toronto Daily Star*, 18 January 1958, LAC, MUS 56, Box 8, File 78.
34 George Kidd, "Dr. Unger Triumphs," *Telegram* (Toronto), 23 January 1958, LAC, MUS 56, Box 8, File 78.
35 John Kraglund, "Music in Toronto," *Globe and Mail* (Toronto), 23 January 1958, LAC, MUS 56, Box 8, File 78.
36 Ibid.
37 Ibid.
38 John Kraglund (attributed), "York Concert Group Told of Mahler Work," *Globe and Mail* (Toronto), MUS 56, Box 8, File 78.
39 Ibid.
40 Susskind lived his life in Czechoslovakia until fleeing the country in 1938 following its annexation by Nazi Germany. Thereafter, he moved to Britain where, among other engagements, he conducted the Carl Rosa Opera Company (1942–1945) and the Scottish National Orchestra (1946–1952). After a spell in Australia, he moved to Canada, where he was appointed conductor of the Toronto Symphony Orchestra, serving in this capacity from 1956 to 1965. See Maria Corvin, "Walter Susskind," in *The Encyclopedia of Music in Canada.*
41 The rest of the program consisted of a selection of arias, the solely instrumental pieces being Weber's *Der Freischütz* Overture, Bach's Air from Suite no. 3 in D (BWV 1068), Liszt's *Les Préludes*, and Strauss's *Roses from the South* Waltz. LAC, MUS 56, Box 8, File 78.
42 Set in the European Renaissance and concerned with the role of music during the Reformation, *Palestrina* (premiered in Munich in 1917) is Hans Pfitzner's (1869–1949) most famous opera. The work, much like Paul Hindemith's opera *Mathis der Maler*, has been the source of much musicological inquiry due to its portrayal of and commentary on musical trends of the period. See Leon Botstein, "Pfitzner and Musical Politics," *Musical Quarterly* 85 (2001): 63–75.
43 Toronto-born Harry Somers (1925–1999) was one of Canada's leading composers during the second half of the twentieth century. The work performed, his *Passacaglia and Fugue*, was written in 1954.
44 Reviewers for this final concert held on 13 May complained of the raggedness of the ensemble, poor string tone, and Unger's occasional tendency to "over-conduct." See Hugh Thomson, "All-Beethoven Concert Dr. Unger's York Finale," *Toronto Daily Star*, 14 May 1958; John Kraglund, "Music in Toronto," *Globe and Mail* (Toronto), 14 May 1958; George Kidd, "Dr. Unger Interprets Beethoven," *Telegram* (Toronto), 14 May 1958. All LAC, MUS 56, Box 8, File 78.

45 The official letter of invitation from Alma Mahler-Werfel, signed in her large script, lies in LAC, MUS 56, Box 1, File 4. The letter is accompanied both by a personal note to Heinz Unger as well as a letter to Hella Unger, indicating that all three knew one another and shared, at the very least, a cordial friendship. See also "Mahler Society," *Globe and Mail* (Toronto), 3 June 1958, MUS 56, Box 8, File 78.

46 "Conductor to be Honoured Wednesday," *CBC Times*, February 1959, LAC, MUS 56, Box 8, File 78.

47 The entire Massey Hall concert began with Mozart's *Marriage of Figaro* Overture, continued with Beethoven's Piano Concerto no. 4 (with Moura Lympany as soloist), and only continued on to Mahler's Fifth Symphony after an intermission. Needless to say, the brunt of the interest in the concert lay with the Mahler premiere.

48 Transcription of Unger's broadcast speech on receiving the Mahler Medal, *CBC Wednesday Night*, 25 February 1959.

49 See John Kraglund, "Music in Toronto," *Globe and Mail* (Toronto), 26 February 1959; George Kidd, "A Lavish Attention to Detail," *Telegram* (Toronto), 26 February 1959; Hugh Thomson, "York Series Opens Honor Heinz Unger," *Toronto Daily Star*, 26 February 1959. All LAC, MUS 56, Box 8, File 78.

50 Kraglund, "Music in Toronto," *Globe and Mail* (Toronto), 26 February 1959.

51 Kidd, "A Lavish Attention to Detail," *Telegram* (Toronto), 26 February 1959.

52 Kerry Olitzky and Marc Lee Raphael, *The American Synagogue: A Historical Dictionary and Sourcebook* (Westport, CT: Greenwood Press, 1996), 51.

53 Acting independently, Dubin put the word in the ear of Mrs. Chandler – actually Dorothy Buffum Chandler (1901–1997), the wife of the publisher of the *Los Angeles Times* from 1945 to 1960 and a woman who would spend much of her life revitalizing the Los Angeles arts scene – that Unger was a "conductor of outstanding ability [that] would bring to our Orchestra the stature and leadership it requires." Letter from Rabbi Dubin to Heinz Unger, 12 May 1959, LAC, MUS 56, Box 1, File 12.

54 Letter from Maxwell Dubin to Sol Hurok, 9 September 1959, LAC, MUS 56, Box 1, File 12.

55 Ibid.

56 There is a vast literature on Furtwängler and even today a debate rages over whether his partaking in what he called an "internal migration" to distance himself from the regime under which he lived and worked represents a morally acceptable course of action. More recent scholarship – led by Austrian historian Oliver Rathkolb – has been particularly condemnatory of musicians such as Furtwängler who remained in Nazi Germany and Austria and by doing so directly or indirectly advanced the reputation of the Nazi regime. I would, however, argue that the resulting debate fails to provide

a nuanced assessment of Furtwängler beyond moral abstractions. To my mind, the most reflective assessment of Furtwängler comes from Michael Kater, who positions the conductor on an abstract moral plain while also recognizing how many of his choices during the Third Reich do not point to an altruism but to a man "who always had to be at the center of things." Michael H. Kater, *The Twisted Muse: Musicians and their Music in the Third Reich* (Oxford: Oxford University Press, 1997), 196. For details pertaining to Furtwängler's denazification, see David Monod, *Settling Scores: German Music, Denazification and the Americans, 1945–1953* (Chapel Hill: University of North Carolina Press, 2005), especially ch. 4: "Learning to Keep Quiet: Wilhelm Furtwängler and the End of Denazification."

57 Howard Taubman, "Musicians' Ban on Furtwaengler Ends His Chicago Contract for '49," *New York Times*, 6 January 1949.

58 Heinz Unger, "Furtwaengler Ban Discussed: Chicago Action Criticized By Former Conductor of Berlin Philharmonic," *New York Times*, 13 January 1949.

59 "Rabbi Hits Furtwaengler: Says Token Saving of Few Jews Does Not Excuse His Role," *New York Times*, 14 January 1949.

60 "It is inconceivable that artists should perpetuate hatred indefinitely, while all the world is longing for peace. In order to spare the Chicago Orchestra further difficulties, I withdraw herewith from the already concluded contract." From "Dr. Furtwaengler Drops Chicago Bid: Cables Withdrawal as Guest Conductor – Deplores the Perpetuation of Hatred," *New York Times*, 20 January 1949.

61 "Threaten to Boycott Menuhin," *New York Times*, 21 January 1949.

62 Heinz Unger, *Gustav Mahler Centenary Concert: The Song of the Earth* (24 February 1960 program notes), LAC, MUS 56, Box 3, File 39.

63 The letter, sent by the council's secretary, Dr. van Dam, explicitly mentions that the money will be used for the training and education of a Jewish teacher ("für die Ausbildung eines jüdischen Lehrers verwandt"). Letter from the Zentralrat der Juden in Deutschland to Heinz Unger, 15 December 1960, LAC, MUS 56, Box 1, File 13.

64 Bialystock, *Delayed Impact*, 72.

65 Only during the 1960s would Jews – and the world at large – openly address the significance of the Holocaust. Such new understandings began only with the kidnapping, trial, and execution of Adolf Eichmann, who was captured in Argentina by Mossad agents in May 1960, faced trial beginning in April 1961, and was hanged on 31 May 1962. During the trial the Holocaust received extensive public attention, and this interest continued on through the 1960s as Israelis and Jews around the world internalized the 1967 Six Day War as a desperate battle for survival against Arab states seeking the destruction of the Jewish state.

66 Having received a favourable reply only from the BBC, the following year Unger wrote to other ensembles in the hopes of securing concerts. The organizations that he contacted in 1959 to arrange Mahler centenary concerts included: the CBC, Vancouver International Festival, and the Oslo Philharmonic (Norway). LAC, MUS 56, Box 1.

67 See letter from Heinz Unger to Bernard Keefe of the BBC, 25 April 1959, LAC, MUS 56, Box 1, File 12.

68 The concert began with a performance of Schubert's Symphony no. 8 (*Unfinished*).

69 Blaik Kirby, "Tenor .22 Calibre in Big Gun Role," *Toronto Daily Star*, 25 February 1960; George Kidd, "Fine Mahler Work Opens New Season," *Telegram* (Toronto), 25 February 1960, LAC, MUS 56, Box 8, File 78.

70 The concert was aired at 9:00 p.m. on a Friday in April, possibly the fifteenth, on CBC Radio. See *CBC Times*, week of 15 April 1960, LAC, MUS 56, Box 9, File 79.

71 Mahler's First Symphony was performed on Sunday and Monday, 20 and 21 November 1960, LAC, MUS 56, Box 9, File 79.

72 Heinz Unger, *Gustav Mahler Centenary Concert: The Song of the Earth* (24 February 1960 program notes), LAC, MUS 56, Box 3, File 39.

**5. The Final Years and a Farewell to the World (1961–1965)**

1 John Kraglund, "Music in 1961: Unger has Birthday with Mozart on BBC," *Globe and Mail* (Toronto), 4 January 1961, LAC, MUS 56, Box 9, File 79. Harry Newstone (b. Winnipeg, MB 1921, d. Victoria, BC 2006) was a Canadian-born conductor who lived much of his life in England, founding the highly rated Haydn Orchestra in 1949.

2 Ibid.

3 Ibid.

4 Ibid. Other early reports were just as clear if not even more condemnatory of the particular reason for the season's cancellation, laying the blame squarely on the recently created Canada Council itself: " 'With no Canada Council Grant, the situation was hopeless,' said Mr. Moysey." See "Financial Difficulties for York Concert Society: Cancel Concert Series," *Telegram* (Toronto), 13 January 1961.

5 John Kraglund, "Music in 1961: York Concerts Will Return Next Year," *Globe and Mail* (Toronto), 10 May 1961.

6 Ibid.

7 The Canada Council, in fact, commissioned two reports at this time: Heinze was responsible for "the artistic part of the survey, the economic part being the responsibility of Mr. Kenneth Carter." In his report, Heinze states that, as of 1959, the Canada Council was "helping 10 of some 25 Orchestras

and the amount available, $200,000, was falling short of the needs of this small number." He continues: "The Council wished to reconsider if it was directing its help to the orchestras most meriting its assistance." Sir Bernard Heinze, "Survey of Canadian Symphony Orchestras," Canada Council, June 1960. Unpublished report from the Canada Council Library.

8 Heinz Unger, "Has the Canada Council Hit a Wrong Note?" *Globe Magazine*, 22 July 1961, 11–12, 23–4, LAC, MUS 56, Box 9, File 79.

9 Ibid, 24.

10 "Dr. Unger is Honoured," *Globe and Mail* (Toronto), 2 September 1961, LAC, MUS 56, Box 9, File 79.

11 Ibid.

12 Unger conducted four concerts in Valencia between 28 October and 11 November 1962. The details on the remainder of his European concert dates for that season are lost. See "Mahler's Ninth," *CBC Times*, 26 January–1 February 1 1963, LAC, MUS 56, Box 9, File 79.

13 John Kraglund, "Music in 1963: York Rehearsal Worth Hearing," *Globe and Mail* (Toronto), 23 January 1963, LAC, MUS 56, Box 9, File 79.

14 John Kraglund, "Music in 1963: Mahler Symphony no. 9 Excellent," *Globe and Mail* (Toronto), 24 January 1963. For further reflections on the success of the performance, see George Kidd, "York Musical Society: An Evening of Musical Excitement," *Telegram* (Toronto), 24 January 1963.

15 For further detail on Udo Kasemets, see Alan M. Gillmor and Evan Ware, "Udo Kasemets," in *The Encyclopedia of Music in Canada.*

16 Udo Kasemets, "Mahler Symphony no. 9 Unreciprocated Love," *Toronto Daily Star*, 24 January 1963.

17 Heinz Unger, letter to the editor of the *Toronto Daily Star*, 24 January 1963, LAC, MUS 56, Box 1, File 16. Unger's letter did not appear in print.

18 Indeed, Unger, despite desperately desiring to have the great honour of presenting the Canadian premiere of Mahler's Ninth Symphony, had been uncertain whether he would be able to do so in the summer of 1962. Unger's pessimism in regards to his health had compelled him to write to his younger colleague and fellow Mahler specialist, Leonard Bernstein, in the hopes that he might fill in to conduct the premiere had his own health been found wanting. Letter from Heinz Unger to Leonard Bernstein, 4 August 1962, LAC, MUS 56, Box 1, File 15. After receiving a negative reply from Bernstein and on Bernstein's advice, Heinz Unger immediately wrote a letter to John Barbirolli, asking him if he might be available instead. See Letter from Heinz Unger to John Barbirolli, 9 October 1962, LAC, MUS 56, Box 1, File 15.

19 John Kraglund, "Music in 1963: York Rehearsal Worth Hearing," *Globe and Mail* (Toronto), 23 January 1963, LAC, MUS 56, Box 9, File 79.

20 Letter from Hella Unger to her friends George and Gladys (last names unknown), 9 October 1962, LAC, MUS 56, Box 1, File 15.

21 Ibid.

22 "CBC Sunday Night," *CBC Times*, 8–14 February 1964, LAC, MUS 56, Box 12, File 89. The work had received its Canadian premiere on 9 April 1963, the Austrian conductor Hans Swarowsky (1899–1975) leading the Montreal Symphony Orchestra.

23 The participating choirs were the Toronto Mendelssohn Choir (sopranos and altos) and the Boys' Choirs of St. Clement's and St. George's (under the direction of choir masters John Sidgwick and Lloyd Bradshaw).

24 Letter from Heinz Unger to Robert Syrett, 7 February 1964, LAC, MUS 56, Box 1, File 16.

25 Ibid.

26 George Kidd, "Enthusiastic Reception for Unger with TSO," *Telegram* (Toronto), 5 February 1964.

27 John Kraglund, "TSO Rendition of Mahler's 3rd Symphony Engrossing," *Globe and Mail* (Toronto), 5 February 1964.

28 Letter from Heinz Unger to Norbert Prefontaine (executive director of the Canadian Centenary Council), 14 June 1963, LAC, MUS 56, Box 1, File 16.

29 Letter from Robbins Elliott to Heinz Unger, 9 October 1964, LAC, MUS 56, Box 1, File 16.

30 The contract between Heinz Unger and Daniel Attractions was signed on 20 April 1964 and came into force that very same day. The contract was signed for a period of three years, to lapse on 19 April 1967, with an option to extend the arrangement for a further three years (until 19 April 1970). Little is known concerning Aladar Ecsedy, barring the fact that he had been born in Hungary and had, between 1950 and 1952, served as a piano teacher for the Oshawa-born Canadian composer Norma Beecroft (b. 1934). See Kenneth Winters and Betty Nygaard King, "Norma Beecroft," in *The Encyclopedia of Music in Canada.*

31 Letter from Aladar Ecsedy to Heinz Unger, 18 September 1964, LAC, MUS 56, Box 1, File 16.

32 "Charge Pianist in Admission of Hungarians," *Globe and Mail* (Toronto), 21 December 1964.

33 Ibid.

34 Letter from Heinz Unger to Peter Johnston (first secretary to the Canadian High Commissioner in London), 9 December 1964, LAC, MUS 56, Box 1, File 16.

35 Ibid.

36 Letter from Heinz Unger to Peter Johnston, 22 January 1965, LAC, MUS 56, Box 1, File 16.

37 Heinz Unger's speech to the consul general of the West German Republic, 28 January 1965, LAC, MUS 56, Box 1, File 16.
38 Ibid.
39 Ibid.
40 Ibid.
41 Letter from Heinz Unger to Leon Weinstein, 12 February 1965, LAC, MUS 56, Box 1, File 16. The letter is marked as follows: "Absolutely confidential, until we jointly decide that it should be otherwise."
42 Ibid.
43 See "Song of the Earth," *CBC Times*, 6–12 February 1965, LAC, MUS 56, Box 12, File 89.
44 John Kraglund, "Mahler Recording Memorial to Unger," *Globe and Mail* (Toronto), 2 March 1965, LAC, MUS 56, Box 12, File 89.
45 Ibid.
46 Ibid.
47 Heinz Unger, *Gustav Mahler Centenary Concert: The Song of the Earth* (24 February 1960 program notes), LAC, MUS 56, Box 3, File 39.

**Conclusion**

1 The Heinz Unger Award is today administered by the Ontario Arts Council and, according to the organization's dictates, and in keeping with the philosophy of the scholarship at its inception, "is given to an individual to encourage and highlight the career of a young to mid-career Canadian professional conductor who has professional experience at a professional, semi-professional and/or community orchestra." http://www.arts.on.ca/awards/ontario-arts-council-awards/heinz-unger-award (accessed 7 September 2019).
2 Letter from Oskar Morawetz to Hella Unger, 2 March 1965, LAC, MUS 56, Box 1, File 19.
3 Documents pertaining to Unger's early career, for example, were lost when the old Berlin Filharmonie was destroyed during the Second World War. Whether records pertaining to Unger's time in the Soviet Union exist is an intriguing question that might be answered if someday a researcher with the requisite knowledge of the Russian language and byzantine archival system takes on the daunting task of seeking out the existence of such material.
4 Of course, recordings by better-established names such as Bruno Walter did continue to circulate, but these recordings bore the authority that Walter commanded as a "first-generation" disciple of Mahler's as well as his having settled in the United States and forging close ties with major American recording companies such as Columbia.

5 In a letter sent by chapter president Judge Harry Waisberg to Hella Unger, he notes that the donation was specifically earmarked "for Student Aid to the Hebrew University in Jerusalem." Letter from Judge Harry Waisberg to Hella Unger, 26 February 1965, LAC, MUS 56, Box 1, File 19.

6 Mr. and Mrs. Orliffe, for example, would make a contribution in Heinz Unger's name to the National Council of Jewish Women of Canada (Toronto Section), the donation contributing to the council's Scholarship Fund. Clare and Joseph Sera, meanwhile, would make a donation to Toronto's Mount Sinai Temple Student's Library Fund in Unger's name, while Leo Weil would make his donation to Clanton Park Synagogue's Doreen (Dolly) Edell Memorial Library. See LAC, MUS 56, Box 1, File 19.

7 Letter from Rabbi Gunther Plaut to Hella Unger, 11 March 1965, and letter from Rabbi Maxwell Dubin to Hella Unger, 15 April 1965. Both LAC, MUS 56, Box 1, File 19.

8 It should be noted that Adara Goldberg's recent book on the immigration of Holocaust survivors to Canada is one of the works that has helped to reshape our understanding, bringing into question the monolithic nature of Canadian Jewry, albeit during a short window of time. See Adara Goldberg, *Holocaust Survivors in Canada: Exclusion, Inclusion, Transformation, 1947–1955* (Winnipeg: University of Manitoba Press, 2015).

# Bibliography

**Fonds and Unpublished Sources**


Heinze, Bernard. *Survey of Canadian Symphony Orchestras.* Canada Council, June 1960. Unpublished report from the Canada Council Library.

Israel Philharmonic Archive.

Library and Archives Canada, MUS 56 (Heinz Unger Fonds).

Library and Archives Canada, MUS 305 (Helmut Kallmann Fonds).


**Secondary Sources and Published Material**


Abella, Irving, and Harold Troper. *None is Too Many: Canada and the Jews of Europe, 1933–1948.* Toronto: Lester and Dennys, 1986.

Aberbach, David. "Nationalism, Reform Judaism and the Hebrew Prayer Book." *Nations and Nationalism* 12, no. 1 (2006): 139–59.

Adler, H.G. *The Jews in Germany: From the Enlightenment to National Socialism.* Notre Dame, IN: University of Notre Dame Press, 1969. (Originally published as *Die Juden in Deutschland: Von der Aufklärung bis zum Nationalsocializmus.* Munich: Kosel Verlag, 1960.)

Adorno, Theodor. *Mahler: A Musical Physiognomy.* Translated by Edmund Jephcott. Chicago: University of Chicago Press, 1996.

Alderman, Geoffrey. *London Jewry and London Politics 1889–1986.* London: Routledge, 1989.

Anderson, Benedict. *Imagined Communities: Reflections on the Origin and Spread of Nationalism.* London: Verso Press, 1996.

Aschheim, Steven E. *Culture and Catastrophe: German and Jewish Confrontations with National Socialism and Other Crises.* New York: New York University Press, 1996.

Aster, Misha. *Sous la baguette du Reich: Le philharmonique de Berlin et le national-socialisme.* Munich: Siedler Verlag, 2007.

Bahr, Eberhard. *Weimar on the Pacific: German Exile Culture in Los Angeles and the Crisis of Modernism.* Berkeley: University of California Press, 2007.

Baigell, Mathew, and Milly Heyd. *Complex Identities: Jewish Consciousness and Modern Art.* New Brunswick, NJ: Rutgers University Press, 2001.

Band, Arnold J. "Kafka: The Margins of Assimilation." *Modern Judaism* 8, no. 2 (1988): 139–55.

Barsova, Inna. "Mahler and Russia." In *The Mahler Companion,* edited by Donald Mitchell and Andrew Nicholson, 517–30. Oxford: Oxford University Press, 1999.

Bassler, Gerhard P. *The German Canadian Mosaic Today and Yesterday: Identities, Roots, and Heritage.* Ottawa: German-Canadian Congress, 1991.

Bekker, Paul. *Gustav Mahlers Sinfonien.* Berlin: Schuster and Loeffler, 1921.

Berghahn, Klaus L., ed. *The German-Jewish Dialogue Reconsidered: A Symposium in Honor of George L. Mosse.* New York: Peter Lang, 1996.

Berghahn, Marion. *Continental Britons: German-Jewish Refugees from Nazi Germany.* New York: Berghahn Books, 2006.

Biale, David, Michael Galchinsky, and Susan Henschel. *Insider/Outsider: American Jews and Multiculturalism.* Berkeley: University of California Press, 1998.

Bialystock, Franklin. *Delayed Impact: The Holocaust and the Canadian Jewish Community.* Montreal and Kingston: McGill-Queen's University Press, 2000.

Blaukopf, Kurt. *Gustav Mahler.* Translated by Inge Goodwin. New York: Limelight Editions, 1985.

Bohlman, Philip. *Jewish Music and Modernity.* Oxford: Oxford University Press, 2008.

– *The Land Where Two Streams Flow: Music and the German-Jewish Community of Israel.* Chicago: University of Illinois Press, 1989.

Bolkosky, Sidney M. *The Distorted Image: German Jewish Perceptions of Germans and Germany, 1918–1935.* New York: Elsevier Scientific, 1975.

Botstein, Leon. "Pfitzner and Musical Politics." *Musical Quarterly* 85 (2001): 63–75.

– "Whose Gustav Mahler? Reception, Interpretation, and History." In *Mahler and His World,* edited by Karen Painter, 1–54. Princeton, NJ: Princeton University Press, 2002.

Braun, Joachim. *On Jewish Music: Past and Present.* Frankfurt am Main: Peter Lang, 2006.

Bredin, Jean-Denis. *The Affair: The Case of Alfred Dreyfus.* New York: George Braziller, 1986.

Brennan, James F. *The Reflection of the Dreyfus Affair in the European Press.* New York: Peter Lang, 1998.

Brenner, Michael. *After the Holocaust: Rebuilding Jewish Lives in Postwar Germany.* Translated by Barbara Harshav. Princeton, NJ: Princeton University Press, 1997.

– *The Renaissance of Jewish Culture in Weimar Germany.* New Haven, CT: Yale University Press, 1996.

Brenner, Michael, Vicki Caron, and Uri R. Kaufmann, eds. *Jewish Emancipation Reconsidered.* Tübingen, DE: Mohr Siebeck, 2003.

Brod, Max. *Israel's Music.* Tel Aviv: Sefer Press, 1951.

Bryn, Robert J., William Shaffir, and Morton Weinfeld, eds. *The Jews in Canada.* Toronto: Oxford University Press, 1993.

Caplan, Usher, and M.W. Steinberg, eds. *A.M. Klein: Literary Essays and Reviews.* Toronto: University of Toronto Press, 1987.

Cardus, Neville. *Gustav Mahler: His Mind and His Music.* London: Gollancz, 1965.

Cesarini, David. *The Jewish Chronicle and Anglo-Jewry, 1841–1991.* Cambridge: Cambridge University Press, 1994.

Chickering, Roger. "'War Enthusiasm?' Public Opinion and the Outbreak of War in 1914." In *An Improbable War: The Outbreak of World War I and European Political Culture Before 1914,* edited by Holger Afflerbach and David Stevenson, 200–12. New York: Berghahn Books, 2007.

Cohen, Richard. "Celebrating Integration in the Public Sphere in Germany and France." In *Jewish Emancipation Reconsidered: The French and German Models,* edited by Michael Brenner, Vicki Caron, and Uri R. Kaufmann, 55–73. Tübingen, DE: Mohr Siebeck, 2003.

Cooke, Deryck. *Gustav Mahler: An Introduction to his Music.* Cambridge: Cambridge University Press, 1988.

Cresti, Sylvia. "German and Austrian Jews' Concept of Nation, Culture and *Volk.*" In *Towards Normality? Acculturation and Modern German Jewry,* edited by Rainer Liedtke and David Rechter, 271–90. London: Leo Baeck Institute/ Tübingen, DE: J.C.B. Mohr, 2003.

– "Kultur and Civilisation after the Franco-Prussian War: Debates between German and French Jews." In *Jewish Emancipation Reconsidered: The French and German Models,* edited by Michael Brenner, Vicki Caron, and Uri R. Kaufmann, 93–110. Tübingen, DE: Mohr Siebeck, 2003.

de la Grange, Henry-Louis. *Gustav Mahler, Vol. 2: Vienna: The Years of Challenge, 1897–1904.* Oxford: Oxford University Press, 1995.

– *Gustav Mahler, Vol. 3: Vienna: Triumph and Disillusion, 1904–1907.* Oxford: Oxford University Press, 2000.

– *Gustav Mahler, Vol. 4: A New Life Cut Short, 1907–1911.* Oxford: Oxford University Press, 2008.

Ditzler, Kirk. "Tradition ist Schlamperei: Gustav Mahler and the Vienna Court Opera." *International Review of the Aesthetics and Sociology of Music* 29, no. 1 (1998): 11–28.

Draughon, Francesca, and Raymond Knapp. "Gustav Mahler and the Crisis of Jewish Identity." *ECHO: A Music-Centred Journal* 3, no. 2 (Fall 2001).

http://www.echo.ucla.edu/article-gustav-mahler-and-the-crisis-of-jewish-identity-by-francesca-draughon-and-raymond-knapp/.

Dubnow, Simon. *History of the Jews: From the Congress of Vienna to the Emergence of Hitler.* Volume 5. Translated from the Russian by Moshe Spiegel. Cranbury, NJ: Thomas Yoseloff, 1973.

Dwork, Deborah, and Robert Jan van Pelt. *Flight from the Reich: Refugee Jews, 1933–1946.* New York: W.W. Norton and Company, 2009.

Eatock, Colin. "Classical Music Criticism at the *Globe and Mail*: 1936–2000." *Canadian University Music Review* 24, no. 2 (2004): 8–28.

Fernandez-Cid, Antonio. *La Musica Española en el Siglo XX.* Madrid: Rioduero, 1973.

Fifield, Christopher. *Ibbs and Tillett: The Rise and Fall of a Musical Empire.* Aldershot, UK: Ashgate, 2005.

Filler, Susan. "Mahler as Jew in the Literature." *Shofar* 18, no. 4 (2000): 62–78.

Fishman, David. "The Bund and Modern Yiddish Culture." In *The Emergence of Modern Jewish Politics: Bundism and Zionism in Eastern Europe,* edited by Zvi Gitelman, 107–19. Pittsburgh: University of Pittsburgh Press, 2003.

Frankel, Jonathan. *Prophecy and Politics: Socialism, Nationalism, and the Russian Jews, 1862–1917.* Cambridge: Cambridge University Press, 1981.

Freund, Alexander. "Troubling Memories in Nation-Building: World War II Memories and Germans' Interethnic Encounters in Canada after 1945." In *Histoire Sociale/Social History* 39, no. 77 (2006): 129–56.

Furtwängler, Wilhelm. *Notebooks, 1924–1954.* Edited by Michael Tanner. London: Quartet Books, 1989.

Gay, Peter. *Freud, Jews, and Other Germans: Masters and Victims in Modernist Culture.* New York: Oxford University Press, 1978.

Gerson, Judith M. "In between States: National Identity Practices among German Jewish Immigrants." In *Political Psychology* 22, no. 1 (2001): 179–98.

Gilman, Sander L. "Are Jews Musical? Historical Notes on the Question of Jewish Musical Modernism and Nationalism." *Modern Judaism* 28, no. 3 (2008): 239–56.

Ginzburg, Carlo. *The Cheese and the Worms: The Cosmos of a Sixteenth-Century Miller.* Baltimore, MD: Johns Hopkins University Press, 1980.

Gitelman, Zvi. "A Century of Jewish Politics in Eastern Europe: The Legacy of the Bund and the Zionist Movement." In *The Emergence of Modern Jewish Politics: Bundism and Zionism in Eastern Europe,* edited by Zvi Gitelman, 3–19. Pittsburgh: University of Pittsburgh Press, 2003.

Goldberg, Adara. *Holocaust Survivors in Canada: Exclusion, Inclusion, Transformation, 1947–1955.* Winnipeg: University of Manitoba Press, 2015.

Greene, Daniel. "A Chosen People in a Pluralist Nation: Horace Kallen and the Jewish-American Experience." *Religion and American Culture* 16, no. 2 (summer 2006): 161–93.

Grover Rich, Samuel, Jr. "Franco's Spain: A Reappraisal." *Political Science Quarterly* 67, no. 3 (1952): 378–98.

Hahn, Hans Joachim. *Education and Society in Germany.* Oxford: Berg Publishers, 1998.

Hefling, Stephen E. *Mahler, Das Lied von der Erde.* Cambridge: Cambridge University Press, 2000.

Heilbut, Anthony. *Exiled in Paradise: German Refugee Artists and Intellectuals in America, 1930s to the Present.* Boston: Beacon Press, 1983.

Helmer, Paul. *Growing with Canada: The Émigré Tradition in Canadian Music.* Montreal: McGill University Press, 2009.

Heskes, Irene. *Passport to Jewish Music: Its History, Traditions, and Culture.* Westport, CT: Greenwood Press, 1994.

Heyworth, Peter. *Conversations with Klemperer.* New York: Faber and Faber, 1985.

Holde, Arthur. *Jews in Music: From the Age of Enlightenment to the Present.* New York: Philosophical Library, 1959.

Howe, Irving. *World of our Fathers.* New York: Simon and Schuster, 1976.

Hundert, Gershon David. *Jews in Poland-Lithuania in the Eighteenth Century: A Genealogy of Modernity.* Berkeley: University of California Press, 2004.

Idelsohn, Abraham. *Jewish Music: Its Historical Development.* New York: Dover Publications, 1992. First published 1929 by Henry Holt and Co. (New York).

Isenberg, Noah. *Between Redemption and Doom: The Strains of German-Jewish Modernism.* Lincoln: University of Nebraska Press, 1999.

Johnson, Julian. "Mahler and the Idea of Nature." In *Perspectives on Gustav Mahler,* edited by Jeremy Barham, 23–36. Aldershot, UK: Ashgate, 2005.

Jütte, Daniel. "His Majesty's Mahler: Jews, Courts, and Culture in the Nineteenth Century." *Simon Dubnow Institute Yearbook* 11 (2012): 149–62.

Kallen, Evelyn. *Spanning the Generations: A Study in Jewish Identity.* Don Mills, ON: Longman, 1977.

Kallmann, Helmut. "Mapping Canada's Music: A Life's Task." In *Music in Canada/La Musique au Canada: A Collection of Essays,* vol. 1, edited by Guido Bimberg, 11–34. Bochum, DE: Universitatsverlag Dr. N. Brockmeyer, 1997.

Kallmann, Helmut, Gilles Potvin, and Kenneth Winters, eds. *The Encyclopedia of Music in Canada.* Toronto: University of Toronto Press, 1981.

Kater, Michael. *The Twisted Muse: Musicians and their Music in the Third Reich.* Oxford: Oxford University Press, 1997.

Keillor, Elaine. "Auf Kanadischer Welle: The Establishment of the German Musical Canon in Canada." In *Music in Canada/La Musique au Canada: A Collection of Essays,* vol. 1, edited by Guido Bimberg, 49–76. Bochum, DE: Universitatsverlag Dr. N. Brockmeyer, 1997.

Kennedy, Michael. *Mahler.* London: J.M. Dent, 1990.

Kennedy, Michael. "Mahler's Only Opera?" Liner notes to Carl Maria von Weber (Completed by Mahler) *Die Drei Pintos.* National Philharmonic Orchestra of Belarus, Paolo Arrivabeni, cond. Naxos: 8.660142–43, 2004.

Klein, A.M. "Music Hath Charm: Review of Jewish Music and Other Essays on Musical Topics (in Yiddish) by Israel Rabinovitch." In *A.M. Klein: Literary Essays and Reviews,* edited by Usher Caplan and M.W. Steinberg, 19–22. Toronto: University of Toronto Press, 1987.

Klier, John D. "From 'Little Man' to 'Milkman': Does Jewish Art Reflect Jewish Life?" In *The Jews of Eastern Europe,* edited by Leonard Greenspoon, Ronald A. Simkins, and Brian J. Horowitz, 217–32. Omaha, NE: Creighton University Press, 2005.

Kushner, David Z. "Religious Ambiguity in the Life and Works of Ernest Bloch." http://www.biu.ac.il/hu/mu/min-ad04/BLOCH-1.pdf (accessed 2 November 2007).

Lamb Crawford, Dorothy. *A Windfall of Musicians: Hitler's Emigres and Exiles in Southern California.* New Haven, CT: Yale University Press, 2009.

Lea, Henry A. *Gustav Mahler: Man on the Margin.* Bonn: Bouvier Verlag Herbert Grundmann, 1985.

Lepore, Jill. "Historians Who Love Too Much: Reflections on Microhistory and Biography." *Journal of American History* 88, no. 1 (2001): 129–44.

Levenson, Thomas. *Einstein in Berlin.* New York: Bantam Dell, 2003.

Levi, Erik. "The German-Jewish Contribution to Musical Life in Britain." In *Second Chance: Two Centuries of German-Speaking Jews in the United Kingdom,* edited by Werner E. Mosse (co-ordinating editor), Julius Carlebach, Gerhard Hirschfeld, Aubrey Newman, Arnold Paucker, and Peter Pulzer, 275–96. Tübingen, DE: J.C.B. Mohr (Paul Siebeck), 1991.

Liedtke, Rainer, and David Rechter. *Towards Normality? Acculturation and Modern German Jewry.* London: Leo Baeck Institute/Tübingen, DE: J.C.B. Mohr, 2003.

Loeffler, James Benjamin. "Do Zionists Read Music from Right to Left? Abraham Tsvi Idelsohn and the Invention of Israeli Music." *Jewish Quarterly Review* 100, no. 3 (2010): 385–416.

– "Jewish Participation in German Culture." In *German-Jewish History in Modern Times, Volume 3: Integration in Dispute 1871–1918,* edited by Michael A. Meyer, 305–35. New York: Columbia University Press, 1997.

– "Richard Wagner's 'Jewish Music': Antisemitism and Aesthetics in Modern Jewish Culture." *Jewish Social Studies* 15, no. 2 (2009): 2–36.

London, Louise. "British Immigration Control Procedures and Jewish Refugees, 1933–1939." In *Second Chance: Two Centuries of German-Speaking Jews in the United Kingdom,* edited by Werner E. Mosse (co-ordinating editor), Julius Carlebach, Gerhard Hirschfeld, Aubrey Newman, Arnold Paucker, and Peter Pulzer, 485–518. Tübingen, DE: J.C.B. Mohr (Paul Siebeck), 1991.

Lowenstein, Steven M. "Ideology and Identity." In *German-Jewish History in Modern Times, Volume 3: Integration in Dispute 1871–1918*, edited by Michael A. Meyer, 281–304. New York: Columbia University Press, 1997.

Mahler, Alma. *Gustav Mahler: Memories and Letters*. Translated by Basil Creighton. New York: Viking Press, 1969.

McClatchie, Stephen, ed. *The Mahler Family Letters*. Oxford: Oxford University Press, 2006.

Mendelsohn, Ezra, ed. *Modern Jews and their Musical Agendas*. New York: Oxford University Press, 1993.

– "On the Jewish Presence in Nineteenth-Century European Musical Life." In

Mendes-Flohr, Paul. "Between Germanism and Judaism, Christians and Jews." In *German-Jewish History in Modern Times, Volume 4: Renewal and Destruction 1918–1945*, edited by Michael A. Meyer, 157–69. New York: Columbia University Press, 1998.

– *German Jews: A Dual Identity*. New Haven, CT: Yale University Press, 1999.

– "Jewish Cultural and Spiritual Life." In *German-Jewish History in Modern Times, Volume 4: Renewal and Destruction 1918–1945*, edited by Michael A. Meyer, 127–56. New York: Columbia University Press, 1998.

– "Jews Within German Culture." In *German-Jewish History in Modern Times, Volume 4: Renewal and Destruction 1918–1945*, edited by Michael A. Meyer, 170–94. New York: Columbia University Press, 1998.

Meyer, Michael A., ed. *German-Jewish History in Modern Times, Volume 3: Integration in Dispute 1871–1918*. New York: Columbia University Press, 1997.

–, ed. *German-Jewish History in Modern Times, Volume 4: Renewal and Destruction 1918–1945*. New York: Columbia University Press, 1998.

Mitchell, Donald. "Mahler's Fifth Symphony." In *The Mahler Companion*, edited by Donald Mitchell and Andrew Nicholson, 236–325. Oxford: Oxford University Press, 1999.

– "The Mahler Renaissance in England." In *The Mahler Companion*, edited by Donald Mitchell and Andrew Nicholson, 545–64. Oxford: Oxford University Press, 1999.

Mitchell, Donald, and Andrew Nicholson, eds. *The Mahler Companion*. Oxford: Oxford University Press, 1999.

Monod, David. *Settling Scores: German Music, Denazification and the Americans, 1945–1953*. Chapel Hill: University of North Carolina Press, 2005.

Moricz, Klara. *Jewish Identities: Nationalism, Racism, and Utopianism in Twentieth-Century Music*. Berkeley: University of California Press, 2008.

Mosse, George L. *Confronting the Nation: Jewish and Western Nationalism*. Hanover, NH: University Press of New England, 1993.

– *German Jews beyond Judaism*. Bloomington: Indiana University Press, 1985.

– *Germans and Jews*. New York: Howard Fertig, 1970.

Muck, Peter. *Einhundert Jahre Berliner Philharmonisches Orchester: Darstellung in Dokumenten*. Tutzing, DE: Hans Schneider, 1982.

Nelson, Amy. *Music for the Revolution: Musicians and Power in Early Soviet Russia.* University Park: Pennsylvania State University Press, 2004.

– "The Struggle for Proletarian Music: RAPM and the Cultural Revolution." *Slavic Review* 59, no. 1 (2000): 101–32.

Niewyk, Donald L. *The Jews in Weimar Germany*. Baton Rouge: Louisiana State University Press, 1980.

Painter, Karen. "Jewish Identity and Anti-Semitic Critique in the Austro-German Reception of Gustav Mahler, 1900–1945." In *Perspectives on Gustav Mahler*, edited by Jeremy Barham, 175–94. Aldershot, UK: Ashgate, 2005.

–, ed. *Mahler and His World.* Princeton, NJ: Princeton University Press, 2002.

Payne, Stanley. *Franco and Hitler: Spain, Germany and World War II.* New Haven, CT: Yale University Press, 2008.

Pecker Berio, Talia. "Mahler's Jewish Parable." In *Mahler and his World*, edited by Karen Painter, 87–110. Princeton, NJ: Princeton University Press, 2002.

Pekacz, Jolanta, "Memory, History and Meaning: Musical Biography and its Discontents." *Journal of Musicological Research* 23 (2004): 39–80.

–, ed. *Musical Biography: Towards New Paradigms.* Aldershot, UK: Ashgate, 2006.

Peukert, Detlev J.K. *The Weimar Republic: The Crisis of Classical Modernity.* Translated by Richard Deveson. New York: Hill and Wang, 1987.

Portero, Florentino. "Spain, Britain and the Cold War." In *Spain and the Great Powers in the Twentieth Century*, edited by Sebastian Balfour and Paul Preston, 210–28. London: Routledge, 1999.

Potter, Pamela. "Jewish Music and German Science." In *Jewish Musical Modernism, Old and New*, edited by Philip Bohlman, 81–102. Chicago: University of Chicago Press, 2008.

– *Most German of the Arts: Musicology and Society from the Weimar Republic to the end of Hitler's Reich.* New Haven, CT: Yale University Press, 1998.

Presner, Todd Samuel. *Mobile Modernity: Germans, Jews, Trains.* New York: Columbia University Press, 2007.

Raab Hansen, Jutta. *NS-verfolgte Musiker in England: Spuren deutscher und österreichischer Flüchtlinge in der britischen Musikkultur.* Hamburg: von Bockel, 1996.

Rabinovitch, Israel. *Of Jewish Music, Ancient and Modern.* Translated by A.M. Klein. Montreal: Book Center, 1952.

Rathkolb, Oliver. *Führertreu und Gottbegnadet: Künstlerelite im Dritten Reich.* Vienna: Osterreichischer Bundesverlag, 1991.

Rein, Raanan. *In the Shadow of the Holocaust and the Inquisition: Israel's Relations with Francoist Spain.* London: Frank Cass and Co, 1997.

Ridout, Godfrey, and Talivaldis Kenins. *Celebration: Essays on Aspects of Canadian Music Published in Honour of the 25th Anniversary of the Canadian Music Centre.* Toronto: Canadian Music Centre, 1984.

Romberg, Otto R., and Susanne Urban-Fahr, eds. *Jews in Germany after 1945: Citizens or "Fellow" Citizens?* Frankfurt am Main: Tribune, 2000.

Rosenfeld, Paul. *Musical Portraits: Interpretations of Twenty Modern Composers.* New York: Harcourt, Brace and Howe, 1920.

Rother, Bernd. *Franco y el Holocausto.* Tübingen, DE: Max Niemeyer Verlag, 2001.

Sacks, Adam J. "Toward an Expansion of the Critique of the Mahler Revival." *New German Critique* 40, no. 2 (2013): 113–36.

Schabas, Ezra. *Sir Ernest MacMillan: The Importance of Being Canadian.* Toronto: University of Toronto Press, 1994.

Scholem, Gershom. "Against the Myth of the German-Jewish Dialogue." In *On Jews and Judaism in Crisis: Selected Essays,* edited by Werner J. Dannhauser, 61–4. New York: Schocken Books, 1976.

– *On Jews and Judaism in Crisis: Selected Essays.* Edited by Werner J. Dannhauser. New York: Schocken Books, 1976.

Schwartz Seller, Maxine. *We Built Up Our Lives: Education and Community among Jewish Refugees Interned by Britain in World War II.* Westport, CT: Greenwood Press, 2001.

Schwarz, Boris. *Music and Musical Life in Soviet Russia, 1917–1970.* London: Barrie and Jenkins, 1972.

Shirakawa, Sam. *The Devil's Music Master: The Controversial Life and Career of Wilhelm Fürtwangler.* New York and Oxford: Oxford University Press, 1992.

Solvik, Morten. "The literary and philosophical worlds of Gustav Mahler." In *The Cambridge Companion to Mahler,* edited by Jeremy Barham, 21–34. Cambridge: Cambridge University Press, 2007.

Speisman, Stephen A. *The Jews of Toronto: A History to 1937.* Toronto: McClelland and Stewart, 1987.

Steinberg, M.W., and Usher Caplan, eds. *A.M.: Klein Beyond Sambation: Selected Essays and Editorials 1928–1955.* Toronto: University of Toronto Press, 1982.

Stent, Ronald. "Jewish Refugee Organizations." In *Second Chance: Two Centuries of German-speaking Jews in the United Kingdom,* edited by Werner E. Mosse (co-ordinating editor), Julius Carlebach, Gerhard Hirschfeld, Aubrey Newman, Arnold Paucker, and Peter Pulzer, 579–98. Tübingen, DE: J.C.B. Mohr (Paul Siebeck), 1991.

Strauss, Herbert A. "Jewish Emigration in the Nazi Period. Some Aspects of Acculturation." In *Second Chance: Two Centuries of German-speaking Jews in the United Kingdom,* edited Werner E. Mosse (co-ordinating editor), Julius Carlebach, Gerhard Hirschfeld, Aubrey Newman, Arnold Paucker, and Peter Pulzer, 81–100. Tübingen, DE: J.C.B. Mohr (Paul Siebeck), 1991.

Tobias, Henry J. *The Jewish Bund in Russia from its Origins to 1905.* Stanford, CA: Stanford University Press, 1972.

Tulchinsky, Gerald. *Branching Out: The Transformation of the Canadian Jewish Community.* Toronto: Stoddart, 1998.

– *Canada's Jews: A People's Journey*. Toronto: University of Toronto Press, 2008.

– *Taking Root: The Origins of the Canadian Jewish Community*. Hanover, NH: Brandeis University Press, 1993.

Turchyn-Duvirak, Dagmara. "Kyiv, the 1920s, and Modernism in Music." In *Modernism in Kiev: Kyiv/Kyïv/Kiev/Kijów/Ķiev: Jubilant Experimentation*, edited by Irena R. Makaryk and Virlana Tkacz, 322–41. Toronto: University of Toronto Press, 2010.

Unger, Heinz. *Hammer, Sickle and Baton*. London: Cresset Press, 1939.

– "Has the Canada Council Hit a Wrong Note?" *Globe Magazine*, 22 July 1961.

Volkov, Shulamit. "The Ambivalence of Bildung: Jews and Other Germans." In *The German-Jewish Dialogue Reconsidered: A Symposium in Honor of George L. Mosse*, edited by Klaus L. Berghahn, 81–98. New York: Peter Lang, 1996.

Wagner, Richard. Translated by William Ashton Ellis. *Judaism in Music and Other Essays*. Lincoln: University of Nebraska Press, 1995.

Ward, Seth. "The Liturgy of Bloch's 'Avodath Ha-Kodesh.' " *Modern Judaism* 23, no. 3 (2003): 243–63.

Warren, Richard S. *Begins with the Oboe: A History of the Toronto Symphony Orchestra*. Toronto: University of Toronto Press, 2002.

Wasserstein, Bernard. *Vanishing Diaspora: The Jews in Europe since 1945*. Cambridge, MA: Harvard University Press, 1996.

Werner, Eric. "Felix Mendelssohn – Gustav Mahler: Two Borderline Cases of German-Jewish Assimilation." In *Yuval: Studies of the Jewish Music Research Centre, Volume IV*, 240–264. Jerusalem: Magnes Press, The Hebrew University, 1982.

# Index of Composers

Entries for works that have a large number of page references have subheadings for the various orchestras that performed the works. Single-letter abbreviations are used for common words in orchestras' names (for example, C = Chamber or Community, O = Orchestra, P = Philharmonic, S = Symphony). Entries containing the full names of all the orchestras appear in the General Index (see pp. 250–60). Works by Gustav Mahler are included in this index, but subject entries relating to Mahler are located in the General Index. Page numbers in italics refer to illustrations.

# General Index

Page numbers in italics refer to illustrations.